THE CEDAR

NUMBER TWENTY-FOUR

Sam Rayburn Series on Rural Life

Sponsored by Texas A&M University–Commerce

M. Hunter Hayes, General Editor

THE CEDAR CHOPPERS

LIFE ON THE EDGE OF NOTHING

KEN ROBERTS

Foreword by M. Hunter Hayes

TEXAS A&M UNIVERSITY PRESS   COLLEGE STATION

Second printing, 2019

This paper meets the requirements
of ANSI/NISO Z39.48-1992 (Permanence of Paper).
Binding materials have been chosen for durability.
Manufactured in the United States of America

Library of Congress Cataloging-in-Publication Data

Names: Roberts, Kenneth D., 1945- author.
Title: The cedar choppers: life on the edge of nothing / Ken Roberts.
Description: First edition. | College Station: Texas A&M University Press, [2018] | Series: Sam Rayburn series on rural life; number twenty-four | Includes bibliographical references and index.
Identifiers: LCCN 2017036270 (print) | LCCN 2017038250 (ebook) | ISBN 9781623496081 (ebook) | ISBN 9781623496074 | ISBN 9781623496074q(cloth :qalk. paper) | ISBN 9781623498207 (paper)
Subjects: LCSH: Loggers—Texas—Texas Hill Country—Social life and customs. | Loggers—Texas—Texas Hill Country—Economic conditions. | Charcoal burners—Texas—Texas Hill Country—Social life and customs. | Charcoal burners—Texas—Texas Hill Country—Economic conditions. | Cedar—Texas—Texas Hill Country. | Self-reliant living—Texas—Texas Hill Country. | Texas Hill Country (Tex.)—History. | Texas Hill Country (Tex.)—Biography.
Classification: LCC HD8039.L92 (ebook) | LCC HD8039.L92 R63 2018 (print) | DDC 305.9/634975609763—dc23
LC record available at https://lccn.loc.gov/2017036270

Cover image: Earl and Leona Townsend. Photo courtesy of Ann Townsend Darragh.
Back cover: Goot Hight, about 1945. Photo by Virginia Clarke, courtesy of *The Cattleman.*

This book is dedicated to
Ronnie Glenn Roberts
(1950–2014):
cedar chopper, firefighter,
friend. I would be proud
if we were kin.

Contents

Foreword

Previous volumes in the Sam Rayburn Series on Rural Life have depicted accounts of individuals, families, and even segments of communities who have migrated to and from Texas, discussing the traditions and ways of life that these people brought with them. Other volumes have looked more specifically at how people connect to the land and a sense of a faded agricultural past, including the grassland prairies and cotton fields that were once readily identifiable with the regional landscape. In *The Cedar Choppers: Life on the Edge of Nothing*, Ken Roberts brings together in an engaging, cohesive narrative the stories of a group of Appalachian migrants in the Hill Country around Austin, families that followed land suited to their lives until arriving "at the edge of nothing." It is a pleasure to be able to present this as the twenty-fourth volume in the Rayburn Series.

Roberts skillfully addresses the economic influences of the cedar choppers and a history of the plant that allowed them to find sustenance. As Roberts reminds readers in chapter five, cedar itself has changed through farming and other practices; now considered by some people to be a nuisance, cedar was vital to many of the foundations on which modern Texas was built. Its value extended beyond transactional economy, especially for those whose lives centered on its harvesting. By demonstrating how deeply the lives of the cedar choppers connect to the land, Roberts also sends a poignant reminder of how shared histories can vanish in the face of development and progress, making his book all the more powerful and important. Additionally, Roberts presents the cedar choppers in a way that confronts stereotypes—that of the "hillbilly" and "hardscrabble" rural families—and addresses the essential individuality of members of this particular group.

Since 2000, when the Sam Rayburn Series on Rural Life published its initial volume under the editorship of James "Bo"

Grimshaw and under the auspices of Texas A&M University Press, the series has continuously sought to represent the complex interconnections between the land and its people, presenting a crazy quilt of history and personal tragedies and triumphs. These books serve as testaments to these relationships and as reminders that, as the novelist William Faulkner expressed it in his *Requiem for a Nun*, "The past is never dead. It's not even past." But ways of life can disappear, and understanding the past enriches us all.

Ken Roberts's *The Cedar Choppers* is a book that captures many of the themes and issues the Sam Rayburn Series on Rural Life has presented since its inception, and it provides a fresh perspective on these matters of shared importance. It is with tremendous appreciation for Roberts's sensitive eye for detail, his ability to craft a seamless story from disparate histories and facts, and his skill in reminding us to observe and scrutinize our own surroundings, that I welcome this book to the series.

M. Hunter Hayes
General Editor, Sam Rayburn Series on Rural Life

Acknowledgments

One of the most enjoyable aspects of writing this book was all the wonderful people I met. I was a newcomer to the field of Texas history and much more, but once I mentioned the topic, everyone enthusiastically supported my research with suggestions for approaches to the material, places to visit, and people to see. Historians Neil Foley, Dan Utley, and John Leffler were very helpful in identifying sources. I learned about cedar from Robert Adams of Baylor University and about literature of the Southwest from Cory Locke of St. Edward's University. Lois Myers of the Baylor Institute for Oral History showed me how to do oral history, and it was there that I discovered a transcript of an oral history project set in rural Texas and one of its authors, Thad Sitton. More than anyone else, Thad guided my research, not only with his expertise in oral history but with his knowledge of marginalized rural peoples. Our conversations over coffee at Quack's in Hyde Park shaped the evolution of my thinking and became important touchstones in the research process.

Another natural beginning for a project on cedar choppers was to talk to the few people who had already written about them: Mark Lisheron, Barbara Langham, Linda Vance, John Kelso, and Clay Coppedge. These writers shared insights and contacts that guided the initial stages of the research. It was in Barbara Langham's research notes that I found the letter leading to the Lomax collection and recordings by the hill people.

Through the historical commissions of Hill Country counties, I met local historians who were treasuries of information. They include Gary Spivey of Liberty Hill, Irene Varan of Cedar Park, Sami Devillier of New Braunfels, Frederica Wyatt of Junction, Carole Goble of Burnet, Jeff Jackson of Lampasas, Louis Stephens of Kerrville, and Chris Dyer of the Williamson Museum and Linda Scarbrough of the *Williamson County Sun*, both in Georgetown. I want to give special thanks to Jane Knapik of Marble Falls and Milli Williams of Burnet, who both gave me amazing contacts and constant encouragement.

Texas has not only a rich history but also excellent collections of historical resources, and while all the staff were helpful in each of the institutions I consulted, I want to single out a few: Rusty Heckeman of the Austin History Center; Bob Brinkman, Texas Historical Commission; Sara Hayes, Texas State Library and Archives; Margaret Schlankey, Dolph Briscoe Center for American History; Nicci Hester, Southwest Collection at Texas Tech University; Warren Stricker, Panhandle-Plains Historical Museum; and especially Dita Dauti of the Eanes History Center, who on several occasions helped me scour the old records. Other people and places providing information include Deborah Holley at the Balcones Canyonlands National Wildlife Refuge, Jean Flahive at the Lower Colorado River Authority, and Tina Rodriguez in the Criminal Division archives, Travis County District Court. Finally, Todd Harvey, curator of the Lomax collection at the American Folklife Center, Library of Congress, provided invaluable assistance in searching that vast collection.

While these repositories provided documents, photographs, recordings, and data, insights into the lives of cedar choppers came from talking directly with them and people who knew them well. I interviewed forty-four of the persons listed in appendix 1, "Voices." They gave me their time and permission to quote them, even when talking about topics that were uncomfortable. These men and women are the heart of the book. I like to think that the timing of my research happened to be perfect: the cedar choppers among them were finally given an opportunity to share the uniqueness of their upbringing and what it was like to work in the brakes—they were proud of their fortitude and far enough from some of the painful aspects that they could talk openly about their lives. Two decades earlier, I might have encountered defensiveness and mistrust; a decade later would have been too late. In addition to the people listed in appendix 1, I talked to Jay Thompson from Bull Creek, Virginia Turner and Gail Gonzales from Buda, Leslie Reaves from Cedar Park, Lonnie Whitt from Marlin, and Tommy and Mary Lou Ward from Camp Wood.

The early drafts of the book received excellent suggestions and encouragement from a number of astute readers, including my friends Rich Peavey, Carl Fink, and Mark Price; my wonderful wife, Duchess; and my sister, Barbara Boyd. But most of all I would like to thank Walt Herbert, longtime friend and colleague at Southwestern University and scholar extraordinaire, for his insights; and Sam Pfiester, who shares with me a passion for fly fishing and much else. Reading each chapter hot off the press, Sam always knew what I wanted to say and would often say it better. By constantly pushing me for the next installment, he collapsed into months what could otherwise have been a long, painful process. And he introduced me to Steve Davis, curator of the Wittliff Collections of Southwestern Writers at Texas State University and current president of the Texas Institute of Letters. Steve has read the manuscript and generously given his time and advice on a number of occasions, greatly facilitating the road to publication.

I appreciate the support of Southwestern University during the early years of research, and useful suggestions from many colleagues there, including Shana Bernstein, Doug Wixson, Dan Hilliard, Ed Kain, Gwen Kennedy Neville, Elizabeth Green Musselman, and Kathryn Stallard. Kelly Lessard, faculty administrative assistant, transcribed the interviews. Although she sometimes missed the words because of the accent, her hillbilly heritage from Appalachian New York meant she usually got the meaning.

THE CEDAR CHOPPERS

INTRODUCTION

The Balcones Fault

Let me start with a confession: I am not a cedar chopper. My father, born in 1878, was from a large family of cowboys who worked on a horse ranch near Eagle Lake, Texas. He was the only one to go to college, and he became a successful businessman. He met my mother, born in Austin's Hyde Park to German immigrants, after his first wife died. They would ride horses together during the 1930s in the area west of Austin that was to become Tarrytown, and they built one of the first houses there. They lived in style during the late 1940s and early 1950s, when he was still young enough to make a living.

With some exceptions, Tarrytown wasn't much back then, but it was better off than most of Austin. Austin in the early 1950s was off the map to people in the rest of the country; it bore no resemblance to the hip city it was to become. It had less than 150,000 people, and the few rich residents were somewhat embarrassed by its provinciality and went to Dallas or Houston to shop. The only big employers were the state and the university, and these jobs could be pretty dull and boring. It was mostly a middle-class town where middle class meant you had a job and could raise a family but had no luxuries or travel. A fairly large black population lived in East Austin, and although the schools were not integrated, there didn't seem to be the same virulent racism that existed in places like East Texas. Austin, on the edge of the Balcones Fault, faced West, not South.

If you were to walk west from the university, you would cross Shoal Creek and go up the hill, past the big houses in Pemberton Heights and then down streets of small houses and tidy green lawns until you reached the golf course. All that green on a hot summer day didn't seem like much until you were deprived of it. After spending a week in the cedar brakes of the Boy Scout camp on Bull Creek, I was so happy to be back where there were lawn sprinklers that I rolled in the grass like a puppy.

Past the golf course was Lake Austin and the Tom Miller dam. There was no reason to go farther up into the dry hills when there were so many opportunities for a boy to swim and fish nearby. My neighbor Dudley Morse and I built a houseboat that sat on six 55-gallon drums and had a little outboard motor. We anchored it in Taylor Slough at the end of Windsor Road and lived like Huckleberry Finn for a summer.

One of my favorite ways to spend a few hours was to ride my bike down to the low-water bridge below Tom Miller dam and go fishing. I could usually catch enough bluegills and bass for dinner, and sometimes even a catfish. One afternoon when we were ten or eleven, Dudley and I rode there to fish. When we got off our bikes and scrambled down from the road with our poles, three boys were standing in the middle of the path. I remember how different from us they looked: they were barefoot; their pants were too short, their shirts ragged. And they looked hard—tanned, skinny, dirty. These were not kids you would see in Austin. In a few years we would go to O. Henry Junior High, which had opened right across the low-water bridge from where they lived, and we would see some of them in school. But before that few went beyond the seventh grade at Eanes school, and they mostly stayed in the cedar hills on the other side of the Colorado River.

The three kids we met were smaller than we were and looked younger. They stood abreast, held up a stringer of bluegills, and one said in a hard, flat voice, "You wanna buy some fish?" I was speechless. We were going fishing, and if we didn't catch anything we'd still have dinner waiting at home. It was about catching fish, not about eating them. But Dudley, a tough kid even back then, popped back, "If we wanted to buy fish, we'd go to the H-E-B," dragging out the initials of the grocery store with sarcasm. There was a long pause, and they turned around and left. I told Dudley, "I don't think you should have said that to those boys," not because I was offended but because I knew that this level of disrespect would likely arouse a response. And sure enough, in a couple of minutes they were back, and one of them was carrying a club. It was clear to me—although Dudley remembers it a little differently—that whatever happened, we were going to lose. Dudley was strong and quick, and with any normal West Austin kids, the odds would have been in our favor. But these weren't West Austin kids, and there was nothing normal about the look in their eyes. They were going to fight without rules until one or the other of us was badly hurt. So we ran.

That was the first time I asked the question, "*Who are these people?*" It wouldn't be the last.

1

Who Are These People?

I found out that I wasn't the only one to ask this question. Several good Texas writers noticed that Austin, alongside the normal diversity of a Texas town with its mix of whites and blacks and Hispanics, of lawyers and merchants and clerks and mechanics, had something else, something not seen in other towns or in most other states. The early newspaper articles called them "mountaineers." You might see them in South Austin buying supplies or selling cedar, in the beer joints west of Austin, peddling charcoal in East Austin during the years when the poor didn't have electric irons, or on Sixth Street on a Saturday night. But then they might be cleaned up and could blend in with the rougher sort of city folk.

Over the years some of Texas' best journalists have had their turn at trying to depict these people. In 1947 Roy Bedichek, at the urging of J. Frank Dobie and Walter Prescott Webb—the trio of Texas writers memorialized by a statue at Barton Springs pool in Austin—went into seclusion at Friday Mountain Ranch in the hills west of Austin. This story is from one of Bedichek's long walks.

> I saw through an opening in the cedars a sight I shall never forget—an aged man cutting cedar. It was obviously the weight of years upon the trim, streamlined axe which had slowed it down. After a dozen strokes or so he leaned heavily on a tree, his chest heaving. As soon as his breathing quieted a little, he resumed his chopping, slow, steady, and accurate to a hair, like the slow-motion of a woodchopper to show correct form. His gigantic frame was stripped to the waist. He was at least

> six-feet-two, broad-shouldered, tapering at the hips, with an almost wasp-like waist accentuated by a belt drawn tightly above the bony hips.[1]

This period, the 1940s and early 1950s, was probably the best ever for the cedar choppers. Trucks provided a way to get the cedar posts out of the hills and long-hauled to ranchers, and for the first time they could make good money. The cutters brought their cedar into town and they stood out. A 1941 article marveled that "within sight of the Capitol dome the people depend for their water supply on the natural springs or creeks, speak a mountain dialect, and depend for their education on a short term in a one-room school."[2] Another article, written in 1946, talked about a sixty-year-old chopper named Goot Hight in Palo Pinto County, an outpost of cedar country in north-central Texas: "The chopper who cuts today and lives in the cedar is as true a mountaineer as his forefathers, who perhaps hailed from the Ozarks or the Blue Ridge Mountains in pioneer days. He has not been noticeably touched by what is known as present-day civilization."[3]

By 1960 a few local journalists began to notice that this way of life

Goot Hight, about 1945. Photo by Virginia Clarke, courtesy of The Cattleman.

was coming to an end. A. C. Greene, who like Bedichek wrote in the hills west of Austin, observed: "The cedar choppers and their families stay to themselves and live in a tribal fashion, most of them handing on the trade to sons or sons-in-law. They work when they want to or need to. . . . It is hard, low-paying work whose rewards seem to be in the way of life it allows you to lead—although Texas writers have tended to be too romantic about the cedar choppers and their ways, confusing lack of contact with splendid solitude."[4] Winston Bode told stories in the *Texas Observer* about a seventy-five-year-old charcoal burner called Uncle Buck Maynard, "the last of a dying breed."[5] In the same magazine Bob Sherrill talked about the Teagues and the Maynards and "a couple dozen other clans of their type who made cedar chopping a legendary occupation in these parts." He lamented that they were abandoning the brakes because good timber was running out and steel posts were coming in, and that "town folks are moving into the hills, squeezing the choppers out."[6]

Gary Cartwright wrote a couple of stories for *Texas Monthly* in the 1970s that took the legend in a darker direction, stories of welfare and dog fights and a type of life that readers of the upscale magazine could find appalling. But if they did, they might be missing the point, for Cartwright came to respect the cedar choppers. He wrote, "I gradually came to see them as a tribe, a class of people who had never joined mainstream culture or had the least desire to. . . . They drive broken-down pickup trucks, deal in cash, preach self-reliance, and maintain a fundamental faith in the use of physical force."[7]

In 1985 Barbara Langham used oral interviews from the Austin History Center to write a long article for *Texas Highways* that put names and faces to a lot of the cedar chopper families, such as Ollie Roberts and his son Wilburn.[8] The title of the article came from an interview with a chopper who decided to move one night for no other reason than "a man's got a right to his own mind."

A lot of Austinites have probably been introduced to cedar choppers by John Kelso, humor columnist for the *Austin American-Statesman*. In a 2013 column he talked about Marie Boatright, "the last person in the area with cedar chopper roots who still maintains that rugged lifestyle," hanging three coyotes on her fence on Spicewood Springs Road.[9] When the newspaper hired Mark

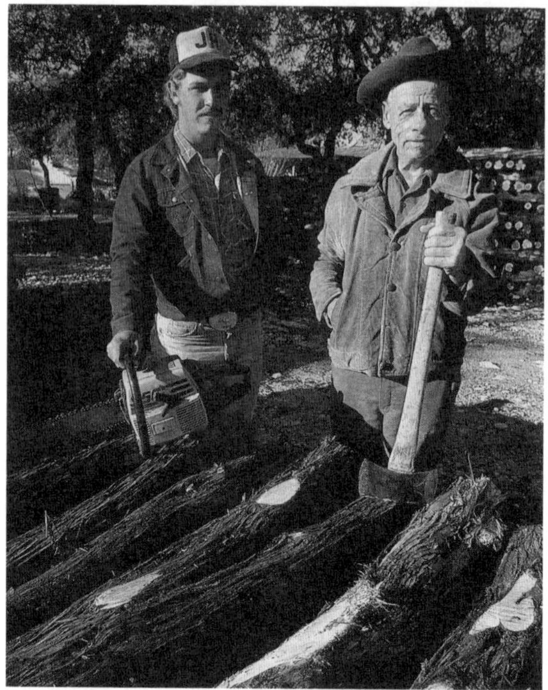

Wilburn and Ollie Roberts, about 1984. Photo by J. Griffis Smith, courtesy of TxDOT.

Marie Boatright, 2013. Photo courtesy of Austin American-Statesman.

Lisheron right out of journalism school to write in-depth interest pieces, he came to John for suggestions. John told him to write about cedar choppers, and Mark did a big story on Frank and Marie Boatright called "Sundown of the Cedar Choppers."[10]

Thus over the years there have been several articles written about cedar choppers. These articles have two things in common. The first is that they are written by people who are local. To write about cedar choppers, you had to notice them and talk to them, and there were no cedar choppers anywhere else. Sure, there were hillbillies in Appalachia and the Ozarks, but the mountain cedar that made the best fence posts grew only in Central Texas. Almost nowhere else or under any other circumstances could a group of rural people make an independent living with no land, little capital, and no boss.

The second thing these articles have in common is that each zeroes in on specific people—Goot Hight, Buck Maynard, Ollie Roberts, Frank Boatright. Generalities—that they lived in big families under hard conditions, cut cedar with an axe, drove old trucks—don't convey the uniqueness of their lives in mid-twentieth century, when mainstream America was immersed in a world of suburban houses, automobiles, and the benefits of modernity made possible by an eight-to-five job. The cedar choppers followed a different path, and it is only by telling the stories of real people that the uniqueness of their lives can be illustrated and authenticated.

Therefore, before delving into their roots—who they were and where they came from—I will follow the example of these authors and anchor the narrative in two people and their families. The first is the person to whom this book is dedicated, Ronnie Roberts. The second is Luther Pierce, a classmate at O. Henry and Austin High. Ronnie was one of the first people I interviewed, and Luther was one of the last. Luther's mother was also interviewed in 1981, and a transcript of that interview is at the Austin History Center. The sources of the quotes by participants in this and subsequent chapters, as well as information on the speakers, are presented in appendix 1, "Voices," and referencing of the interviews is explained at the opening of the endnotes.

Cecil Roberts with Ronnie and brother. Photo courtesy of Gail Roberts Gonzales.

Ronnie Roberts described his life as a little kid in the early 1950s on the forks of the Guadalupe River as a kind of paradise. "Back then, that was my heyday, I mean I was about five years old, and I used to run around. I looked like a little Mexican boy, no shirt, no shoes, you know. And I'd go either way, I could go the North Fork or the South Fork, I could go fishing and do all that stuff."

Ronnie's dad Cecil had followed in the steps of his own father, Joe L. Roberts, who owned a ranch on Nutty Brown Road and a cedar yard in Oak Hill. Cecil started his own yard outside Kerrville; he was an upstanding citizen and a deacon of the church. But Ronnie's older brother died at six of a brain tumor, and things fell apart. His dad started drinking and his mom committed suicide. In 1958 Ronnie and his three sisters moved in with their grandparents.

Joe L. Roberts was married to Mary Patterson. They were both in their mid-fifties when they took in their grandkids. Joe L. was blind but still sharp and working. Mary did the grading of cedar, and within a few years grandson Ronnie was loading the long-haul trucks. "He'd work my ass to death, I mean, boys were like—boys were like mules, you know. I'd tell everybody I always thought my name was 'goddammit boy' until I was ten years old."

Mary Patterson's sister Edna married Litten Pierce, and by the

Joe L. Roberts. Photo courtesy of Gail Roberts Gonzales.

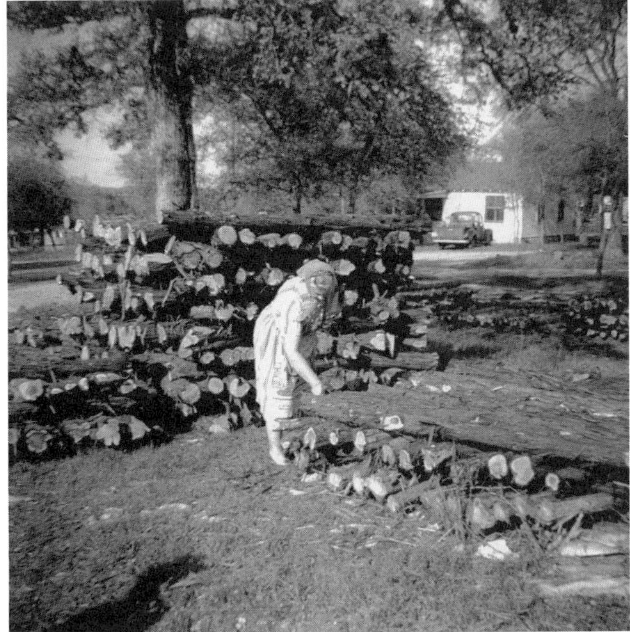

Mary Patterson grading cedar, 1969. Photo courtesy of Gail Roberts Gonzales.

time of her death she was a celebrity in Westlake. In what is now one of the ten richest zip codes in Texas, she cooked on a wood stove and lived without running water all her life. When she died in 1992, her little rock house was converted into a studio for the main house, but they planned to tear down the outhouse. John Kelso's column called for a "Save the Westlake Outhouse" movement, and Luther Pierce got a call from his sister: "Hey, Luther, you ain't gonna believe this. They've got a picture of Old George on the front page of city-state." Old George was the name of their outhouse.

Luther Pierce, born in 1945, was the youngest son of Litten and Edna. Twenty-two years and eight other children were between him and his oldest brother Ed. The epitaph on the graves of Ed and his wife in Tucker Cemetery reads, "The Best Cedar Choppers." That's saying a lot, because the Robertses, Pierces, and Pattersons were all skilled cedar choppers.

Mary and Edna's dad Pate Patterson owned a large ranch off Bee Cave at Patterson Lane, but it was worthless for anything except a few goats. To provide for his family, he sold charcoal and wood in Austin during the early part of the century. He took Edna out of school after the eighth grade to help with the work. She remembers getting up at daybreak to help gather fodder for an hour or so, and

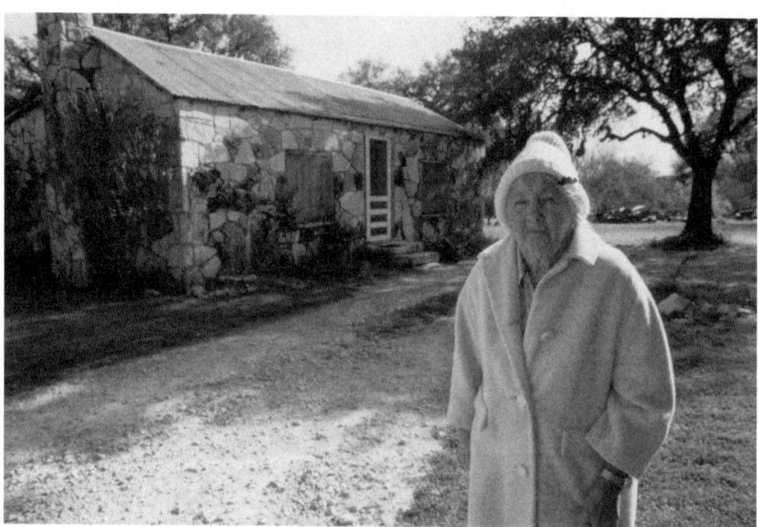

Edna Patterson in front of her house, about 1984. Photo by Randy Greene, courtesy of TxDOT.

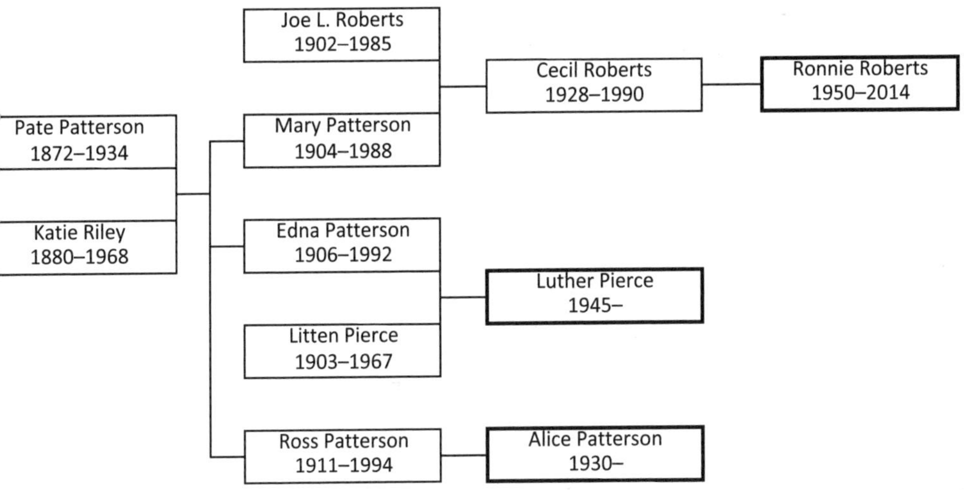

This tree includes only the people discussed here and excludes many family members. I interviewed the three people highlighted.

Patterson tree. Drawn by author.

then Pate would say to his wife, "'Well, Katie, wake 'er up. I got ya a fire built. Have breakfast in 'bout a hour, we'll be back.' Then we'd go chop wood, make us a load of wood to buy our groceries. Double bed load of wood." They made money and spent it, day by day, living on the edge of nothing.

Edna Patterson met Litten Pierce at church—they called it the Snuff Box church because the preachers dipped snuff—when she was thirteen and he was sixteen. One afternoon, "I seen him coming over the hill in that truck. He was dressed up in the army suit. He wore his soldier suit and soldier hat. Wore wrap leggings." She talked to her mother. "I said, 'I sure do like Litten.' She said, 'Listen, young lady. You're too young.' My daddy told me, 'You ain't startin' to go with no boys. You don't need to think so.' And I said, 'Well, next time I go to church and I meet him I'm going to talk to him.'" A little later she told Litten, "'Oooh, I'd like to get married tonight. If papa don't let you have me, let's run off.' 'Oh no,' he replied. 'Pate Patterson'll kill me.' And next afternoon he asked papa."

Litten Pierce and Edna Patterson, 1920. Photo courtesy of Luther Pierce.

Litten and Edna spent their honeymoon in a tent on Barton Creek. "During the day we would swim in the creek, hunt squirrels and chop a little cedar for cash money." They moved in with his parents, and Ed was born nine months later. All the babies were born at home, and two died shortly after birth. Little Luther, the last, barely made it, weighing only two and a half pounds when he was born. "Doctor said, 'If you can keep him three days you can raise him.'" She put him in an apple crate with his head down and gave him drops of sugar water spiked with whiskey. The doctor returned. "He come back the third day, 'You still got him, ain't ya?' 'Yeah, I got him. I got him laying in an apple box.'"

Luther lived to be a strong healthy boy who graduated from high school, studying for years by a kerosene lamp. His mother had to "pack water outta these hollers" and take her washing down to the creek half a mile away. Luther would try to get her to use a gas stove or do anything to make her life easier. He said, "Mama had a really,

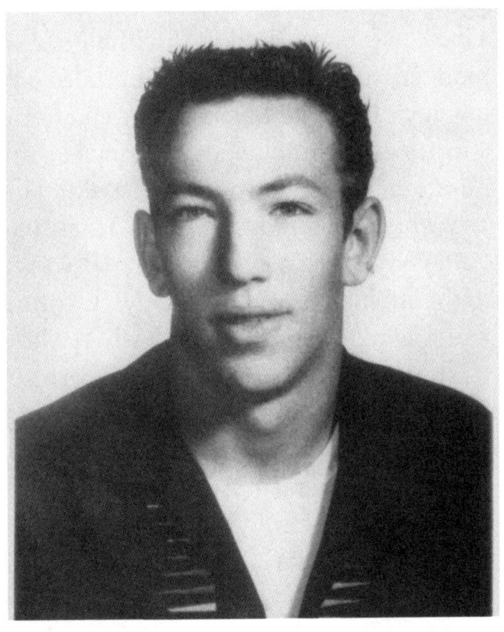

Luther Pierce, 1963. Photo courtesy of Luther Pierce.

really hard life. It didn't have to be that hard. I mean, she would pack her clothes down there, so that she had to tie Cooter (the baby) up to keep him from jumping in there and stirring up—you know how the water gets muddy looking? And then hang them clothes out on them bushes to dry. It shouldn't have been that way."

Luther became a rock hauler and eventually owned a quarry. Ronnie Roberts said, "A few years ago we lived in Oak Hill and I had some rock work done there, and this guy drove up with a load of rock, and I looked at him and I said, 'Man, you look like a Patterson.' Pattersons have a certain look. They kind of have these little beady eyes. I said, 'Man, you look like a damn Patterson,' you know, and this guy got out of his truck. And it was, I can't remember his name right now, but he was a Pierce. He had a rock quarry out there in Liberty Hill, somewhere down in that area. And, uh, I couldn't believe it, man, it's like I could recognize it, yeah, see them eyes, you know."

Tiney Teague was married to Charlie Roberts, the uncle of Joe L. Roberts. The Teagues were another big Westlake cedar family, and

Tiney, like Edna, lived in the middle of the twentieth century like pioneer women in the nineteenth. She kept her little house in a hollow near the Wild Basin until well after land in the hills was worth a fortune. But unlike Edna, Tiney had an attitude. When she got a phone call, she answered it, "Driskill Hotel."

Luther Pierce was related to Tiney Teague through his aunt Mary Patterson, and Tiney's son Charlie was his best friend. Charlie told Luther a story about Tiney. In 1981 the Memorial Day Flood had washed down Bee Creek where she lived, carrying a bunch of trash into the lake. The health department found that the source of the trash was Tiney's house and sent a young woman to investigate. "He said that woman made the mistake of going down there to Tiney's by herself. And probably what kept Tiney alive—she had drank three or four beers, Old Milwaukee, in the evening, every evening—and she come out of there with her eyes sparklin,' and Charlie got down there before it was over and said that woman asked Tiney, said 'I just kind-of wondering where you use the restroom at around here?' 'Well, that ain't none of your damn business where I use the restroom.' Said, 'I own this f-ing place, I'll crap behind a cedar bush if I want to.' And Charlie said that woman was shaking like the leaves on the tree. 'You see that road you come down here on, you better get your ass back up that road or I'll run you up it with my double-barrel shotgun.' And she did have a double-barrel 10-gauge. I told Tiney, you cannot—this is the state health department, they'll be back—you can't do that. She said, 'Well, I pay taxes on this damn place. This place is mine.' Well, the way they ended up settling it is she got a port-a-potty. They come out and serviced it and all, and that's how they let her stay there, but Charlie said that same little girl come out there—he lived right up on the hill from her—but she would never go down to Tiney's. She'd park at his house. If he wasn't there she would wait until he come home, and get him to walk down there with her."

When I asked Ronnie about this sort of behavior, he attributed it to their roots. He said, "They were like, they was stuck in little Appalachia over there. They liked livin' kind of under the radar, you know, I mean that's just the Irish. Like there's a lot of Irish culture over there in Eanes, you know. Most of them come like my family from Tennessee. They were all from Appalachia. Yeah, I mean, it's like this Irish shit, they liked livin' out in the woods. And they liked their whiskey."

Ronnie was the first to confirm what I had been reading about their origins in oral interviews at the Austin History Center. One of the best of these was Frank Wilson's interview in 1978, when he was seventy. He grew up in Hyde Park and knew families like the Suttons, who were grandparents of Edna and Mary Patterson. He talked for over an hour about what he called a "very unique bunch of people. I credit that to their Scotch and Irish blood in them 'cause they had known that for centuries back in the old country, 'cause they didn't have anything back there either." He repeated what he was told by one cedar chopper: "They were the same stock that came into the Alleghenies, up in there around Pennsylvania and New York State, came on down this far. And they wouldn't live anywhere except up in the mountains, in the hills. They weren't farmers."

I wondered if this was true, and so I began to research the paths the cedar chopper families had taken to Texas. The Pattersons and the Robertses were from Tennessee, Hamilton County and Hardin County, near the border with Alabama. The first direct ancestor of the Teagues was from Kentucky and showed up in 1810 in Knox County, just west of Harlan County, West Virginia, made famous by the Harlan County (coal) War in the 1930s and the TV series *Justified*. The Pierces were from farther south, Alabama and Mississippi. Of the ten most frequent family names among the cedar chopper clans, four were from Tennessee, two from Kentucky, and two from North Carolina. In a word, from Appalachia. That's where it began.

THE MIGRATION

We held tight to our loved ones and we held on to the promise
And scraped our meager living hand to mouth.
We prayed to what would have us, every doubting John Thomas
Spread through the Appalachia ever south.

Drive-By Truckers, "Ever South"

Appalachia

What does it mean that the cedar choppers had their origins in Appalachia? It identifies them with immigrants whose roots are the borderlands of Ireland, England, Scotland, and Wales. They are often called Scots-Irish (or Scotch-Irish, as my father said of his ancestors), and they certainly include the lowland Scots resettled in Northern Ireland by the British. David Hackett Fischer called them "a double-distilled selection of some of the most disorderly inhabitants of a deeply disordered land."[1] They were a Celtic culture that lived a violent, uncertain life for centuries, and during the 1700s their descendants flowed down through the highland South—the mountainous areas of Pennsylvania, Virginia, Kentucky, Tennessee, and the Carolinas—known as Appalachia. From there they went to the Ozarks and finally to the Hill Country of Texas.

Appalachia defines "a discrete region, in but not of America."[2] It is identified as one of the major regional cultures of the United States by historians David Hackett Fischer in *Albion's Seed* and Colin Woodard in *American Nations*. Woodard draws a clear distinction between the culture of the cotton South, transplanted from the Caribbean slave islands, and that of the "Borderlanders" of Appalachia, asserting that the region did not really join the South until *after* the Civil War.[3] Historian Jack Temple Kirby wrote: "This was a different South, without plantations, many black people, or a palpable Confederate mystique. Vast, it nevertheless seemed singular and simple. The highlands remained hidden behind mountain vastness, serenely beyond the modern world, primitive, clannish, violent, and beautiful."[4]

The images of Appalachia and the Ozarks—"a single fantastical place"—are so cartoonish and ingrained in our imagination that it is difficult to sort fact from fancy.[5] What is true is that the Scots-Irish, or Anglo-Celts as Fehrenbach calls them, came through Philadelphia in the 1720s—Quakers were more accepting of this wild and unruly lot than were the other colonies—and moved west, passing through the good land around Lancaster that was later farmed so successfully by Germans.[6] Subsequent waves moved down into the Shenandoah Valley, to the Appalachian and Allegheny mountains, and to the western Carolinas. They were a warrior culture every bit as ferocious as any of the Native Americans they displaced and were tolerated by the planter class only because they kept the Indians at bay.

The swath of country dominated by the Scots-Irish runs from Appalachia to the Ozarks to Central Texas. It is so geographically elongated because the people were constantly moving. James Leyborn, in his history of the Scots-Irish, wrote that many "seemed to feel a compulsion to move again and again. Long before fertile areas in the Susquehanna and Cumberland valleys had been filled up, scores who had settled here had, for one reason or another—or for no reason at all, so far as observers could perceive—moved on down the great Valley into Virginia, and thence into the Carolinas."[7]

Some claim that this "locational instability" is bred into their Scots-Irish bones.[8] The idea is that the lease system under which they labored or the frequent violence in the borderlands precluded permanent abodes, so that "they became mobile, moving easily from one temporary, hastily built lodging to another."[9] Ronnie Roberts said, "The Germans, they stayed put. But it's like the damn Irish, they were always looking for a little greener pasture, you know, like they just were restless."

Another explanation is that the agricultural system of the American backwoods frontier required frequent movement. Following the Indian method of slash and burn, they girded the big trees and plowed around them to plant small fields of corn, fencing these off and letting hogs and cattle range free.[10] Corn was the ideal frontier crop: it could be harvested without threshing, processed without milling, and it was food for animals as well as people. But this system depleted the land; the forage and game became scarce, so that it was common for persons to move several times during their lives.

A fascinating hypothesis is that this agricultural system is an adaptation of Indian methods by settlers in New Sweden on the Delaware River. These were Savo-Karelians, who had lived independently in the woods of Finland for hundreds of years by hunting, planting rye, and raising cattle, and had later been invited to Sweden to tame its interior frontier. They were banished to America for poaching—"banishment of backwoods Finns to America was a bit like tossing Br'er Rabbit into the briar patch"—and brought with them methods and tools for forest cultivation, including the worm rail fence, notched log construction and, of course, the axe.[11] Having lived among the Lapps in Scandinavia, they sought good relations with the Delaware Indians, intermarrying, learning their language, and adopting Indian methods and crops, especially corn. This Finnish-Indian agricultural system had been fully developed for half a century when the Scots-Irish landed in the Delaware Valley and adopted it so wholeheartedly.[12]

Animals were a central component of the forest agricultural system. These people weren't really farmers; they were stockmen. While corn made bread and grits and whiskey, it was also a feed to keep the free-ranging hogs and cattle from going completely feral. Thad Sitton says the appearance of the houses and little patches of corn led observers "to drastically misinterpret a whole social class. Considered as agriculturists, these folks looked like 'poor white trash,' but they were stockmen, not agriculturalists. The weedy corn was intended for their animals. The men seen taking their ease on their porches often had hundreds, perhaps thousands, of hogs and cattle on the open range. Their real wealth was invisible. Typically, they owned only a hundred acres or so because they did not need to own more."[13]

Worm fence and barn in Appalachia. Photos by author.

Back in Scotland, stealing cattle was a favorite sport, and there was little law to protect one's property. The only means of enforcing order was *lex talionus*, the rule of retaliation. This could be the reason for one of the defining characteristics of the Scots-Irish: extreme aggression in response to perceived injury. They "rushed straight to the isolation of the eighteenth-century frontier to found a society that was . . . modeled on the anarchical world they had left behind," where central authority was scorned and personal honor sanctified with violence.[14] "There's an old saying in the mountain

Worm fence and cabin in the Hill Country. Photos by author.

South. Insult a Yankee and he'll sue you. Insult a mountain boy and he'll kill you."[15]

From Appalachia the migratory trail moved west to a similar mountain environment in the Ozark region of Arkansas and Missouri. The Texas frontier was still a dangerous place before the

Civil War, and although backwoodsmen arrived before mid-century, they were likely to have to fight Mexicans or Indians to carve out their settlements.

But after the Civil War the Comanche threat dissipated, and many in the Ozarks joined their cousins from Tennessee and Kentucky and migrated west of the Balcones Fault to the Hill Country of Texas. And though it was drier than Appalachia and the Ozarks and the hills and trees were not as tall, the rivers and springs ran clear, and the canyons provided shade and patches of good soil. The geographer Terry Jordan wrote, "The southern mountain folk found enough of the familiar about the Texas hills to make them feel at home. The hillbillies passed through and rejected the splendid rolling lands east of the Texas Hill Country and deliberately chose . . . areas inferior in quality but similar in appearance."[16] This was just what they had done in Pennsylvania, and as had also happened there, in Texas immigrants filled in behind them to farm the rich Blackland Prairie east of the Balcones Fault and turn it into one of the most productive cotton growing areas of the nation.

Jordan's thesis—that "the central Texas hill area is a transplant of the economy and culture of Ozarkia and Appalachia"—is supported by their common woodland subsistence economy, their buildings and fences, and their speech.[17] They planted less land per person than in regions to the east, and on this land they planted more corn. They had many more animals per person and depended upon abundant game for food as well. They built double-pen log barns and worm fences from the plentiful cedar. They gave the same names to geographical features, like gap, cove, and hollow, and their speech had a cadence and rhythm that some people called Elizabethan.

Contemporaries noticed the uniqueness of this culture. A rural school teacher during the 1930s wondered why the mountaineers of Appalachia and the Ozarks had received so much attention when "Americans of the oldest stock with their special culture and customs are to be found also in an intact community in the Texas hills near Austin."[18] Harold Preece, born of cedar chopper parents in western Travis County, wrote, "Traditional ballads and folksongs still survive among these Texas highlanders. I once heard a toil-worn, soot-begrimed mountain woman sing a very old version of 'Barbara Allen' as she attended to her charcoal kiln . . . [and people sing] old songs from England such as "King William was King James' Son," "The Irate Chief," and "Bonnie Prince Charles."[19]

It was one of those remarkable moments of serendipity that sometimes happens during research that led me to confirm this and perhaps to find this very woman. I was going through the notes Barbara Langham had collected for a 1985 article in *Texas Highways* and came across the following letter, written to her by a reader:

> In 1936, Alan Lomax found a three-generation family of charcoal burners out in the hills from Austin who were singing Elizabethan ballads very nearly as they had been sung in Elizabethan times. These people could not read or write, and could not read music of course, but they could play guitars and sing.
>
> One song had the lead sung by a late teenage man—18 or 19 years old. The song had a 'damn' in it, and when he got to that word, he scuffed his toe and dropped his head and blushed. They were extremely sensitive people. Through Alan, you could get them into town to perform. They approached the whole set-up as though they were friends coming into town to entertain your guests. They did not like to take money, but there was a young child who had impetigo. In those days, impetigo could not be cured, only held in check, and the treatment was expensive. So they took the money to pay for the treatment for the child.
>
> They were real charmers—low key and with a marvelous sense of humor. And they were almost totally independent—living off what they made from charcoal burning, taking care of their own, and taking very little from the twentieth century.[20]

Alan Lomax was the son of musicologist John Lomax and became a famous folklorist himself. He was born in Austin and, while still a teenager, went with his father to collect music from across

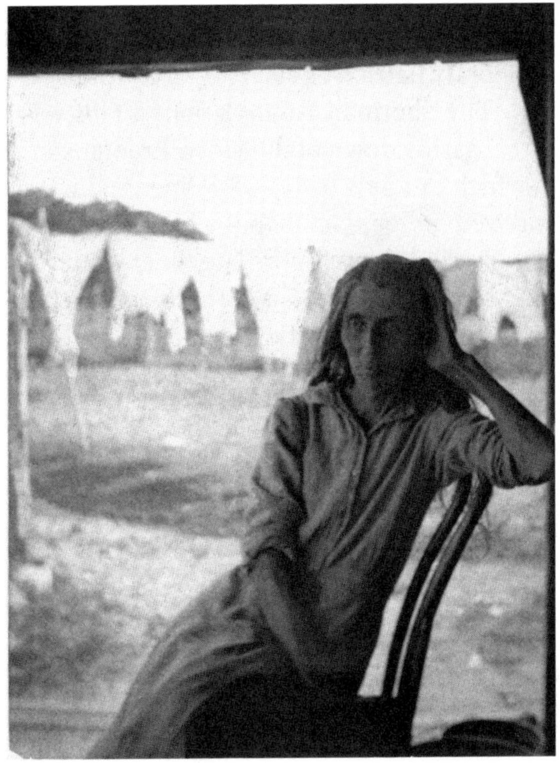

Mountain woman in the Hills near Austin, 1934. Photo courtesy of Library of Congress, Prints and Photographs Division, Lomax Collection, LC-DIG-00281.

the South. It was while Alan was completing his education at the University of Texas that these recordings were made. Just as with the writers, you had to be local to know the cedar people were unique.

The Lomax Family Collection is housed in the Library of Congress, and I went to their website to see if I could find these recordings. But there were hundreds of songs recorded around Austin, and at the time I did not know which ones were relevant. But I did come across a remarkable picture of a woman with the caption "Mountain woman in the hills near Austin, Texas," reproduced here.

Later I was to learn the names of the big cedar chopper families, and I searched for these names among the recordings done around Austin. I found fifteen songs recorded in 1937 by Dave and Hallie May Preece, an old Bull Creek family, about whom more detail follows in the next chapter. The songs included not only old English ballads like "Barbara Allen" and "The Romish Lady" but more contemporary narratives such as "Cole Younger" (of the James gang) and "The Sherman Texas Cyclone." This was still an illiterate culture, passing down oral history through stories and songs, some of which can now be heard online. And it was a culture that had survived more intact than that of Appalachia and perhaps that of the Ozarks as well. In the late nineteenth century Appalachia was often portrayed by outsiders as an untouched wilderness, peopled by "a folk so isolated they seemed trapped in a time capsule from the eighteenth century or earlier."[21] But these romantic characterizations of a pre-industrial paradise, if they were ever true, ignored the dramatic social change caused by mining and timber and railroads. Many people in the hills of Appalachia were dispossessed of their land and means of subsistence and became wage workers in mills and coal mines. But the Texas hills did not have resources attracting modern exploitation and were spared the extractive capitalism that so ravaged parts of Appalachia.

What was it about this land that attracted them so?

The Hill Country of Texas

The streams, these men discovered, were full of fish. The hills were full of game. . . . And as the men sat their horses, staring, flocks of wild turkeys strutted in silhouette along the ridges. Honeybees buzzed in the glades, and honey hung from the trees for the taking. Wild mustang grapes plump and purple, hung down for making wine. Wrote one of the first men to come to the Hill Country: It is a Paradise.

Robert Caro, *The Path to Power*

Before it was worn out, the Hill Country must have taken your breath away. To get there from the east, you had to pass through 250 miles of low humid country. Sometimes the trees closed in and you slogged through mud; other times you walked endlessly on a featureless plain. Even back in the Ozarks and Appalachia, whenever you got to the top of one hill there was another right in front of you, and the land closed in upon you. But in the Texas Hill Country the mountains and valleys stretched out and you could see for miles.

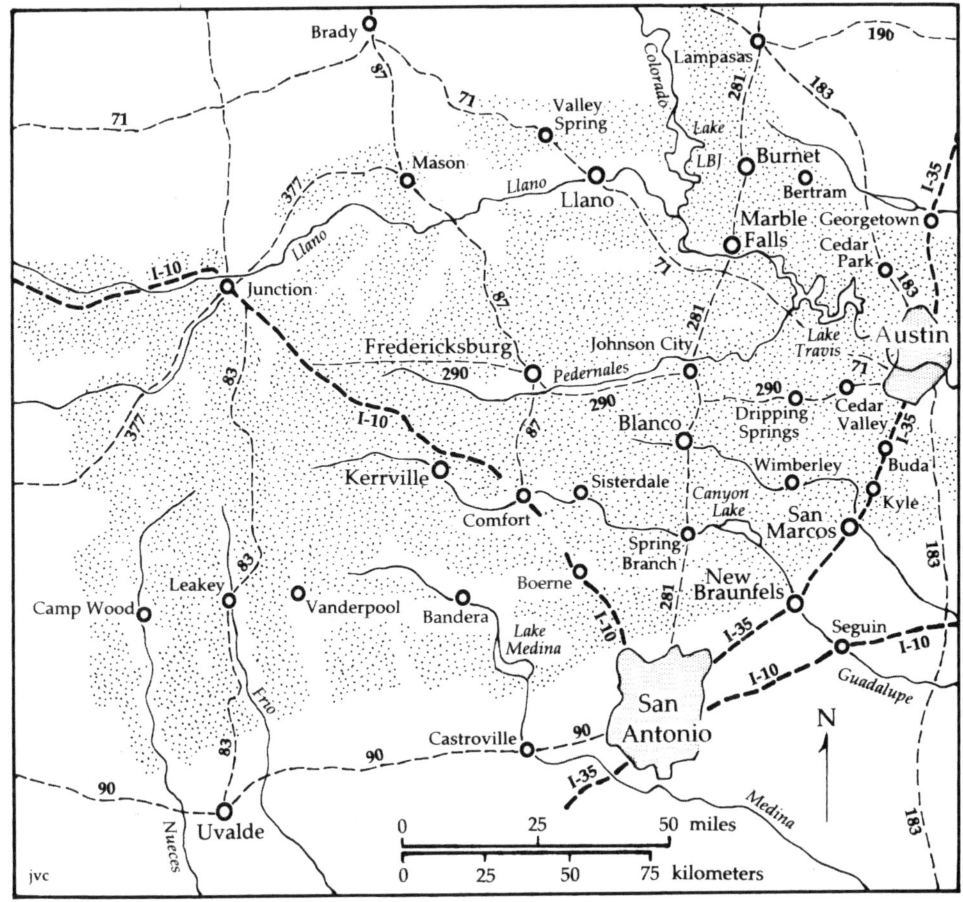

The Hill Country and cedar coverage. Cedar distribution from B. W. Allred, "Distribution and Control of Several Woody Plants in Texas and Oklahoma," Journal of Range Management, *Archives 2, no. 1 (17-29). Map drawn by John Cotter.*

You climbed up off the prairie onto a limestone escarpment with water so clear that you could see the fish below as if they were frozen in space. You could drink the water without the fear of diseases that were common back East, like cholera and typhoid. The air was cooler and drier, and the sky seemed higher. The early settlers called it a sapphire sky, and on some evenings about sunset there would be a belt of lavender that was glorious, earning Austin the name "City of the Violet Crown."

The early chroniclers of this land were impressed. The German geologist Ferdinand von Roemer spent 1845 to 1847 in Texas and said that if someone were suddenly transported to the hills from the plains below, "such a person would firmly believe he was in another country."[22] Frederick Law Olmsted, the designer of New York's Central Park, described the country between the Colorado and Nueces rivers in 1857:

> For sunny beauty of scenery and luxuriance of soil, it stands quite unsurpassed in my experience. I believe no region of equal extent in the world can show equal attractions. The whole extent . . . is covered with the finest and most nutritious grasses. . . . The streams which, in other parts of the State, are thick and discolored with mud, flow here clear as crystal.

And the wildflowers!

> Today . . . three or four more species opened into bloom. After this hardly a day went by without some addition, and very soon it was impossible to welcome each newcomer. . . . The beauty of the spring prairies . . . is inexpressible.[23]

The eastern edge of the Hill Country is a sweeping arc from north of Austin to near Del Rio, closely following the route of Interstate 35. There was an old road there long before the automobile, for it sits atop a formation called the Austin chalk. To the east is the Black Waxy, fertile land that is practically impassable when wet, and to the west is the Balcones Escarpment, where the land is too rugged for north-south travel. It is a fundamental geographical boundary in the United States, near the 98th meridian, often considered the dividing line between the South and the West. And in Texas this divide is pronounced: to the east the soil is deep and the rainfall sufficient in most years to grow crops; to the west is the Edwards Plateau, where thin soil barely covers a bed of limestone and the rainfall is less than 30 inches per year. East is farm country, west is ranch country—the rural road numbers are prefixed with FM or RM, farm roads east and ranch roads west of the interstate. East there was cotton, west there were cows. East the predominant minority was African American, west it was to become Hispanic. Walter Prescott Webb saw the 98th meridian as a fundamental institutional fault in the nation where everything changed—environment, economy, society, and culture.[24]

If you kept going west on the Edwards Plateau you eventually came to what the Spanish called the Llano Estacado and geographers called the Great American Desert. Albert Pike, on a journey from Missouri to Taos in 1831, described it thus: "Imagine yourself . . . standing in a plain to which your eye can see no bounds. Not a tree, nor a bush, not a shrub, not a tall weed lifts its head above the barren grandeur of the desert; not a stone is to be seen on its hard beaten surface; no undulation, no abruptness, no break to relieve the monotony; nothing."[25] The great migratory trail from Pennsylvania through Appalachia and the Ozarks to Texas ended there. Beyond there was no wood, no water, no game—no means of survival for a mountain boy. They had gone as far as they could go and had arrived on the edge of nothing.

Like the Comanches raiding to the south, the cedar choppers would occasionally make forays west to work in the fields, but they rarely moved there. Keron Cantwell, from a cedar chopper family who lived near Austin, recalls the family going west to pick cotton. It was 1917, and her mother died in the influenza epidemic. Her father "had to bury my mother in west Texas, a place that was foreign to us all."[26]

The Hill Country was home. The families moved beside the creeks and rivers, and for the first time in a century and a half they went no further. The climate was mild. There was enough fertile land in the valleys to grow a little corn and plenty more for grazing. But most of all, there was good water; the name given the country by the indigenous Tonkawa meant "Land of Good Water."

The limestone cliffs seeped water—more than two hundred springs flowed within seven miles of Georgetown as late as 1960.[27] They ran down the limestone and trickled though the crevices, joining into small rivulets that flowed over rock beds to form creeks with waterfalls and deep, cool pools. Roemer found water so transparent that he could see every leaf of the aquatic plants on the bottom twenty feet below. He said, "I have seen nowhere in America or Europe more beautiful water."[28]

These creeks flowed into rivers that ran swift and clear: the Nueces, Frio, Sabinal, Medina, Guadalupe, Blanco, Pedernales, Llano, Colorado, San Gabriel, and Lampasas. Fed by springs, they ran almost continuously. The 1887 agricultural census describes the Pedernales as "a bold, rapidly running stream, making its way through wild and almost trackless mountain gorges."[29] Olmsted remarked that the upper Guadalupe was "quick and perfectly transparent . . . the rocky banks are clean and inviting; the cypresses rise superbly from the very edge like ornamental columns."[30]

But more than beautiful, the abundance of good water was essential to the cedar chopper way of life. David Hackett Fischer attributes the independent lifestyle of the Appalachian settlers to mountain springs that never ran dry, similar to those in Scotland that had nourished such stubborn defiance of authority.[31] It is no coincidence that the demise of the cedar choppers took place during the decade of one of the worst droughts in Texas history, when the springs ran dry.

The Hill Country on which this book is focused consists of all or parts of fifteen counties west of Austin and San Antonio: Bandera, Blanco, Burnet, Gillespie, Kendall, Kerr, Kimble, Llano, Mason, Real, most of Lampasas and western parts of Comal, Hays, Travis, and Williamson. This is cedar country, home of the golden-cheeked warbler, an endangered species that builds its nests from the bark of mature cedar trees. Its range includes these counties and runs northward through Coryell to Palo Pinto County west of Fort Worth. That northern outpost of cedar country—the country of John Graves's *Hard Scrabble*—is not examined in this book. More than just sharing an occupation, the cedar choppers I profile were like a tribe, all connected through marriage, and all tied to the Hill Country of Central Texas.[32] Like the Tonkawa and the Penateka Comanches before them, they moved freely between Austin, Dripping Springs, Leakey, Kerrville, Junction, and Lometa. These were their boundaries, and this was their territory.

3

The Clans in the Hills

When I first started this project I knew little about the origins of the cedar choppers or even if they were in any sense a "people" or just a bunch of individuals thrown into a similar situation. My best guess, knowing what had happened to farmers in the hardscrabble South during the early twentieth century, was that they were sharecroppers who could not make it in cotton and had turned to cedar to survive. Since sharecroppers tended to move frequently, this would make it unlikely that they had a strong attachment to the hills. Another hypothesis I heard was that they were charcoal burners who had been drawn from afar by the prospects on the Hill Country rivers like the Guadalupe and had only later turned to cutting posts.

But as soon as I began to talk to people I began to see that the family ties went much further back than the early twentieth century. For generations these people had lived west of Austin on the Colorado River and the creeks feeding into it, especially Barton Creek south of the river and to the north along Shoal Creek, Bull Creek, Cypress Creek, Sandy Creek, and Cow Creek (see map of western Travis and Williamson counties). Most of them had come to Central Texas shortly after the Civil War, though some came earlier and had fought on the frontier as Texas Rangers. They shared a common Appalachian heritage, lived near one another in similar circumstances, and intermarried. Over the decades the family bonds grew tighter; by the 1940s and 1950s—what I call the heyday of the cedar choppers—many of them were kin, and it was rare to find someone from the hills whom all the others didn't know. As Ronnie Roberts's sister Mary said, "Everybody knew each other back then. Especially the hillbillies on the outskirts. Even the Oak Hill South Austin ones [like herself] knew the ones out here in North Austin." She proved this by marrying Johnny Boatright, the grandson of Dick Boatright from Bull Creek.

Their memories of these family relationships appeared to be integral to their culture, and it became obvious that to get inside this culture I had to know how people were related—that is, I had to create some semblance of a family tree. By this time many of the names were familiar, and I used Ancestry.com to find ancestors of the people I knew to be cedar choppers and to see whom they had married. For each of these families I created a tree, usually beginning during the mid-nineteenth century and going through the 1940 census, tracing the descendants of these original families, where they lived, and their occupations. Then I connected these family trees through marriage; think of each family tree as a page with ancestors at the top and their descendants below, and parallel to this page are other pages (families) living in the same place during the same period. These pages are linked by marriage. The tree grew until it encompassed more than 2,500 related individuals, and it demonstrated that most of the cedar choppers in the Hill Country counties really were kin to one another (see appendix 2 for more on methodology).

While all the families in the tree were related, certain families had much closer ties with one another. For instance, three of the children of Joseph Almar Roberts, the patriarch of the Roberts family and Ronnie's great-great-grandfather, married Hutsons, and two married Teagues, cementing the bonds among these three families who lived along Barton Creek before the beginning of the twentieth century. Marriages of their children brought in other big families—the Simpsons, the Browns, and the Cantwells, to name a few. A lot of these people, including Tiney Teague, Joseph Almar Roberts, and his great-great-grandson Ronnie, are buried in the Roberts-Teague Cemetery off Bee Cave Road.

I came to call these groups of closely interrelated families "clans," although they did not act as one with established leaders, as had the clans of the Scottish Highlands. But when people talked, "clan" was a word they used. Ronnie Roberts said, "Boatrights—actually one

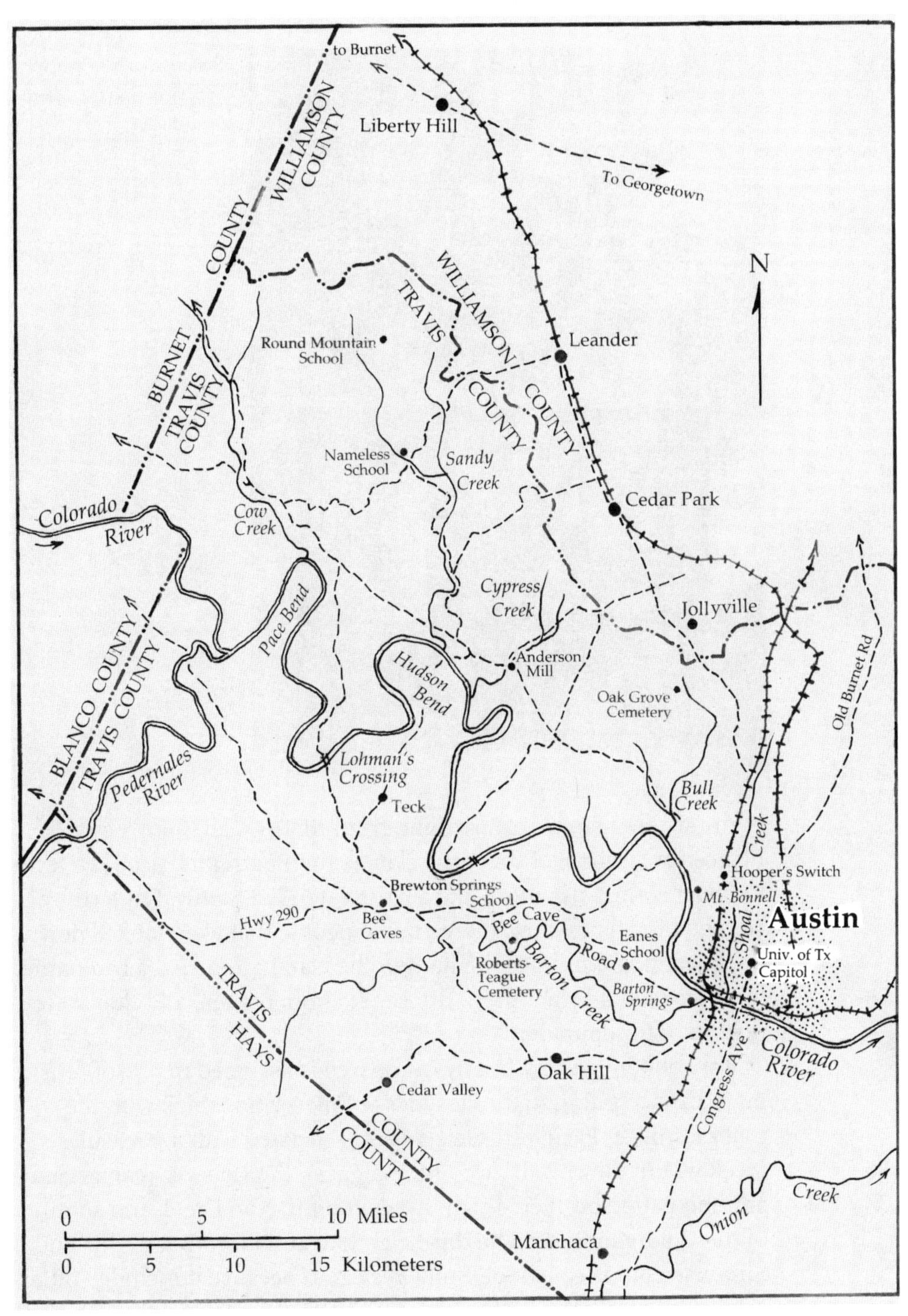

Western Travis and Williamson counties. Map drawn by John Cotter.

HISTORIC TEXAS CEMETERY
TEXAS HISTORICAL COMMISSION
ROBERTS-TEAGUE CEMETERY
IN THE 1860s, THE ROBERTS AND TEAGUE FAMILIES CAME TO THE BEE CAVE AREA WHERE, FOR GENERATIONS, THEIR SKILLS AS FARMERS, RANCHERS, CEDAR CHOPPERS, COAL KILN BURNERS, AND HOMEMAKERS HELPED TO SHAPE ITS DEVELOMENT AND CULTURE. IT IS SAID THAT THIS CEMETERY WAS ESTABLISHED IN 1898 WHEN JOSEPH ROBERTS (1843-1925) OFFERED THE SITE TO THE GRIEVING SIMONS FAMILY FOR AN INFANT'S BURIAL. A NUMBER OF VETERANS ARE LAID TO REST HERE, INCLUDING ALFRED R. (BUCK) SIMPSON (1895-1961), THE SECOND MOST DECORATED SOLDIER OF WORLD WAR I. THIS BURIAL GROUND RECORDS THE LIVES OF THE PIONEERS AND FAMILIES OF THESE ONCE ISOLATED CANYONS OF TRAVIS COUNTY.
HISTORIC TEXAS CEMETERY · 2001

Roberts-Teague Cemetery historical marker. Photo by author.

of my sisters married a Boatright, from that—I call them a clan." Princeton Simons, of the same clan as the Boatrights, used the term to mean something more like a large extended family: "In terms of stereotyping, you know, there's some people that were looked down on, but it was more like the name. The clan had earned a bad name, but here would be another clan, cedar choppers too, and they were held in high reputation."

Consequently every family in the tree is assigned to one of four big clans according to the closeness of its relationships with the other families. Each of these clans is associated with a particular creek where they lived. Two of the biggest, the Roberts-Teague clan and the Patterson-Pierce clan, lived along Barton Creek and south of the Colorado River. The third clan had at its core Boatrights and Simonses but is called the Bull Creek clan because it included other important families who lived there. The fourth clan lived north and west along Sandy Creek and the upper stretches of the Colorado River and is called the Whitt-Maynard-Bonnet clan. The following pages trace the history of each of the four clans in the nineteenth century and show how they ended up in the Austin hills.

The first of the three Austin clans is called the Bull Creek clan because to name just the major families it would have to be called something like the Boatright-Preece-Shannon-Simons-Toungate clan. They lived not only along Bull Creek to Jollyville but also along Shoal Creek into West Austin and along Cypress Creek to Anderson Mill and the Colorado River. Like the Roberts-Teague clan, many of them are buried together, in this case in the Oak Grove Cemetery on Bull Creek Road, where for years there has been a big Fourth of July picnic to celebrate their heritage.

One reason for beginning with the Bull Creek clan is that its roots were in the Hill Country by the mid-nineteenth century. Dick Preece (1833–1906) shows up in the hills west of Austin in 1850 at age seventeen. He and his brothers came to Texas in 1838 from Floyd County, Kentucky—the heart of Appalachia—with their Scots-Irish father and Scots-Cherokee mother. They settled on a crystal clear creek in the hills twelve miles northwest of Austin, where it is said that Dick killed the last male buffalo in Travis County. They named it Bull Creek.

The early history of the Preeces and Shannons illustrates the uniqueness of the Hill Country relating to the big issues of the time—Indians, slavery, and the Civil War. Dick and little brother Will became Texas Rangers, fighting the Comanches during the 1850s under Unionist Governor Elisha Pease. (Pease bought a mansion in West Austin that still stands, and sold the rest of the 365-acre estate to Charles Clark, a freedman, who developed it into Clarksville.) With the expulsion of the Comanches from Central Texas and the beginning of the Civil War, all pro-Union Rangers—and there were many recruited from the raw frontier who had no sympathy for aristocrats and planters—were decommissioned. Dick and his brothers, as well as their brother-in-law Mark Shannon, refused to fight for the Confederacy and took to the hills, branded

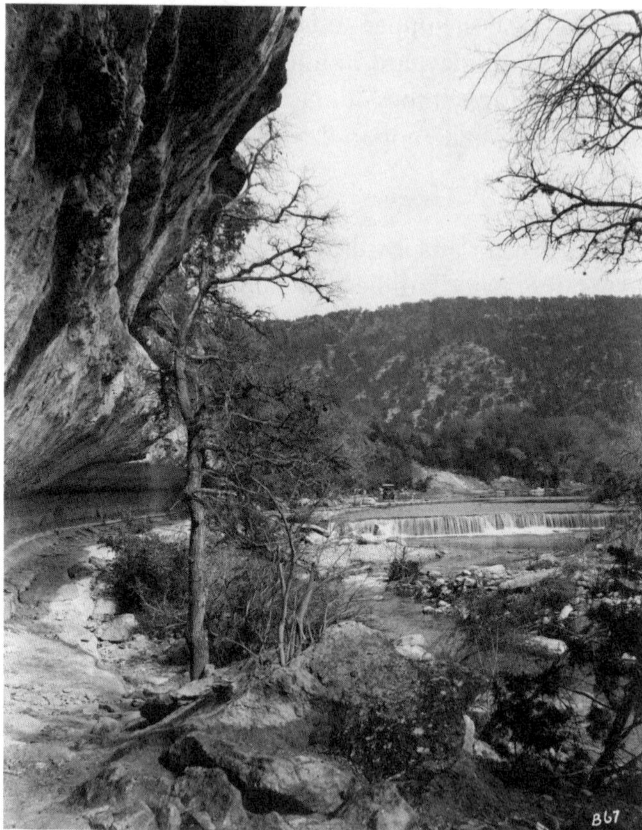

Bull Creek, 1920s. Photo courtesy of Austin History Center, Austin Public Library.

as "deserters from conscription." For two years they used the hollows and caves of Bull Creek to wage guerilla warfare against the Confederate home guard, calling themselves the Mountain Eagles. Dick Preece "turned caves into citadels which belched death on the mounted thugs every time they rode into the hills," wrote his grandson Harold. They "never conquered that detached, unsurrendering patch of the United States which was Bull Creek."[1] This would not be the last time that the hills west of Austin would be a dangerous place for an outsider to enter.

The Preeces and the Shannons eventually joined the First Texas Cavalry of the Union Army, which one source said "consisted primarily of Mexicans, Germans, and Irishmen."[2] They weren't the only men in the clans to fight against the Confederacy: the two sons of Lenearce Boatright of the Bull Creek clan fought on opposing sides—Elisha from northwestern Missouri for the Union and Alexander from Texas for the Confederacy. Joseph Almar Roberts, the patriarch of the Roberts side of the Roberts-Teague clan, fought for the Union in the 29th Illinois Infantry. The Teague side fought for the Confederacy—but some perhaps not wholeheartedly: it appears that the patriarch of one of three branches of Hill Country Teagues, William Marion, was kept from fighting by understating his age. The 1850 census shows him to be five years old, but the 1860 census shows his age as only eleven, not fifteen. In the other clans, the patriarch of the Pierces was a Confederate, as were the Whitts.

The Hill Country of Texas, like the Appalachian counties of Tennessee and Kentucky, was divided on the issue of secession. All but 18 of 122 Texas counties approved secession in the 1861 Referendum; only in the Hill Country did a major block of counties oppose it.[3] The heavily German counties of Gillespie, Kendall, and Mason voted against secession, but so did Burnet, Uvalde, and Medina and even populated Travis and Williamson.[4] Many residents of the Hill Country did not support slavery because there were very

A Bull Creek family. Photo courtesy of Austin History Center, Austin Public Library.

few slaves west of the Balcones Fault. The issues of the deep South and the lowland plains of Texas were not the issues of the Hill Country—the immediate danger lay to the west, beyond the edge of nothing on the Llano Estacado. That area was called Comanchería, and men who could fight were needed at home.

Partly because of their heritage from a land with few slaves, race does not appear to have been a central issue in cedar chopper culture. Living out in the hills, they did not have much association with African Americans.[5] There appears to be little evidence of the overt racism that might be expected from a people some might place at the low end on a scale of whiteness. While they might have called a slingshot a "nigger shooter" without missing a beat, and would undoubtedly have used the same word as a central marker of identity, like "banker" or "one-armed," there does not seem to be much more to it than that. It did not hurt that Bill Pickett, who invented bulldogging and was the first black inductee into the National Rodeo Cowboy Hall of Fame, came from a family of cowboys in the Jenks Branch community between Leander and Liberty Hill that was well known to residents of the area, many of whom were cedar choppers. In 1941 Babe Pickett brought supplies for the war effort to nearby Nameless school; the teacher Easter Whitt told her students that he was a gentleman from whose example they could all learn.[6] And when push came to shove, as in the 1920s when the Ku Klux Klan tried to intimidate Emmett Shelton's brother, Emmett said, "All of Papa's friends in Bee Cave, Creedmoor and around, including the Simpsons, they wanted Pap to point these Ku Klux out to them so they could start shooting 'em. . . . Buck [Simpson] had it in his craw that he wanted to whip a Ku Klux . . . most Austin police were Ku Klux."

One of the few places where cedar choppers and blacks did meet was in parts of Austin like Clarksville, the community in West Austin that Gary Cartwright said was "comfortably integrated, making it unique in Austin and probably anywhere else in Texas." He wrote a 1977 article in *Texas Monthly* about a cedar chopper he called Henry Polk—a real person but a fictitious name—who grew up in Clarksville in the 1930s. "We played and fought with the niggers just like they was our own," Henry said. "There was two old ex-slaves, Aunt Eady and Aunt Jenny Moe, lived just down the street from our place. My daddy used to make us call all old folks uncle or aunt no matter what color they was."[7]

Two important families in the Bull Creek clan are the Simonses and the Boatrights. D. D. Simons (1856–1919) came from Michigan and started a large family on Bull Creek, listing his occupation in 1900 as "manufacturing charcoal." Lenearce Boatright followed the more typical route to Texas: he was born in central Virginia in 1798, married in Warren County, Kentucky, lived for a while in Missouri, and finally came to Williamson County after the Civil War. More than one of his sons came to Texas, and there are a lot of Boatrights who are related to this branch of the family. But it is his grandson Lee (1860–1943) who is the major figure of the Bull Creek Boatrights. He married Annie Williams, the daughter of Evan Williams from Wales, one of the few non-native-born ancestors of the clans (but of the same Celtic heritage). Evan owned several hundred acres of land along Bull Creek in 1850, and the marriages of his children acted like glue uniting Boatrights, Simonses, Shannons, Cantrells and Waechters.

The Waechters were very much a part of the Bull Creek community despite the fact that the old man had come directly from Germany. As we will see in chapter 4, his son Paul would be the central figure in the "Travis County Dog Wars" of 1902, when once again the Bull Creek community resisted incursions from Austin. Not many German families in the hills married into cedar chopper families. Joseph Almar Roberts married Henrietta Freitag, and some of the Marx boys of Oak Hill and Bonnets of Leander became cedar choppers themselves. But generally the feeling was one of mutual incompatibility. The Germans worked even harder than the cedar choppers, fencing off the valleys with stone walls built with thousands of hours of family labor, while the grandparents of the cedar choppers were free-grazing the hills and not worrying much about any crop except a little patch of cotton for spending money. When Charlie Marx wanted to marry Edna Patterson, "Papa say, 'You needn't think you gonna marry a Dutchman. Cause you're not—he'll work you to death.'" On the other side Lorenz Bading's father, a farmer in Comal county, called the cedar choppers coming into New Braunfels from the western hills "dreckig Amerikaner," or "dirty Americans." During the 1960s anyone growing up in the Hill Country could have pointed out the difference between a German farm and an "American" one, because the former was tidy with good stone walls and outbuildings, while the latter was probably overgrazed and had generations of farm and household equipment rusting in the fields surrounding a run-down house. But the cost of this neatness was, of course, work. By no means were the cedar choppers lazy, but when they worked, they made money. Neatness was not nearly as desirable as leisure.

Dick Boatright, one of Lee's kids, was a contemporary and friend of Dick Simons, one of D.D.'s kids, during the heyday of the cedar choppers in the 1940s and 1950s. Not only were they first cousins by marriage, but both had ancestors prominent in the Indian wars. I interviewed Don Simons, Dick Simons's nephew, and he was proud that his great-grandfather was Texas Ranger Jim King, a man with sparkling blue eyes, reddish brown hair, and an Irish brogue. The great-grandfather of Dick Boatright's wife was Tsa'l-au-te (Cry-of-the-Wild-Goose), an army scout and the favorite son of the famous Kiowa chief Satanta. The roots of these families were on the Texas frontier, and they were proud of their warrior heritage.

Two of the biggest clans—Roberts-Teague and Patterson-Pierce—lived along Barton Creek and south of the Colorado River in what are now the Rollingwood, West Lake Hills, Oak Hill, and Bee Cave areas. The first direct ancestor of the Teague side of the Roberts-Teague clan was William Marion Teague, born in Kentucky in 1796. He married Elizabeth Bales of Scots-Irish descent when they were both twenty-two, and he either died or divorced, for it was she who took her children to Missouri in 1834 in a wagon. She left Missouri about 1853 with six of her sons and two daughters, settled for a while near Fort Worth, and then moved to Travis County. Three of the children—Wesley, William Riley, and Hulda– would start three major branches of the Teagues. The first two settled along Barton Creek and the last in the western Hill Country.

Wesley's son William Teague married an immigrant from

Tsa'l-au-te (Kiowa), early 1870s. Photo by William S. Soule, from Wikimedia Commons.

Prussia named Sophia, who got separated from her father upon landing at Galveston at age fifteen and walked to Austin. There she married a Swedish man named Anderson, who had land near Barton Springs but died during the war, and she then married William in 1868 at age twenty-eight. William and Sophia bought 500 more acres of land from the Eanes ranch, two acres of which they later donated for Eanes school, and they had seven children. One of William's children married the daughter of the patriarch of the Roberts family, Joseph Almar, and three more of Joseph Almar's children married children of William's sister Rhoda (these relationships are shown in the Teague family tree on page 216).

The other Teague brother whose family settled along Barton Creek was William Riley, who died while serving as a blacksmith for the Confederacy. His first son, John Malcolm, bought 1,400 acres that stretched from Barton Creek to the Colorado River, including 60 acres of good bottomland, for fifteen to twenty-five cents an acre. John Malcolm and his wife had three sons whom we will meet

Joseph Almar Roberts and son Henry (right). Photo courtesy of Gail Roberts Gonzales.

again—John, Tom, and Homer Teague. Son John's trial for murder in 1911 was one of the most spectacular court cases in Travis County history, and his story later this chapter illustrates the violence of the time. Homer was probably the most famous cedar chopper on Bee Cave Road in the years when Austin began to move west into the hills, and we will learn more about him later in the book.

William Riley Teague's daughter Mattie, through children from her two marriages, integrated some of the most notorious of the Westlake families into the Roberts-Teague clan. Her marriage to Henry Tucker in 1872 produced only daughters, one every year for six years. Annie Mae, the oldest, married Charlie Pierce of the Patterson-Pierce clan and had son Litten, whom we met in chapter 1. Lula married Duff Short, whose sons Walter, Earl, and Charlie got into serious trouble and became infamous but never served time. Earl was a bootlegger, and his story is told in that context. Mary Francis married Jim Plumley, who died violently in 1935. Mattie, the youngest of the Tucker sisters, married Buddy Brown, whose family at one time owned lots of land and had a registered cattle brand, but they lost it and became one of the iconic cedar chopper families along Bee Cave Road. Buddy often carried a rifle, rode a big white horse, and wore a black hat with the band made of rattlesnake skin decorated with the rattles.

The most notorious of the families that came from Mattie Teague's first marriage were the Youngs. Kate Tucker married Ol Young in 1897, and in 1906 Ol's brother Tom was hanged for the brutal murder of a young girl near Florence. The trial of the "desperate mountaineer" received a lot of coverage in the papers, partly because Tom Young was so violent and unrepentant. His hanging, the last in Williamson County, was attended by thousands. There was fear among lawmen that a rescue attempt might be made by Tom's friends from the hills, but his crime was so beyond the pale that he had no support. Even his uncle, a Baptist preacher, said it was "far better he should die" than to go on in the life he was

Mattie Teague, Charlie Pierce, and Annie Mae Tucker. Photo courtesy of Janet Taylor-Carusi.

leading.[8] Later Ol himself was killed over a minor incident. Several of their boys were involved in violence during the 1930s, including the killing of a federal agent, and these incidents are discussed in later chapters. Of the Youngs, the lawyer Emmett Shelton said, "The reputation that the family had was that there hadn't been a natural death among the male members for three generations."

The third branch of the Hill Country Teagues was started by Hulda, who married Tim Ratliff (1830–1904). Tim fought for the Confederacy, and he was the great-grandfather of Simon Ratliff, one of the last of the true cedar choppers among my interviewees. The Ratliffs moved around a lot, living as far west as Vanderpool and Uvalde and north to San Saba and Lometa, probably following the cedar. Tim's father was from Tennessee, and in 1818 he married Jane Tumlinson from North Carolina. Her father was one of Stephen F. Austin's Old Three Hundred, and her brothers became famous during the Texas Revolution and later as Rangers. In 1836 her brother John led a company of Rangers to build the first Anglo-American post in Williamson County, on what is now called Block House Creek in Leander.[9]

Tom Young (bowtie), 1906. Photo courtesy of Williamson Museum, 2012.018.004.

Closely related to the Roberts-Teague clan, because Mary Patterson married Joe L. Roberts and Charlie Pierce married Annie Tucker, is the Patterson-Pierce clan. They form the second of the Barton Creek clans. Charlie Pierce's father had moved from Mississippi to Travis County by 1859 and fought as a sergeant in the 30th Texas Cavalry. His son Litten married Edna Patterson, Mary's sister and Luther's mother.

The plight of the Pattersons exemplifies an important element of the violence prevalent in Texas during the latter half of nineteenth century: the feuds of the Reconstruction era. Three of my own father's older brothers were killed in Colorado County in incidents related to the Jaybird-Peckerwood feud. But the deadliest Texas feud, with as many as eighty persons killed between 1867 and 1880, was the Sutton-Taylor feud in DeWitt County southeast of San Antonio.[10] On one side were the Texas State Police and the county law of the Sutton faction, which included one of Jane Tumlinson's brothers, who commanded a group of vigilante lawmen called Tumlinson's Regulators. When Peyton Patterson married Annie Sutton in 1869, he became a part of that faction. On the other side were the Taylors and eventually the gunman John Wesley Hardin, called the most dangerous man in Texas. Peyton Patterson was killed by Hardin's cousin Manning Clements in 1872, shot off his horse, unarmed, just a couple of months after his son Pate was born. Mack Sutton, whose great-grandfather was in the feud, said, "The Taylors and Suttons waylaid one another—man, it was like guerrilla warfare, just kill 'em any way you could. Ambush 'em and shoot 'em off their horses, any way you could." The violence escalated until Annie and some of the Suttons moved west. Thus Pate Patterson, the father of Edna and Mary, escaped with his mother, living in Luling as a child and moving to Travis County by 1900.

The last clan, the Whitt-Maynard-Bonnet clan, lived northwest along Sandy Creek and the Colorado River and from there north into the hills toward Leander and Liberty Hill. John Wesley Whitt grew up in the heart of Appalachia. He was born in 1823 in Russell County, Virginia, and married sixteen-year-old Rhoda in 1848 in Wayne County, West Virginia. After fighting for the Confederacy he and his family moved to northwestern Williamson County near the little town of Bagdad, on the stage line from Austin to Lampasas. When the census was taken in 1870 John and Rhoda had nine children, one born about every two years since she was sixteen. By 1880 they would have three more.

John Wesley's younger sister Nancy married Martin Maynard in 1854. He was born in Kentucky and moved to Wayne County, West Virginia, before joining the 167th Regiment of the Virginia Militia, a Confederate unit in the heavily divided county. The couple stayed in West Virginia after the war and moved to Travis County in the 1880s.

Martin Maynard appears in the census of western Travis County in 1890 on an addendum listing veterans of the Civil War. Below him on the Veterans Schedules is his brother George W. Maynard, who was a corporal in "45 Ky Cav," the 45th Kentucky Mounted Infantry, a Union regiment.[11] He is shown as having been a prisoner of war at Andersonville, the Confederate prison where conditions were so dire that a third of the prisoners died, and as having gone to Minnesota with his wife after the war. Thus it appears that Martin and George are another set of brothers in the clans who fought on opposite sides of the Civil War. This branch of the family were called the "Bloody Holler Maynards," because they lived in Bloody Hollow off RM 1431.

John Whitt's grandson Connie Whitt (1881–1978) raised a big family near Liberty Hill: his daughter Edna married a Turner from Cow Creek, whom I interviewed, and I now live on the ranch formerly owned by Connie Whitt's son Bernard Whitt. Another daughter, Lorna Whitt, married Frank Maynard, further cementing relationships between these two families, and Katy Whitt married Zeke Bonnet. The Bonnets are the last big family in the clan. Zeke's grandfather Heinrich came to Texas from Germany at age ten and fought in a Union cavalry regiment, rising to the rank of captain.

Arvil Maynard family. Photo from a public member tree on Ancestry.com, attached to Arvil Maynard in the Krenek Family Tree on May 26, 2012, consent D. Krenek.

Katy Whitt and Zeke Bonnet. Photo from a public member tree on Ancestry.com, attached to Arvil Maynard in the Bonnet Family Tree on March 25, 2008, consent Carolyn Bonnet.

The stories of the clans settling in the hills west of Austin has as its backdrop the drama of nineteenth-century Texas history. Some, like the Tumlinsons, came early and fought in the Texas Revolution and on the frontier as Rangers. Most came right after the Civil War, having fought on one side or the other. The violence continued into Reconstruction-era Texas, sometimes escalating into deadly situations like the Sutton-Taylor feud that caused Pate Patterson's mother to escape to the hills with her family.

The violence of this period was formative for the clans. When members of the clans emerge on the Austin scene at the turn of the century, it is in stories of violence, and well into the next century there seems to have been a violent streak running through cedar chopper culture. Their response to insult was an almost instinctive resort to deadly force, sometimes with a knife or a gun. Fistfights, if not for fun, were brutal, with the desire to hurt. Their Scots-Irish background has something to do with it, but this cultural disposition was almost certainly hardened by the lawlessness of the Texas frontier. Immediate and brutal retaliation was the only effective response to a world without order.

The Civil War was dehumanizing to all who fought in it, but not enough has been reported about the real menace to Texans on the frontier, undoubtedly told and retold to children of the clans in graphic detail. The Civil War drew soldiers and Rangers east, leaving scattered settlements west of a line through the Hill Country vulnerable to lightning raids by mounted warriors. In just two years beginning in the summer of 1865, 163 Texans were killed and 43 more were captured by the Kiowas and Comanches.[12] While there were certainly other tribes in the American West that were a menace to whites, only in Texas was there a large population of farm families within reach of a warrior tribe that could strike swiftly from hundreds of miles away and then escape back into the unknown. Texas historian T. R. Fehrenbach observes, "For forty years, this bleeding ground was filled with men and boys, wives and sons, who had kinfolk carried off, never to be heard from again or to be ransomed . . . teen-age girls and women returned to their relatives with demented stares."[13]

After the Civil War the Comanches and Kiowas were assigned to reservations, but their lifestyle and livelihood were based on raiding to steal horses and captives, and their hatred for Texans made it seem unreasonable to stop because of a treaty made with the Americans. In May 1871, only hours after General William

Tecumseh Sherman had passed by on a tour of the frontier, Satanta led a raid by 150 Kiowas on a wagon train supplying the forts. The carnage they left made Sherman listen to the pleas from Texans; he changed his mind regarding the policy of tolerance and arrested Satanta and two others who led the raid.[14] Satanta's death by diving from a high window at Huntsville prison was the inspiration for the scene of Blue Duck's death plunge in Larry McMurtry's *Lonesome Dove*.

The following story was told by Serilda Cox, a cousin of Hugh Cox, a Ranger in the western Hill Country. He married the daughter of a Cantrell of the Bull Creek clan, and his granddaughter married a Maples of the Roberts-Teague clan. Stories like this were probably often heard among the clans in the hills during evenings before radio.

In 1865 the Cox family moved to a branch of the Nueces River, the most westerly of the Hill Country rivers. They and the Binghams were the first settlers in this rough country, and they lived in tents for two months without seeing any Indians. Then one morning about twenty-five Indians came yelling and running toward the tents. Hugh's grandfather grabbed his flintlock but had failed to load it after shooting a turkey, and as he reloaded he was shot in the leg with an arrow. John Bingham and his wife were also wounded, and Serilda's little sister was grabbed. When old man Cox saw the chief exposed through the brush, he shot and mortally wounded the leader. In retaliation the Indians killed the little girl and dragged the chief away in silence. Henry followed their trail, found the dead chief, and scalped him. Serilda was fourteen. Her little sister was four.[15]

The Comanche menace ended with Quanah Parker's surrender in 1875, but that decade was still violent on much of the Texas frontier. Lipan Apache and Kickapoo renegades were raiding across the Rio Grande until finally stopped by Rangers. A confederation of outlaws took over Kimble County on the western edge of the Hill Country until a concerted effort by lawmen led to the arrest of forty men.[16] Mason County had the Hoodoo War in 1875–76, and DeWitt and Gonzalez counties suffered the Sutton-Taylor feud.

In 1878 a dog brought a human head with a bullet hole in

the back to Jasper Brown's house on the road to Bee Cave. They believed it to be the stepson of Sparlin Young, the father of Ol and Tom Young.[17] A decade later Wesley Collier of the Bull Creek clan was shot in his bed near Liberty Hill by a Ranger who had been chasing him for months. He was one of four men who had killed an old German in Fredericksburg. Two others were caught and one of them was burned alive in his cell by another of the killers to keep him from talking.[18] And there was plenty of accidental violence. In 1876 Bennie Anderson, son of the immigrant Sophia who married William Teague, accidentally killed his younger brother Willie while playing "sheriff and outlaw."

This was also the period of famous outlaws such as Jesse James, Sam Bass, and John Wesley Hardin. Many people were sympathetic to these men: Jesse James was sometimes portrayed as a victim of discrimination against Confederates, and the Taylors of the Sutton-Taylor Feud were the good ol' boys who stood up to the Texas Police. In 1877 the James boys stayed the night with the family of Rufus Moore of the Roberts-Teague clan and the grandfather of one of my interviewees. "The law was chasing 'em across Texas and my dad put 'em up for the night," recalled Moore's grandfather. "They were real gentlemen and never did a poor man a bit a harm in their lives."[19] Sam Bass was known to tip porters on the trains he robbed, and he once paid the mortgage of a poor widow and then robbed the bank to steal it back.[20] As the "Ballad of Sam Bass" goes, "A kinder-hearted fellow, you'd scarcely ever see. He always drank good liquor, and spent his money free." And none other than Bob Dylan assures us, despite evidence to the contrary, that "John Wesley Hardin was a friend to the poor . . . he was never known to hurt an honest man."

Kids on the violent frontier looked up to these outlaws. When the families on the frontier were becoming increasingly marginalized by the pace of postwar economic change, they sympathized with outlaws who stood up against the official system of law. William and Sophia Teague moved from Austin about 1888 because, according to Fred Teague, their boys "were getting so rough and uncontrollable they decided to get them away from the city. They took as heroes the early outlaws such as Sam Bass."[21]

It is in the context of this late nineteenth-century culture of violence, both real and romanticized, that we can begin to understand two widely publicized stories around the turn of the century about men in the cedar chopper clans. The first, in 1896, involved the Browns and the second, in 1911, the Teagues.

It was on a Sunday morning in early May of 1896 that Dempsey Brown and Jim Nixon gunned each other down in the middle of the Colorado River. Dempsey Brown was the son of Jasper Brown, whose dog had found the human head, and the older brother of Buddy Brown, the man with the rattlesnake hatband. Dempsey was crossing the river in his wagon at McGill's Ford, a couple of miles west of Austin at the end of Pecan Street, past the Deep Eddy that is the site of the historic swimming pool. He was taking his wife Sallie and her sister Jennie on an outing when Jim Nixon, Jennie's estranged husband, drove up beside the wagon and shot Brown. Brown had instinctively raised his shotgun at the same time, emptying both barrels at Nixon. He was trying to reload when he fell forward in the wagon, shot through the heart. Nixon was peppered with buckshot and floated down the river until he could pull himself up on the sand. He died two weeks later in jail. The newspaper said Dempsey Brown had persuaded Jennie to leave Nixon and live with them, and he had publicly threatened to kill Nixon on sight if Nixon tried to take her back.[22]

A year before, another story, "An Exciting Elopement," said that Dempsey and a bunch of men who lived west of Austin had awakened the sheriff at 3:00 a.m. to report that forty-six-year-old Nixon had just run away with Dempsey's "niece, only thirteen years old," begging the sheriff to arrest him.[23] He had actually run away with Dempsey's wife's sister Jennie, and she was probably just a little over fifteen years old.

The bad blood between Dempsey Brown and Jim Nixon went way back before that. Twenty years earlier Jim Nixon had married Mary Brown, Dempsey's sixteen-year-old younger sister. The next year he was convicted of cattle theft. By the time he ran away with young Jennie years later, he was a "a well-known character in criminal circles and a married man."[24] There was no way Dempsey was going to let him take the girl back, and he died trying to prevent it. When burying Dempsey, his wife Sallie threw his gun into the grave, saying "Dempsey can finish this fight in Hell."[25]

The second story of turn-of-the century violence follows a similar theme, the protection of a woman's honor. It concerns the trial of John Teague (1872–1963) for the murder of John Gest and a deputy sheriff.[26]

John Gest and his bartender Max Himmelreich ran a saloon in 1911 at the southwest corner of South Congress and Monroe Street. Bars like his were abundant in what is now downtown Austin: the 1910 city directory lists two beer gardens and over forty saloons for a town of less than 30,000 people. Many of the owners, like forty-two-year old Gest, were of German origin. Over half the saloons were between First Street and Sixth Street; there were only a couple south of the river on Congress and a couple more as far north as 38th Street and West Avenue. West of that, both north and south, was nothing but hills, canyons, and cedar brakes.

John Teague and his wife Mattie had been married about three years when they moved to Austin from Caldwell with their fourteen-month-old baby on a Sunday afternoon in September, 1911. They had nowhere to stay, and so camped on a vacant lot on First Street for a night. Money did not seem to pose a big problem, because the following week they rented a house, and John was back trading horses, which he was good at. John may have been illiterate, but he was smart.

Two of John Teague's sisters lived at the Gest household. John's oldest living sister, Mamie, had been married to Gest for seventeen years. His youngest sister Myrtle, not yet sixteen though she claimed to be older, was a live-in housekeeper for Gest (see Teague family tree in appendix 2). When John and his wife came back to live in Austin, Gest's wife Mamie was nowhere to be found.

John's wife Mattie went to the Gest house after the trip to do laundry, and found young Myrtle Teague outside hanging up clothes. Mattie said at the trial, "Mr. Gest came in his buggy. He passed her just as she was hanging out a garment. He punched her in the side. He had his back to me and I could not see the expression on his face. Myrtle Teague did not laugh at the man's action. A

South Congress Avenue, 1914. Photo courtesy of Austin History Center, Austin Public Library.

little later, however, he took her into the barn, which is back of the house. They were there about twenty-five minutes."

Mattie didn't immediately tell her husband John what she had seen, but she did say that perhaps John should talk to his young sister. He had been in this position before with his sister Mamie before her marriage to Gest; she admitted in testimony that John had "frequently tried to get her to reform," including taking her into his home in Waco. John and Gest did not get along well—John once said he had "hell with that Dutchman down at the saloon," and Gest resented that John had not paid back the money loaned him by Gest's wife when he got out of Huntsville the second time. John went to Gest's saloon shortly after their return to Austin and had a beer. Neither man said a word to the other.

The following Saturday John heeded his wife's advice and went to the saloon to talk to his young sister Myrtle. He came unarmed and spoke to her from his horse. "I told her that in my understanding she hadn't done the right thing. I told her that she was taking the place of her other sister. I didn't abuse her. I did tell her, however, that she ought to be ashamed of herself. I asked her to get up and go away. I asked her to go to my home." On the stand, Myrtle Teague was asked, "'Didn't your brother tell you that two of your sisters had gone wrong and that he wanted you to live pure and right?' Witness replied to the affirmative. 'I finally promised to go to Irene's (another sister) that night,'" she said. Then Gest appeared in the doorway of the saloon, and it looked to John as if he might be drawing a pistol, so "I dug my spur in the little cow pony I was riding, wheeled and rode off."

John was upset by his talk with his younger sister and the menacing situation with Gest, and on his way home he had several glasses of beer. When he returned his wife related what she had seen earlier in the week. Upon hearing of the interaction between Gest and Myrtle, John drank most of a pint of whiskey and said, "Mattie, you get ready and go with me. I am going over to see if I can't straighten this out. I want you to face Gest and tell him what you have told me." He denied that he was planning to kill Gest, "that is, not if he would do the right thing," but he was carrying his .44 Winchester rifle.

On his way to confront Gest, John Teague stopped at several saloons, leaving his wife outside holding the infant while he went in and had a drink. The third baseman on the Austin team remembered him coming into a saloon drunk and carrying his rifle. Teague used the proprietor's phone to call for a buggy to drive him south of the river.

By this time it was late in the evening, and John was very drunk. He came up to the saloon and saw Gest sitting at a table near the door. He called for him to come out and said he saw him reach into his shirt for a pistol. "Gest cut his eye up at me that way (grimacing) and threw his hand down this way and I ups with my gun and shot him. Before he fell, I shot him again, and after he fell I shot him again." He was heard to say, "God damn you—I'll show you how to insult my sister."

The bartender Max Himmelreich was standing behind the bar witnessing this scene, and John turned on him and said, "I believe

I'll just kill you too." He shot, missing Max's head by only an inch and shattering the mirror behind. Max dropped behind the bar and ran out the back while John fired a couple more shots in his direction. After that John started walking west down Monroe Street toward the cedar brakes, his departure lit by one of Austin's famous moonlight towers.

But the shooting had been heard all over South Austin, and a deputy sheriff named George Duncan pulled on his clothes, grabbed his pistol, and ran out of his house—right into John Teague. He wrestled with Teague, who shot him several times, leaving him writhing in the middle of the road. Teague then stopped at the house of John Freitag, the brother-in-law of Joseph Almar Roberts. A woman at the house recalls, "A man came running up and fell over the partition fence against the house. He ran up the steps and I told him that he couldn't come in. 'Give me some cartridges,' he said. I told him I had no cartridges. He again tried to come into the house. I told him there was a sick woman in the house. He asked for a drink of water and I gave him one. Afterward I gave him three more. He said: 'My name is John Teague. I have killed John Gest, his bartender and another man. He is laying down there in the road.'"

The next morning John was apprehended without resistance. He lay injured, having fallen from a twenty-five-foot cliff during the night as he worked his way west into the cedar brakes. He was avoiding roads because he said he had heard a posse was after him and thought it might lynch him, and he had planned to give himself up the next day.

John Teague's murder trial was said to have been one of the most dramatic in the history of Central Texas: "The eager, curious crowd—one of the largest that has ever crowded into the courtroom—jammed the aisles and pushed its way up against the railing all day long." The state pushed for the death penalty, calling it a "cowardly assassination from the dark." Teague's attorneys based his defense on fits of insanity that ran in the family and the "unwritten law."

The "unwritten law"—the statue in Texas was overturned in only 1974—provided that "homicide is justifiable when committed by the husband upon one taken in the act of adultery with the wife."[27]

In this case it was an older brother defending his young sister from a man older than John himself, and *married* to another of his sisters. He said he wanted her to "live pure and right." His father was too old to do anything to help and his younger brother Tom was in prison. If John was to defend the honor of his sisters—of his family—he had to put a stop to Gest's indecency.

John Teague and Dempsey Brown, each intervening in the relationship of a young sister or sister-in-law, acted the way they did because they were immersed in what has been called a "culture of honor," where "vengeance is not optional; it is obligatory. Some measure of revenge must be taken; it cannot simply be forsaken or ignored."[28] To have a relationship openly with the younger sister of your wife is an insult to each woman and to the entire family, and "since a reputation for strength is of the essence in the culture of honor, the individual who insults someone must be forced to retract; if the instigator refuses, he must be punished—with violence or even death. A particularly important kind of insult is one directed at female members of a man's family."[29] When John's youngest sister Myrtle was on the stand, "she cried as she admitted the love that her brother bore for her and told the jury that she still loved him although she feared him."

The insanity plea was based upon the claim that some members of the family, including John, were prone to "fits of insanity." To substantiate this claim, the defense called each member of Teague's family to the stand, starting with his mother. The *Austin Statesman* covered every moment in lurid detail, presenting the amazing spectacle taking place in the courtroom in a style of newspaper reporting that withheld nothing: "The astonished courtroom attendants and hangers-on were afforded the novel spectacle of a woman, promulgating it for the consideration of all, that her husband was partially insane, that her oldest son, a second son, and at least one daughter were afflicted with the mental defect, and that another daughter was an idiot. Indeed, to make the scene more complete, the woman's sixteen-year-old daughter was marched into the courtroom, stood by her mother's side in front of the jury, and exhibited thus." The mother said, "John has spells of insanity. . . . He gets excited and goes into these spells. . . . Liquor nearly always affects him that way." She related that once "he followed his brother with a gun all night, trying to kill him."

What she did not say was that the reason John had been after his younger brother Tom back in 1903 had likewise involved a woman's honor. His father had testified in that earlier trial that he was "expecting trouble between the boys for some time. They have been at outs for months, and all because Tom is in love with John's stepdaughter. John don't want him to go with her." John waited for Tom at his sister's house on East Fourth Street, and when Tom drove up he asked him if he had his gun. Tom replied, "You bet I have," and both fired. John went down when the shot from Tom's .44 Winchester tore into his shoulder. John was indicted for assault with intent to murder, but was acquitted when their father said Tom was the aggressor: Tom had told John on the morning of the trouble "he had just as well buy a coffin, for Tom intended to kill him on sight." This story, had it been told, would have shown that John's reaction in both cases was not a spontaneous fit of insanity but a calculated response to his obligation as a protector of the family's honor.

The jury in the 1911 case voted eight to four for the death penalty, and later three of the four jurors agreed to go with the majority. But one man whose brother had been spared from death by an insanity plea held out, and John Teague was sentenced to prison for life for killing Gest, and again for killing the deputy. He was pardoned only ten years later, in 1921.

There is a sequel to this story.[30] Mamie Teague, Gest's widow and John's sister, married the bartender Max Himmelreich, and they lived near Second Street. In the early 1930s an old man showed up at Emmett Shelton's law office wanting Shelton to represent him. He said his name was John Teague and that he had been living with his sister Mamie and receiving his old-age pension. One evening soon after he had cashed the check, he drank too much and fell asleep. When he awoke his money was gone, and he figured that Mamie and this man—Emmett Shelton says it was her boyfriend but it could have been Max—went through his pockets and took his money. John knew they were probably in one of the bars on Sixth Street, so he grabbed his shotgun and walked north on East Avenue, where I-35 is today. He saw the man across the wide road and shot him. The shotgun must have been loaded with bird shot, because at that distance it barely pierced his skin. John was charged with assault with intent to murder. His defense was simple and effective; he maintained he had not intended to kill the man, saying, "Now, Judge, you know me, and you've knowed me a long time, and you know I ain't never shot at nobody intending to kill 'em unless I done it." He pleaded guilty to a charge of aggravated assault and was sentenced to thirty days in jail.

Max Himmelreich died just a few years later, in 1937. His wife Mamie Teague Gest Himmelreich lived until 1982. She was 104 years old.

The Early Twentieth Century

Whiskey and posts and a little subsistence farming—those were what you could do in the hills, after the cotton and the grass played out and the cedar moved in. . . . The cedar people asked less of the land and of life than those who had come before; the land had much less to give.

John Graves, *Hard Scrabble*

During the decades of violence at the end of the nineteenth century, economic forces were at work in Texas that would be formative for the people who would become cedar choppers. Recently built railroads began providing a way to move cotton to markets from fields far from the waterways that had been necessary for transport, allowing farming to spread into the fertile Blackland Prairie of Central Texas. After 1880 this area grew 44 percent of the state's cotton and became the most densely populated area of Texas.[1] The population of Williamson County soared, growing from 15,155 to 42,228 between 1880 and 1910.[2] Most of this growth was on the farms in the eastern half of the county—the urban population of Georgetown, Round Rock, and Taylor stayed constant at 20 percent of the total. Many of the newcomers were of German and Czech descent.

Cotton on the Blackland Prairie

It is impossible to overstate the importance of cotton to the lives of rural Texans at the turn of the twentieth century. The average farm in Central Texas was about 100 acres, divided between garden, pasture, corn and cotton. Corn was a staple food and feed for mules and chickens, but only cotton could give small farmers the money to buy a few items—sugar, flour, tobacco, shoes, tools—that were necessary to supplement the food they grew. During these years, a 500-pound bale of cotton would bring $50 at the average price of $0.10 per pound. But the majority of these farmers could only plant about ten acres, for cotton required huge amounts of labor for weeding and picking. At two acres per bale, families without the means to hire labor worked "from can see to can't" to earn $250.[3] Most women did field work, twice as many as northern and western farm women. During peak seasons, three-fourths of white women on the Blackland Prairie were working in the cotton patch seven to nine hours a day.[4]

Early in the twentieth century the price of cotton rose and stayed above $0.15 per pound until the Great Depression. When it reached $0.35 in 1919, some farmers with good land in Central Texas lived "high on the hog," building fine houses and buying cars.[5] But most could not: their land was becoming less productive, and they needed every dollar just to pay back the advances for seed and supplies.

The implicit promise of farming after the Civil War was that a farmer could climb the "agricultural ladder" from farm hand to tenant to owner. But instead of a ladder, after 1880 it was an escalator going down, and small farmers could not run fast enough to keep up. They fell from the status of independent tenant farmer, providing all inputs but the land and giving the landlord a third of the corn and a fourth of the cotton, to the status of sharecropper, working with the landlord's animals and tools and giving the owner half of both crops.[6] It was little different than being a wage laborer, except that it was subject to all the risks of cotton farming, such as the boll weevil and drought. When prices turned down in the Depression, a massive migration from the farms would occur, not only in Central Texas and the cotton-growing South but also in the wheat-growing Panhandle, where low prices and the environmental disaster of the Dust Bowl emptied the Plains.[7]

Farming the Hills

The Hill Country soil was not like the Black Waxy of the prairies to the east. Once you left the fertile bottoms along the creeks and rivers, only a thin layer of soil covered the limestone, just enough to grow grass if every part of the system worked just right. Fire kept the brush from taking over the grass, and grass kept the soil from eroding down to rock. Once the cycle was interrupted, the grass became thin, the soil washed away in the frequent floods that would follow years of drought, and the brush invaded. When the first farmers and ranchers came to the Hill Country, the grass grew thick and stirrup high. They grazed cattle where there had once been bison, and for a while fortunes were made from the combination of virgin grassland and access to northern cattle markets. But this opportunity did not last long on the limestone hills—the cattle overgrazed the land, the brush and cedar moved in, and the thin soil clinging to the hillsides washed away, leaving only rock or hard gray caliche. The Hill Country, wrote Robert Caro, had been a trap that was baited with grass.[8]

When cotton farming moved into the Hill Country, it was even worse for the land than cattle. At first the yields were sufficient for a farmer to make enough cash to buy necessities and even to thrive. There were cotton gins during the 1880s in Bertram, Liberty Hill, and Travis Peak on the upper Colorado. Communities with stores and churches and schools sprang up in close enough proximity that the children could walk to school and the family could take a wagon to church or market. In 1890 the 92 square miles near Belton appropriated for Fort Hood encompassed twenty-eight of these small communities.[9]

But cotton depleted the soil, so that it became thin and powdery after a few years under the plow. In 1890 it took three acres to make a bale of cotton near Johnson City in Blanco County; by 1900 it took eleven.[10] In addition, deflation resulting from linking the dollar to gold caused farm prices to fall more than a third between 1870 and 1890.[11] Farmers in the western hills struggled to survive: it is no coincidence that the Farmers' Alliance—the precursor of the People's Party, the greatest populist movement in American history—began in Lampasas County northwest of Austin.

The Hill Country was poor—Caro called it "one of the most remote, most isolated, most neglected—and most impoverished—areas of a wealthy nation."[12] Cedar had climbed out of the deep canyons and the tributaries of the Colorado and the Pedernales and spread across the once fertile grasslands. In Blanco County old-timers would tell of times in the 1880s and '90s when you could stand on top of one of the hills and see cattle grazing five to ten miles away; forty years later it was covered with cedar, and the ranchers were so poor that none of them had painted their houses in the last fifteen years.[13]

Margie Carlton, born in 1929, was one of the more fortunate children in the Hill Country. Her family owned 1,500 acres where Sandy Creek runs into the Colorado River, including 80 acres of cultivated land, an orchard, garden, and smokehouse. They could eat what they grew and smoke a hog for the winter. But they still had to sell turkeys and pecans on the streets of East Austin for money

Preston, Margie, and Peggy Carlton, about 1941. Photo courtesy of Margie Carlton Simons.

to buy shoes and sweaters.[14] By urban standards, or even by those of Blackland farmers, they would be considered poor. Wanda Jean Faulkes, whose family owned a 700-acre ranch near Nameless school, said that in the 1930s and '40s they were lucky enough to have screens. Most families didn't, and certainly not the cedar choppers. "It was kind of a hard old country," she said.[15]

The Balcones Fault

The cities on the edge of the Balcones Fault boomed. A rail line came to San Antonio in 1877 and another in 1881; its population doubled between 1880 and 1900 and tripled between 1900 and 1920.[16] There and in Austin, streetcars and homes were electrified, and appliances made women's lives a little easier. Austin had built a dam across the Colorado River in 1893 that created a beautiful lake and had celebrated the feat with an international rowing regatta that drew 25,000 spectators.[17] Couples could spend an evening on the steamboats *Ben Hur* or *Belle of the Colorado,* or steam up the lake to the Chautauqua summer camp to hear music and inspiring lectures. After World War I young people in the city could have fun like they had never had before, celebrating a culture geared toward enjoyment and gratification.[18]

But as soon as you crossed the Balcones Fault, everything changed. None of the roads west of Austin were paved. Bull Creek Road was nothing but a rough trail hugging steep bluffs and criss-crossing the water. Bee Cave Road climbed up and down rocky hills so rough that few cars made the journey. If a car passed Brewton Springs school during the 1930s when Alice Patterson was a student, the whole class would run outside and wave. As late as 1937 there was just one mile of paved road in all of Llano County, and that same year less than 1 percent of the homes in LBJ's Tenth Congressional District had a radio. Robert Caro wrote, "The roar of the Twenties was only the faintest of echoes in those vast and empty hills. . . . To the extent that the 1920s were the age of radio and the movies, and of country clubs, golf, joy-riding and cheek-to-cheek dancing—of a new mass culture—the Hill Country was not a part of the 1920s."[19] T. R. Fehrenbach said Texas had entered the

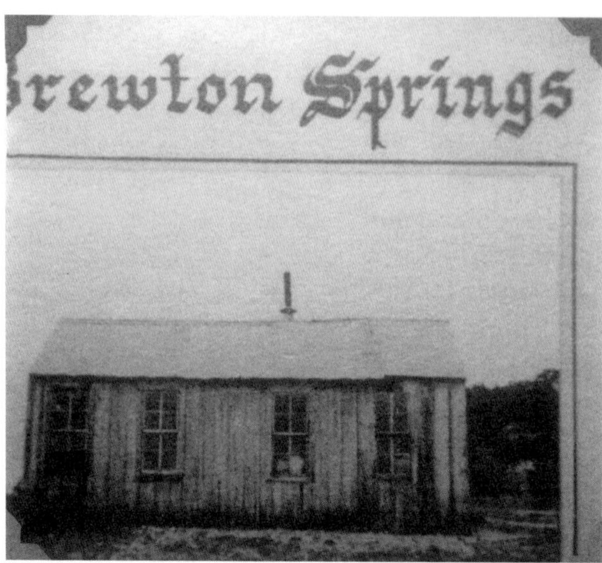

Brewton Springs school. Photo courtesy of Eanes History Center.

twentieth century a full two generations behind the American mainstream.[20] At best, the Hill Country was a generation behind the rest of Texas.

By the end of WWI the people in the hills had abandoned farming, and only a few families had enough land to run cattle or sheep. But everybody in the hills hunted and fished. They were deadly with a slingshot, and squirrel was a regular part of their diet. Floyd Cantwell, who was born in 1932 and grew up on Spicewood Springs Road, said even during those later years, "there were more squirrels and rabbits ate back in them days than there was anything. We had squirrel dogs back in them days, me and my brother. We'd go in the morning and we had two dogs, and we could always catch eight or ten squirrels, every day. We had a nigger shooter. Dogs would tree 'em, when them damn squirrels hit the ground, our dogs would catch 'em." Luther Pierce said, "You had some hillbillies up there that, that's all they hunted with. . . . I was good with one. I could hit a soda can from here to the front porch almost every shot."

Floyd's background illustrates how closely knit the cedar chopper families were to one another. His grandmother on his father's side was Dootie Hutson, the sister of the three Hutson siblings who married Roberts siblings and whose mother was a Teague, so he has ties to all the families in the Roberts-Teague clan. His grandmother on his mother's side was Jennie Pierce, Litten Pierce's aunt and Luther Pierce's second cousin. Everybody knew everybody else, and you stuck by your kin.

Living so near running water, you could always catch fish. As I learned from the incident at the low-water bridge, fishing was not just for sport—it was serious business. Pat Henry, whose family married into the Bonnets of the Whitt-Maynard-Bonnet clan, told John Leffler how he used to grapple for catfish in the creeks near the Colorado River:

> You just go along the banks—we was born and raised along the creeks and fishing was part of our survival. . . . You just go along the banks and find a place . . . and you slide your hand in there. . . . When you slide your hand in there, well you learn real quick not to put your hand in flat, cause he'll run plumb up on your hand up to your wrist, and when he comes off . . . thousands of little teeth just serrate you. . . . When they get you by the hand you've got 'em by the mouth. All you gotta do is just get out of the water . . . and figure out how you're going to get your hand out.[21]

Betty Jo Henry, wife of Pat's cousin Artie Henry, lived near the railroad track in Cedar Park. She pointed west to the hills and told me, "They lived off over there and they shot deer illegally, and lived a lot off the land. But they didn't farm. They fished and they hunted and they sold furs. Back then you could sell coon hides and fox hides."

Andy Preece of the Bull Creek clan said, "We lived good. Lots to eat for free back then. Wild fruit every place: red and black haws, dewberries, mulberries, wild cherries—shoot fire, I've seen 'em so heavy they broke the tree down—wild plums—woods full of 'em."[22]

These men came from three different generations of cedar choppers. Andy Preece was born in 1900, Floyd Cantwell and Pat Henry in the early 1930s, and Luther Pierce in 1945. One of the youngest of the real cedar choppers was Olan Raley, born in 1946 in Junction. That country, especially the headwaters of the Llano River, was still wild and had lots of game. Olan told me, "We were living on Coke's,

Carlton family with deer. Photo courtesy of Margie Carlton Simons, in Leffler interview, 2012.

T. M. Pearson with catfish. Photo courtesy of Dorothy Pearson.

you know [the land of Coke Stevenson, governor of Texas during the 1940s]. Yeah, I mean we had five miles of riverfront. . . . Yeah, we fished and hunted all over that place. Ate deer meat all the time, and had some wild goat. We'd kill a goat every once in a while."

I met with Olan and Arthur Lee Wallace, a cedar chopper in Junction whose grandmother was a Cantwell from west of Austin and Floyd's second cousin, and Charles Hagood, a banker in Junction from an old ranching family. They told me about legendary cedar chopper Johnnie Pale, who had lived on Coke's ranch before Olan's time and swore he could rope an armadillo from a horse at a dead run in a cedar brake. That may be an exaggeration, but C. W. Wimberley, who put together a collection of his stories for a book he called *Cedar Whacker,* said that when the old trucks would roll in with a load of cedar, "usually there was an armadillo or two lying on the floorboards."[23]

Nothing better illustrates how the cedar choppers could live off the land than the story of Bud Tracy. After Mattie Teague had six girls during her eight years of marriage to Henry Tucker, he died and she married Orlando Tracy. She had two children with him, Pearl and Bud. Pearl's story is told later, in her role as the mother of Ernest Thurman, one of the truly bad men in the clans.

In 1926, when Bud was forty, he was charged with stealing a pig. He vanished into the hills, and for six months lived in various hiding places west of Austin. A common question was, "How did I eat? Why, man, that's the easiest thing on earth. Sometimes I'd drop into somebody's house for a meal or two, then again I'd shoot a squirrel or catch a fish. There's plenty of ways of getting plenty to eat."[24]

Even though he avoided caves, Bud did get bitten by a rattlesnake. He went to a neighbor's house and borrowed some kerosene and salt and treated the wound himself. When he was asked if he needed moonshine for the pain, he said, "Man, I never drunk that stuff." He was finally captured when lawmen discovered his hideout between the railroad tracks and Barton Creek. Two teams of deputies watched the place in twenty-four-hour shifts; he surrendered immediately when they drew their guns on him. He was lucky—they thought he had two pistols and a rifle, and he said he had heard they were going to shoot him on sight. He was unarmed, and yet he could still survive in the hills.

As a kid you take things as they are. When I went fishing at the low-water bridge about 1956 and later went to O. Henry Junior High, I didn't know or care that the bridge was completed only in 1949 and the school opened in 1953. The people living in the hills west of there were even poorer and more isolated than in the ranching communities of Blanco County or the farming communities of western Williamson and Burnet counties. Farmers and ranchers looked down on the cedar choppers living in the brakes along the Colorado as an inferior breed.

The Balcones Fault was not only a rupture that separated the South and the West; it was a rift in time. To the east was West Austin, always pretentious, posturing as an island in the wilderness of Texas culture. To the west lay a transplant of Appalachia. These were different worlds at opposite ends of a spectrum of civility. My confrontation with the cedar chopper kids selling fish was like an encounter with people from another country or another time. We were further apart than we could have imagined.

It is hard to put yourself into another person's shoes, to imagine how a kid might feel walking across the bridge into Austin from a shack in the hills. Writer Elroy Bode, who came from a Hill Country farm around 1950 to attend the University of Texas, tells how he felt. He found houses "with lush lawns and gold door-knockers and polished staircases winding to second floors—and the thoughts I had inside me burned so much like hot metal that all I wanted to do was yell out to the surrounding darkness. This is not my life here; I am not of this world. I am of a house that never had the proper thing, where closet doors never shut and faucets always dripped and dogs smelled a little like old grease."[25] And in the hills west of Austin, few of the houses even had running water.

If a kid walked across the low-water bridge into Tarrytown he would follow streets that were straight and clean and tree-lined, with white houses and green lawns and bright beds of flowers. The children there rode bicycles, and people went from house to house on sidewalks wearing nice clothes. If he walked up Exposition Boulevard to Windsor Road, he would pass a gas station and a grocery store and an air-conditioned pharmacy with a soda fountain, and next door a toy store with a sleek replica of a passenger airliner hanging in the window. To a cedar chopper kid, it was another world. When Don Simons went with his dad on the regular Saturday moonshine run from Bull Creek to Sixth Street, he would pass the golf course on Enfield: "I would see all those guys out there with those white golf shoes on, and golf shirts. Man, I wanted to play golf!"

Bob Willess grew up in the cedar brakes of western Bell County, where Fort Hood is now, and at seventy-five was still hauling cedar to different parts of Texas. He told me the story of taking a detour from Interstate 45 outside Houston and coming across a bunch of shacks of cardboard and canvas occupied by families of Mexican laborers. He said, "When I seen that I thought about back when I was a little kid, and then you looked, like, you looked to the left and that's what you'd see. But then you looked to the right and you could see the city, the high—the high buildings and stuff down there. And I always thought, 'We was so close to civilized country, but yet so far away.'"

If the cedar choppers were amazed by the city, the people of Austin were appalled by the stories that came out of the hills, often embellished with the florid language of a dime-store novel. A 1927 article in the *Austin Statesman* tells the story of a public health nurse who went up into the hills, "where the rattle of the diamondback is apt to challenge the occasional visit of the stranger into the backwoods cedar country," and found a family of charcoal burners with an incapacitated husband, a "deranged" wife, and "two tow-headed, sickly little children."[26] It was a scene out of Erskine Caldwell's *Tobacco Road.* The nurse could supposedly tell stories from that "forbidding high place" that "would fill the average resident of this city with amazement and, perhaps, a little horror." The previous time the "demented" woman had been brought to town, her little two-year-old boy watched her go with only a tear, for "the instinct of survival is strong even in the young of his kind."

This time the whole family was brought in, and the paper made a plea for donations to buy milk for the kids, asking, "What is going to be the reaction of the people of Austin when they read of a case such as this one? These hill children are not actually the responsibility of the community, but should the community say: 'We'll take care of our own—those that don't belong to us must live as best they can?'"

If the people of Austin considered the hill people an alien race, the feeling seems to have been mutual. Linda Vance, who wrote *Eanes: Portrait of a Community* for the Texas Sesquicentennial, concluded: "As far as can be determined, the people who lived in Eanes never perceived themselves, either mentally or physically, as Austinites. . . . Through the years, again and again, they deliberately chose to maintain their separateness, even when logic said they should do otherwise."[27]

There was a time when the bankers and doctors and politicians used the hills as their playground. Before a law was passed in 1923 outlawing the practice, they would bring packs of trained dogs to Bull Creek to run down deer, threatening the best source of meat for the residents. Once again, outsiders from the city were invading the hills with guns, and the hill people didn't like it.

They started waiting for the hunters to come. One unidentified Bull Creek resident said, "Whenever we'd see a whole bunch of dog men coming up from town, I'd saddle up my old mare and ride over to my partner's house. Then he'd do the same with the next neighbor, and so on 'til there was a pair of eyes lookin' out at the dog men from pert' near every bush." And they shot the dogs, starting what was called "The Travis County Dog Wars."[28]

The hunters went ballistic: one physician had prize hounds shipped from Kentucky "ambushed by damned hillbillies who pay no taxes." A merchant said, "Those aren't human beings gunning our dogs down. Hell got overpopulated so the Devil moved the worst lot over to Bull Creek and gave them guns to play with."

A reward of $250 was posted, but nobody responded. Finally enough evidence was gathered to indict Paul Waechter of the Bull Creek clan. His brother Lewis was married to a daughter of Lee Boatright, one of the patriarchs of the clan, so Paul was well connected. The article said the "young mountaineer, despite the loss of one arm, had the reputation of a rifleman who could knock a gnat's eyebrows off at a hundred paces." A hundred witnesses were called to the stand during the trial, but nobody would testify against him. Paul's younger brother was asked, "'Son, did you ever see a dead dog in the hills?' 'Yes, sir, judge, I saw one,' the youth replied. 'Well, son, what do you think killed that dog?' 'Judge, I believe that poor hound must of got hooked to death by a buck.'" To mollify the powerful men who demanded retribution, Paul Waechter was fined, but the fine was dismissed "for fear it would arouse the mountaineers' ire, and that the hillbillies would stop shooting dogs and start shooting hunters."

Moonshine

Well my name's John Lee Pettimore, same as my daddy and his daddy before.
You hardly ever saw Granddaddy down here, he only come to town about twice a year.
He'd buy a hundred pounds of yeast and some copper line, everybody knew that he made moonshine.
Now the revenue man wanted him bad, he headed up the holler with everything he had.
It's before my time but I've been told, he never come back from Copperhead Road.

Steve Earle, "Copperhead Road"

Prohibition went into effect in January 1920, and many men in the hills took to making moonshine to sell. It was a skill they had

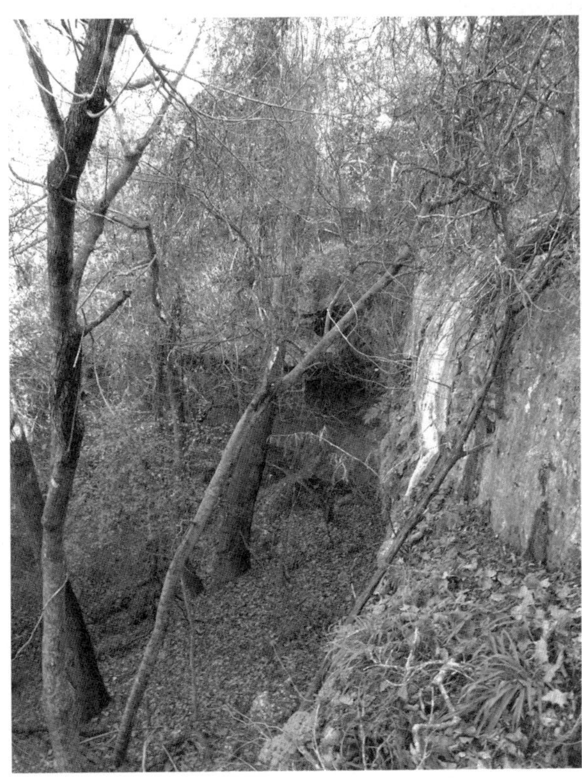

Stillhouse Hollow Nature Preserve. Photo by author.

brought from Appalachia, and at fifty to a hundred dollars a batch, one of the best ways to turn corn into money. The hills west of Austin were perfect—crystal clear water bubbled up from hundreds of springs, caves in the limestone were good hiding places for equipment and barrels of whiskey, and dense cedar brakes in the hollows provided cover for the illegal stills. A newspaper article in 1923 claimed, "The wild mountain fastnesses of Kentucky and Tennessee offer no better places for the concealment of illicit liquor stills."[29] One of the canyons of Bull Creek was called Stillhouse Hollow, and there is a little park there today with that name. A still discovered near Cow Creek was in a cavern thirty-five feet long, eight feet wide, and high enough to walk upright. The entrance was a small hole concealed in the creek bank near a spring that was the source of water to cool the whiskey running through copper lines. The furnace was so well hidden that it could not be spotted from twenty yards away. Dug into the creek bank was a storage space for twenty-five barrels of whiskey, its cedar ceiling covered with brush and dirt, impossible to detect from above.[30]

The hills west of Austin became no-man's land. Frank Wilson, who grew up in Hyde Park and knew some of the families from Bull Creek, said: "Austin people didn't go out in there. No, you stayed out of there. You got to Dry Creek then you'd better slow down, and when you got to Bull Creek you'd better stop" (laughter). He went on to tell a story about Deputy Sheriff Jim McCoy, who wore polished boots and a white Stetson and carried a pearl-handled revolver. This story was told to him by Mack Sutton, whose grandfather was in the Sutton-Taylor feud.

> Jim went up there one time, and right at the mouth of Bull Creek there used to be some great big rocks, and you just had to stop there and walk or ride a horse. Well, Jim went up there and he said he was trying to find this guy and he knew he was making whiskey. And he saw this young fellow lying there on one of the rocks sunning himself, and he looked like he was about twelve or thirteen years old, and he asked him if he knew this man. And the boy raised up off this rock and said, "Yep, I know him." And he asked him, "Do you know where he

> lives?" "Yep, I know where he lives." "Well," he said, "Will you take me up there?" And the boy said, "Well, yeah, for a dollar." And so Jim said, "You take me up there and bring me back here so I can get back down and I'll give you a dollar." And the boy says, "Hell, you're not comin' back."

Jim McCoy would try to locate the stills by the smoke from the fires used to cook the mash, searching with binoculars from a high vantage point. But as soon as the hillbillies found out about it, they started building little fires everywhere. Lawmen—federal agents, sheriff's deputies, and Austin police—would go out in large groups for protection, but they rarely found anything. They went on long searches in the Bull Creek area on the theory that "a veritable nest of stills is in operation in the hill country northwest of Austin." They estimated that one hundred gallons of high-quality moonshine were coming from there into Austin every month, and boasted they would match this "double-poisoned, steel-lined, greased white lightening" against any "squirrel whiskey" from Tennessee and Kentucky. In talking up their adversary's strengths, they appear to have been playing a part in an elaborate game.

Their work finally paid off in February 1923 with the arrest of several men from Bull Creek, including Dick Boatright. His first trial was thrown out and the case does not reappear on the court docket until September, in a trial along with several other men in the clans. But there is no written evidence of a conviction, and the following year Dick was residing in South Austin with his wife.[31]

The Boatright family of the Bull Creek clan has been my source of numerous stories, including those about moonshine. Dick Boatright is the son of Lee Boatright, the patriarch of the family. I got to know Dick's son Jim in 1973 when he did some road work for us, and later I worked for his wife at the Leander Post Office. I interviewed another son, John T., who was very close to Jim. I also interviewed his nephew Albert Boatright Jr. Another nephew, Frank Boatright, was the subject of the article "Sundown of the Cedar Choppers," and I have talked with Frank's daughter Marie.

Jesse Thomas "Dick" Boatright was listed in the 1920, 1930, and 1940 Bull Creek censuses as a wood hauler and rock mason.

Sometime during the 1940s he moved west a few miles and started a cedar yard at the northwest corner of Highway 183 and RM 1431 in Cedar Park. Preston Carlton was a realtor in that area for many years, and he told me that although Dick did not have an education, "he was one of the smartest people I've ever seen." When a truck would bring in a load of cedar of different grades and prices, he would tally up the amounts and prices of each in his head and pay the man right on the spot.

Dick Boatright's son John T. told me stories of Dick's bootlegging during the 1930s. Dick had a 1929 Chevy flatbed truck that he used to haul cedar, charcoal, and whiskey.

> Let me tell ya, my daddy was a good honest man and made lots of whiskey. And we'd load his old truck with about ninety to a hundred bushels of charcoal in tow sacks. And, when he went to town on Monday to peddle his charcoal he'd go right out there to the Capitol, drive up there, this black guy'd swing the gate open. In goes daddy. Then he'd put him under that big ol' tin shed. Daddy'd jump up there and start to digging, and then back out. Unloading the whiskey back there, I'll tell ya. Some of the high-priced Capitol people come out to the place to get whiskey too. . . . But every, everybody bragged on how good daddy's whiskey was. And when, when the Capitol bunch got a hold of it—man, he can't make it fast enough. . . . And they'd come out there in these big, black cars, and they'd get out with their shotguns, they're gonna go hunt doves. But daddy goes the other way and fills their car up (laughter) . . . they'd come out pretty late in the day, and daddy would disappear. And just after dark, well, that car would leave full of whiskey.

I asked John T. if his father was the only one who made whiskey on Bull Creek. He said everybody made it—"everybody that had any ambition." The same question asked of one of the Teagues on Barton Creek brought a similar response: "All of 'em. Anybody. Everybody."[32]

Dick was working with his brothers Albert, Tim, and Floyd, when they got raided one day. Everybody escaped but Albert. His son

Albert Jr. told me that his dad was crippled from polio, and "everybody got away except my Dad 'cause he couldn't run. He couldn't run fast enough! And I think he had spent about a year in jail." Tim and Floyd were arrested around the same time in separate incidents.[33]

Albert probably spent his time at one of the state correctional farms in Fort Bend County that used convict labor to harvest crops. One of the men sentenced for running the elaborate underground distillery on Cow Creek was Carlie Varner, who was related to the Henrys and the Turners of the Whitt-Maynard-Bonnet clan. His incarceration illustrates how the criminal justice system worked in the 1920s. His record shows him to be 5 feet 9 inches tall, with a ruddy complexion and blue eyes. He was sentenced to one year at the Harlem Plantation, a five-thousand-acre unit that included several private sugar plantations leasing convict labor. He served only six months and was pardoned by Governor Miriam "Ma" Ferguson in 1926.[34]

Pardons were often exchanged for favors. There was probably something behind his pardon similar to what happened a few years later. Lawyer Emmett Shelton describes himself as "kind of a fair-haired boy on account of family connections," and he was still in law school when asked to introduce Ma Ferguson during her runoff campaign in 1931. When she became governor, "I was in line to rectify some of these miscarriages of justice that had people in the penitentiary." One of the first pardons he secured was for another bootlegger, John Riley of the Patterson-Pierce clan.

John Riley was not sent to prison for bootlegging but on the more serious charge of pandering (pimping), and was sentenced to Huntsville for a term of five to thirty-five years beginning in March, 1926. He apparently was not too cooperative the first year, because he was given "three hours over the barrel" twice in September for laziness and twenty lashes later the same month.[35] He was moved to the Harlem Plantation late in 1927, made a trustee, and his life improved.

His brother Rush Riley found out that John was entitled to $2,500 from the government for his service during WWI. Rush enlisted the help of Emmett Shelton to get the money, but of course it would not do any good unless he was out of prison. So Emmett went to Governor Ferguson to call in the favor, and she promised to give John a pardon.[36]

In the meantime Emmett and Rush went to visit John and tell him of his good fortune. He was puzzled why the government would give him money for his service, because he said he'd been treated better in the army than he'd ever been his whole life. And he was skeptical about leaving prison during the Depression. He said, "Now, boys, I don't know whether I want out of here or not. I hear times is hard outside. . . . They don't work me, and I'm running the hogs over here on the creek somewhere, and we do a little home-brew making over there, and I'm just having a pretty good time living down here."

Emmett talked him into taking the deal, for it was the only way he was going to get paid $500 for securing the pardon. But John received the money a week before he was pardoned. When Emmett and Rush went to get him out of prison, he was not there: he was partying at the Rice Hotel in Houston, paying the bills for his guards, who would rotate in two-man shifts for as long as the money lasted.

Emmett stopped the party and got his money, and John got the rest, spending it all in a year. When it was gone, he came back to Emmett and said, "Mr. Shelton, you know that money you got from me last year? Well, if you'll get me some more, I'll give you half of it."

John's brother Rush was also a well-known bootlegger, but not a very good one. He sold liquor to Deputy US Marshal Jim Quinlan twice in the same day; Rush did not recognize him because the marshal had worn different hats. When busting him, Marshal Quinlan said, "Rush, you just don't have sense to be a bootlegger."

5

Cedar and Survival

Yeah, that heart cedar, it just don't give up.

John T. Boatright, Interview

Ashe Juniper

When you come to Central Texas from somewhere else it does not take long until you hear about cedar, and all of it is bad. It chokes out the oaks and sucks the aquifers dry. It grows rapidly and takes over the land until nothing will grow under it. It's impossible to get rid of. But worst of all, it reaches into the cities and smites even those who couldn't care less about being outdoors. During the winter months the male cedars explode with red pollen, causing "cedar fever"—burning eyes, a runny nose, and an "insidious malaise." In 1926 J. Frank Dobie wrote an editorial pleading for the city to "compel the cutting down of all male cedars within its limits. . . . No sane and independent person can look forward with equanimity to living permanently in a place where for six weeks or two months out of each year he must endure the tortures of the damned and be so drained of vitality that for weeks afterwards he feels like a cast-off dish rag." Dobie would leave the area every season because there was, and is, no cure.[1]

Whether it deserves its reputation as "the vilest plant living in Texas" is a complicated matter, because the cedar we see today is not like it used to be.[2] When the land became overgrazed and exhausted by cotton, the cedar moved in. It spread until one-third of the 24 million acres in the Edwards Plateau has at least an 11 percent cover of cedar.[3] On the open prairies it grows fast, more like a big bush than a tree, with multiple stalks near ground level. The dense foliage blocks the light and consumes a lot of water, permanently changing the landscape.

But this isn't the way it used to be, and this shrubby cedar doesn't resemble the mountain cedar that started an industry. Periodic fires used to sweep the high grass on the plains, killing the young trees that grew from berries dropped by birds. Cedar was confined to deep canyons and high rocky hills, such as those immediately north and west of Austin.

The trees that grew like this are known as old growth cedar. Roemer, writing in the middle of the nineteenth century, found them to be "stately trees with straight trunks, seldom more than twenty to twenty-five feet in height and one and one-half feet thick."[4] Soft light filters through the sparse foliage to a carpet of fine grass. A century later C. W. Wimberley wrote, "Standing inside one of these brakes gave the feeling of being inside one of Nature's Cathedrals."[5] Two of the women I interviewed talked reverently of the old brakes. Margie Carlton grew up on a Colorado River bottom and described their 25-acre brake as similar to a pine forest,

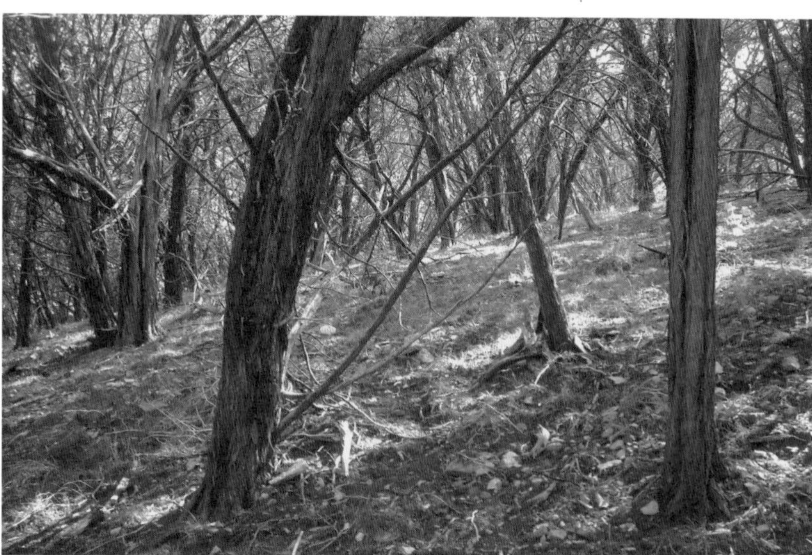

Old growth cedar, Burnet County. Photo by author.

Heart cedar. Photo by author.

with trunks that grew straight up without limbs until reaching the canopy high above. Betty Henry told me, "Back then they were big trees, tall. They'd been there, I guess, hundreds of years. And we just thought they were beautiful."

Old growth cedar has a core of hard reddish brown wood called the heart. The wood of the heart is saturated with an oil that repels insects and makes it highly resistant to rotting. Across the Hill Country you'll find places where the cedar was cut fifty to a hundred years ago, and the old stumps lie there like weathered bones, still with enough oil to make a blazing fire or to extract for perfume and other uses. It's the heart cedar in Ashe juniper *(Juniperus ashei)* that makes it the post that fenced the west, and cedar choppers are contemptuous of new growth cedar, which they call sap cedar.

Lee Cantrell of Liberty Hill, closely related to the Simonses of the Bull Creek clan, was born in 1934 and of the last generation of cedar choppers. He told me that down in Kerr County and Leakey there was still some good heart cedar, but "most cedar we've got now, it just growed up here and is sap. It's got about that much of white and a little bitty ol' heart like that," he said, touching his thumb and index finger.

Another cedar chopper of the same generation was Charlie

Maugham, related to the Bonnets of the Whitt-Maynard-Bonnet clan. Charlie cut near Longhorn Cavern in Burnet County. The very best heart cedar grows slowly in the rocky canyons, reaching up toward the light. He said that down in a canyon about three miles in "was the prettiest cedar you ever laid your eyes on. Some of 'em was tall enough to get two posts out of 'em."

Good cedar meant good posts and good money, but there seems to be more to it than that. Don Simons of the Bull Creek clan said, "I remember my father building roads to get to the good cedar. That was always the deal—the good cedar. Maybe more important than the money." Stanley Allen's family had a yard outside Wimberley. He found some cedar in an inaccessible canyon near the Blanco River that was "some of the prettiest cedar I've seen in my life. Good Lord almighty! I walked that thing, eyes watering, boy. It's some of the prettiest ten- and twelve-foot blocking you ever saw."

Cedar in the Early Days

It was hard to earn cash from the land, and every family needed some cash for what they couldn't grow. In the early days in the hills, cedar and cypress were both good woods, and each started an industry. Cedar had a variety of uses; cypress made great shingles.

Hill Country rivers like the Guadalupe were lined with majestic cypress trees, and as early as 1856 Olmsted noted single men living up and down the river splitting cypress into shingles.[6] Sam Sutton, Pate Patterson's brother-in-law, made shingles on the Medina River. Once about 1880 he and a neighbor made six thousand shingles. They took them to San Antonio and were offered the usual price, five dollars per thousand. When they heard that they could get six dollars in Eagle Pass, ten days south on the Rio Grande, they went for it. After they got their thirty-six dollars, Sam said: "Well, we went to George Hay's saloon and bought a gallon of corn whiskey each; then went to Carmichael's store and bought a supply of coffee, sugar, tobacco, and two sacks of flour, and we went home happy."[7]

Cedar was first used for building cabins, barns, pens, and rail fences. There was a mill on Cypress Creek in Wimberley that sawed 5 x 5-inch cedar posts out of pure heartwood, and even then some of the logs that were brought to the mill were too big for the saw carriage.[8] Farmers came into the hills from the prairie to cut posts, for although there was good pine to the east for building houses, there was really no good wood for posts. Guthrie O'Donnell, from a ranching family outside Marble Falls, told me, "We had a two-story barn. And those old poles, gosh, they were that big around (one foot in diameter) and as straight as an arrow. They'd go up to the second story of that barn, you know, where you built a loft."

The headquarters building of the T Anchor Ranch, built of cedar in 1877, was the first Anglo structure in the Texas Panhandle.[9] The cedar came from Palo Duro Canyon—a name meaning "hard post" in Spanish—and was probably redberry cedar (*Juniperus pinchoti*), according to Robert Adams of Baylor University.[10] Its heart is yellow and not as rot-resistant as that of *Juniperus ashei*, but it grows tall and straight. When famous cattleman Charles Goodnight (the inspiration for Woodrow Call in Larry McMurtry's *Lonesome Dove*) began to fence the JA Ranch in 1880, sixty-seven miles of barbed wire and six months' supplies for fifty men arrived by wagon from Dodge City. In partial payment, Goodnight allowed the wagons to return loaded with cedar logs. His biographer J. Evetts Haley wrote, "The cedars they took on the return trip left the Mulberry barren of its noblest trees, and Goodnight sick at heart over the devastation."[11]

Railroads dramatically increased the demand for cedar. Railroad construction in Texas surged during the late 1870s and '80s, and cedar made excellent railroad ties. On one day in March 1874 forty cars left Austin loaded with 8,000 cedar ties for the western expansion of the Houston and Texas Central Railroad.[12]

Cutters brought the wood to the railhead any way they could. In 1875 some 30,000 cedar logs were rafted down the Colorado River from Burnet County to Austin,[13] and in the early 1880s P. C. Taylor got a big contract for ties and floated logs cut across from Mount Bonnell to a little inlet now known as Taylor Slough.[14] Farther south near Barton Creek, cedar logs were hauled down Bee Cave Road in wagons drawn by oxen. But these were arduous and unreliable means of transport and only gave access to the cedar close by. It took getting rail *into* the Hill Country to make cedar economical, and there were not enough resources there to justify laying the track.

New Braunfels smokehouse. Photo by author.

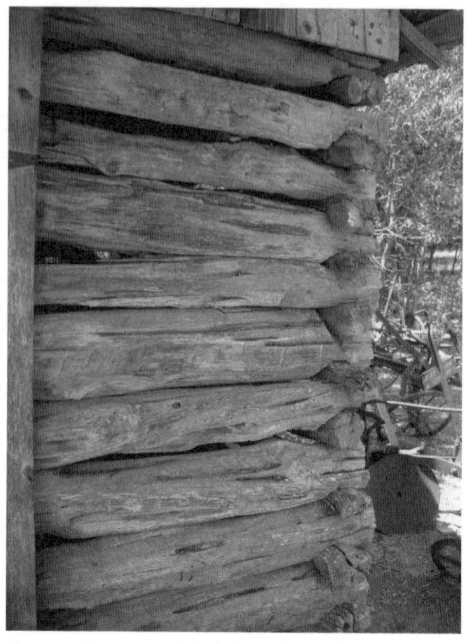

Burnet County cabin. Photo by author.

Kimble County loading chute. Photo by author.

Straight-rail cedar fence. Photo by author.

T Anchor Ranch headquarters, 1873. Photo courtesy of Panhandle-Plains Historical Museum, Canyon, Texas.

In 1882 an event occurred that was one of the defining moments in the cedar industry, one that would increase both the supply of and demand for cedar—the building of the State Capitol. The Capitol was built with red granite from just west of Marble Falls, necessitating a rail line to haul the stone. The Austin and Northwestern Railroad Company built a narrow-gauge line from Marble Falls through Burnet, Bertram, Liberty Hill, Leander, and what was to become Cedar Park. What could haul stone could haul cedar, ensuring a supply of posts.

The payment for building the Capitol was a 3-million-acre parcel in the Panhandle that became the XIT Ranch.[15] The XIT and several other huge ranches were fenced in the 1880s, starting a new way of raising cattle that depended upon windmills and containment in pastures surrounded with barbed wire.[16] That wire was strung on cedar posts, creating a potentially huge source of demand. Though there were lots of posts hauled by rail, the explosion of that demand

Hauling cedar near Austin, 1887. Photo courtesy of Lawrence T. Jones III Texas photography collection, DeGoyer Library, Southern Methodist University.

would have to wait another half century—it came when long-haul trucks could reach farms and ranches far from the rails.

Demand for cedar ties also came from the cities. In 1881 men in Austin erected telephone poles 35 feet tall made of cedar, with crowds gathering to offer advice on the difficult task.[17] An advertisement in the *Austin Daily Statesman* in 1890 invited bids to supply 12,000 mountain cedar ties 7½ feet long and 6 inches in diameter for the electric streetcar. In addition, 500 barked cedar poles 30 feet tall and 5 inches in diameter were needed on which to string the electric wires.[18] Uncle El Preece, who was Dick Preece's nephew and born in 1879, said, "Weren't no fences around here when I was a boy. Only cedar business I knew when I was a boy was chopping ties for the mule streetcar in Austin."[19]

Cutting ties for the track to Marble Falls provided jobs for lots of men. Mack Joseph Sutton (1864–1940) told his grandson Mack Sutton, interviewed in 1978, that he contracted 125 cedar choppers to work cutting ties on land he had leased. A Texas historical marker titled "Cedar Chopping in Central Texas" marks the location of a cedar camp in Williamson County near Highway 183 and Lakeline Boulevard. There A. F. Martin, who owned Austin White

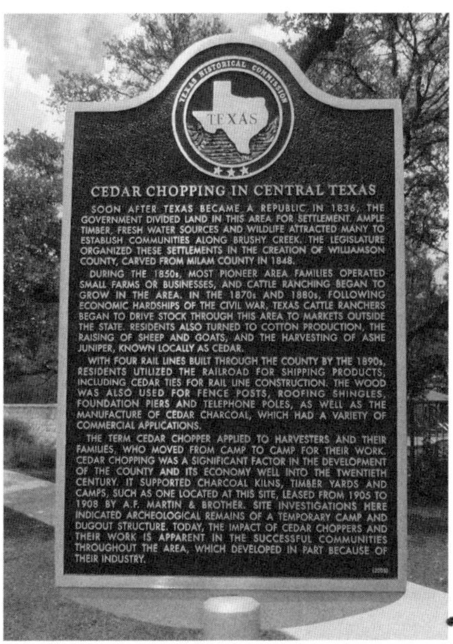

"Cedar Chopping in Central Texas" historical marker. Photo by the author.

Lime Company, paid $500 plus $0.50 per cord for the rights to cut cedar off a couple of hundred acres and hauled it out by rail.[20] Two yards opened on the rail line in Cedar Park; F. W. King's yard shipped 800 boxcars a year from there during the peak years.[21]

After the frenzy of railroad building subsided, and continuing until the 1940s, a big source of the demand for cedar was for rot-resistant pilings as the foundation for frame houses. Zeke Bonnet told his son Morris that the yards would buy a big trunk four feet long with at least a seven-inch top, called "blocking," which would later be cut to the desired length. "They shipped a lot of cedar out of Cedar Park and Whitestone on rails because they shipped to San Antone and Houston and places, they put houses on 'em," Morris said.

There were two attempts to make cedar into big business. The first succeeded for only a few years. In 1911 two brothers from Holland named Scholten built a twenty-five-mile narrow gauge railway from Lometa on the Santa Fe Line into the brakes at Bend on the Colorado River.[22] Before the line was constructed the Scholtens placed an ad in the Austin paper calling for thirty cedar choppers, stating that they would provide the tools and "would prefer Mexicans."[23] Not only could Mexicans be paid less, but they were

Scholten yard and bridge, 1912. Photos courtesy of Southwest Collection, Texas Tech University, Lubbock, Lampasas County SWCPC envelope 62, #27, #28.

considered ideal laborers, especially when compared to the unruly hill people.[24]

For three years the business thrived in this excellent cedar country, each train pulling six flatbed cars piled high with posts. A local historian wrote, "The Scholtens put a small army of men into the brakes to cut cedar by hand, and they organized them into a village of people who shared a common lifestyle and who seldom associated with outsiders."[25]

With the onset of WWI farm prices fell, causing farmers and ranchers near the Santa Fe Line to the west to defer the expense of fencing until times got better. But more than the falling demand for posts, it was the Colorado River that shut down the Scholtens. The first few years had average rainfall, but after that came typical Texas weather when averages meant nothing. Wagons had to cross a low-water bridge over the Colorado to load the cedar on the train; the river flooded twenty-three times, each flood causing large trees to pile up on the bridge or rip it apart.

But even if it failed as a business, the Scholtens' project put a lot of men in the northwestern brakes cutting cedar, and some stayed to become independent cedar choppers. I interviewed the son of one of them, Simon Ratliff, great-grandson of Richard Ratliff and Hulda Teague of the Roberts-Teague clan. Simon grew up in Lometa, and many of his relatives cut cedar in the hills around Lampasas.

The most successful large-scale cedar business was started in 1921 west of Leakey on the Nueces River. A thirty-seven-mile rail line was run north from Uvalde to a rugged area covered with heart cedar, where men lived in a tent city that became known as Camp Wood. At its peak in 1924, the Uvalde Cedar Company shipped 1,342 carloads of cedar posts and other wood products, employing at least two hundred cedar choppers in the brakes near town. Later in the decade three trains per week, with as many as 40,000 posts each, rolled out of Camp Wood. After that the best cedar ran out, and demand fell when natural gas became a common fuel in the cities. The railroad continued running for a few years and was closed for good in 1941.[26]

Uvalde and Northern Railroad. Photo courtesy of Nueces Canyon Chamber of Commerce museum.

Camp Wood store, 1914. Photo courtesy of Nueces Canyon Chamber of Commerce museum.

Charcoal

By far the most important product shaping the lives and culture of the cedar choppers during the early twentieth century was charcoal. Charcoal did not require any capital other than a shovel and a rake, although a wagon and team would allow you to sell it in town rather than to the closest store. Water needed to be handy when charcoal was made, and the mountain people lived near creeks and rivers. Children could peel the bark and sack up the coal, so the whole family could work. When the land wore out and the cities grew, a family could turn cedar into money by selling charcoal in the cities. Unlike cedar posts, charcoal was light, and a wagonload would bring good money.

Perhaps the most significant way that charcoal shaped cedar chopper culture was that making it marked you. Fritz and Emilie Toepperwein wrote a book in 1950 about charcoal burners living on the Guadalupe River at the turn of the century. One man told them, "'I can tell one anywhere.' We asked 'How?' He answered, 'Why, by their dark complexions from working with charcoal and always being out in the sun. Their skin often looks dry and sometimes red. Many of them are bent over from toil . . . and they may still have some cedar wax on their hands.'"[27]

Charcoal was an essential product well into the twentieth century, used to heat stoves and irons, to purify water, and to forge metal. Charcoal made from cedar burned hot and clean. It didn't smoke like other woods, didn't pop, and left no ashes. Good cedar charcoal was light and had a sheen like anthracite coal, and it would ring if you tapped it. Even after electricity had come to parts of Austin, black women who did laundry often heated their irons with charcoal. E. J. Rissman said so much charcoal was used in East Austin for irons and stoves that you could recognize where you were by the smell alone.[28] Henry Roberts's son Lonnie would bring charcoal to Rissman's store and trade for groceries. "His charcoal had to be good or he'd not sell it," wrote the storekeeper, "and the Negro women asked for it by his name."[29]

Making charcoal was an old craft, for it was the major fuel in furnaces producing iron and glass and brick in late medieval times. Perhaps because it was such a dirty occupation, the people who made it in Europe often lived apart from the mainstream and commonly were gypsies.[30] One of the earliest charcoal-fired iron furnaces in the United States was operating at Harpers Ferry in 1740, and later Wheeling, West Virginia, became an important iron center fired with charcoal.[31] Stronger, less brittle, and capable of a finer edge than coke-fired iron, all iron was made with charcoal until 1830, and charcoal-fired iron production continued to grow until 1890.[32]

One theory often repeated is that the charcoal burners came to

Texas to continue the craft they were already doing elsewhere. The Topperweins wrote, "Word spread to Tennessee, Indiana, Georgia, New York, England and Ireland" that Charcoal City on the Guadalupe had everything you needed to burn good coal, and people would arrive and ask, "Is this where they are burning charcoal?"[33]

If this were true, it could be the genesis of the cedar choppers. But I have found no other support for this theory. The stories of the clans living west of Austin in the early days are of farming and ranching, with charcoal and cedar coming later. There was a drought in 1884–86 that was one of the worst in Texas history, causing many people to quit farming and return to the East. But in the Hill Country what had been the plague of small farmers and ranchers became their salvation, allowing them to turn cedar into money and to hang on. In western Travis County "these proud, independent men, who had once been farmers, now became cedar choppers or charcoal burners," wrote Elaine Perkins.[34] John Hoover of Burnet told me, "I think the cedar choppers we had here were more farmers and ranchers that had went broke, whatever you want to call it—they had to have some money so they started chopping cedar." One farmer whose crops failed said, "I can tell you that charcoal meant pure money to many of us."[35] There are reports of charcoal kilns on all the creeks in the Hill Country close to markets in Austin and San Antonio.

By the turn of the century, cutting cedar for charcoal and other uses had become a major source of income to many people living in the hills. This is evident from a page in the 1900 census of northwestern Travis County, where the primary occupations (third column from the right) are wood chopping, wood hauling, and making charcoal. But these are not so much occupations as stages in a process of turning cedar into money. At one time or another, most of the families in the clans did it all—cutting cedar for posts, burning cedar for charcoal, or making moonshine.

On the page pictured from the 1900 census, of the ten men whose occupation was listed as manufacturing charcoal or wood chopping, six are in the family tree I developed, and we can follow the occupations of family members in the censuses of 1930 and 1940. Jason Reeves's daughter Lillie married Jesse Clawson of the Roberts-Teague clan, who was cutting cedar in 1930 and was a mason in 1940. David Bilyeu's daughter Mary married John Walden, and their son Dowell was shown cutting cedar in 1930. Levi Bankston, as well as William and Robert Hickman, all married Preeces of the Bull Creek clan, many of whom were cedar choppers. William's son Nolan and David Whited's son Elmo were both

TWELFTH CENSUS OF THE UNITED STATES. B

SCHEDULE No. 1.—POPULATION.

State: Texas; County: Travis

Supervisor's District No. 10; Enumeration District No. 113; Sheet No. 1

[Towns]hip or other division of county: Precinct No 4 [Insert name of township, town, precinct, district, or other civil division, as the case may be. See instructions.] Name of Institution, ______

[Name] of incorporated city, town, or village, within the above-named division, ______ Ward of city, ______

Enumerated by me on the 4 day of June, 1900, James P Colley, Enumerator. 616

Line	Dwelling (1)	Family (2)	Name (3)	Relation (4)	Color (5)	Sex (6)	Birth month (7)	Birth year (7)	Age (8)	Marital (9)	Yrs married (10)	Mother of how many (11)	Living (12)	Birthplace (13)	Father's birthplace (14)	Mother's birthplace (15)	(16)	(17)	(18)	Occupation (19)	Months not employed (20)	School (21)	Read (22)	Write (23)	English (24)	Owned/rented (25)	Free/mortgaged (26)	Farm/house (27)	Farm schedule (28)
51			—— William M	Son	w	m	June	1892	7	S				Texas	Alabama	Texas													
52			—— Willie M	daughter	w	F	June	1892	7	S				Texas	Alabama	Texas													
53			—— Ab	Son	w	m	June	1895	4	S				Texas	Alabama	Texas													
54			—— Ed	Son	w	m	Aug	1897	2	S				Texas	Alabama	Texas													
55	11	11	Reeves Jason [illegible]	Head	w	m	Aug	1878	21	m	4			Texas	Louisiana	Georgia				wood Hauling	0		yes	yes	yes	O	F	[illegible]	
56			—— Fannie	wife	w	F	Feb	1877	23	m	4	2	2	Texas	Georgia	Georgia							yes	yes	yes				
57			—— Jessie F	Son	w	m	Oct	1897	2	S				Texas	Texas	Texas													
58			—— Tillie M	daughter	w	F	Aug	1899	[illegible]	S				Texas	Texas	Texas													
59	12	12	Pickens Albert B	Head	w	m	Feb	1869	31	m	7			Texas	Tennessee	Arkansas				Mfg charcoal	0		no	no	yes	R		H	
60			—— Mary T	wife	w	F	Aug	1873	26	m	7	4	4	Texas	[illegible]	Arkansas							yes	yes	yes				
61			—— Abberry	Son	w	m	May	1894	6	S				Texas	Texas	Texas													
62			—— Mittie	daughter	w	F	Mar	1896	4	S				Texas	Texas	Texas													
63			—— Minnie A	daughter	w	F	Sept	1897	2	S				Texas	Texas	Texas													
64			—— John F	Son	w	m	Sept	1899	8/12	S				Texas	Texas	Texas													
65	13	13	Waddle Andrew J	Head	w	m	Mar	1845	55	M	0			Alabama	Alabama	Tennessee				Hauling wood [illegible]	0		yes	yes	yes	O	F	[illegible]	
66			—— Sandra [illegible]	wife	w	F	Dec	1854	45	M	0	0	0	Arkansas	Louisiana	Louisiana							yes	yes	yes				
67			—— John A J	Son	w	m	Mar	1876	24	S				Texas	Alabama	Louisiana				Stock drover	3		yes	yes	yes				
68			—— Frank M	Son	w	m	July	1886	13	S				Texas	Alabama	Louisiana				at School		2	yes	yes	yes				
69			Whited, Daved M	step son	w	m	Apr	1879	21	S				Texas	Louisiana	Arkansas				wood choping	4		yes	yes	yes				
70			—— Enzly	step son	w	m	Oct	1881	18	S				Texas	Louisiana	Arkansas				wood Choping	3		yes	yes	yes				
71			—— Susie E	step daughter	w	F	Mar	1884	16	S				Texas	Louisiana	Arkansas				at School		2	yes	yes	yes				
72			—— Bazora L	step daughter	w	F	Apr	1886	14	S				Texas	Louisiana	Arkansas				at School		2	yes	yes	yes				
73			—— Perlee	step daughter	w	F	Aug	1888	11	S				Texas	Louisiana	Arkansas						0	no	no	yes				
74			—— Bunk A	step son	w	m	Nov	1891	8	S				Texas	Louisiana	Arkansas						0							
75			—— Lillie M	step daughter	w	F	Mar	1895	5	S				Texas	Louisiana	Arkansas													
76	14	14	Bates Danel D	Head	w	m	June	1845	54	m	31			Texas	N Carolina	Mississippi				Farmer	0		yes	yes	yes	O	m	F	6
77			—— Mary	wife	w	m	Oct	1844	55	m	31	10	9	Tennessee	Tennessee	Tennessee							yes	yes	yes				
78			—— Minnie	daughter	w	F	Mar	1878	22	S				Texas	Texas	Tennessee							yes	yes	yes				
79			—— Alice	daughter	w	F	Jan	1880	20	S				Texas	Texas	Tennessee							yes	yes	yes				
80			—— Ida	daughter	w	F	Jan	1883	17	S				Texas	Texas	Tennessee							yes	yes	yes				
81			—— Rosey	daughter	w	F	Nov	1886	13	S				Texas	Texas	Tennessee				at School		9	yes	yes	yes				del
82			—— Quincy	daughter	w	F	Nov	1889	10	S				Texas	Texas	Tennessee						0	no	no	yes				
83	15	15	Hancock Reuben [illegible]	Head	w	m	Nov	1870	29	m	3			Texas	Arkansas	Texas				wood Hauling	0		yes	yes	yes	O	m	F	7
84			—— Lelar L	wife	w	F	Feb	1878	22	m	3	2	2	Texas	Missouria	Missouria							yes	yes	yes				
85			—— Elmer A	son	w	m	July	1897	2	S				Texas	Texas	Texas													
86			—— Mary N	daughter	w	F	Jan	1899	1	S				Texas	Texas	Texas													
87	16	16	Conner Loui[illegible]	Head	w	F	June	1852	47	wd		6	4	Texas	Georgia	Arkansas				farmer	0		yes	no	yes	O	m	F	8
88			—— William A	Son	w	m	Sept	1889	10	S				Texas	Arkansas	Texas				at School		1	no	no	yes				
89			—— Perry	son	w	m	Apr	1891	9	S				Texas	Arkansas	Texas													
90			—— Wesley	son	w	m	Jan	1894	6	S				Texas	Arkansas	Texas													
91			—— Dee L	Son	w	m	Apr	1897	3	S				Texas	Arkansas	Texas													
92	17	17	Bankston Levi	Head	w	m	July	1842	57	m	26			Arkansas	Illinois	Arkansas				wood coper	3		yes	yes	yes	O	m	H	
93			—— Rachel L	wife	w	F	May	1840	60	m	26	1	0	Kentucky	W. Virginia	Kentucky							yes	yes	yes				
94	18	18	Hickman William H	Head	w	m	Feb	1873	27	S				Texas	Kentucky	Missouri				Manufacture [illegible]	0		yes	yes	yes	O		H	
95			—— Robert E	Brother	w	m	July	1877	22	S				Texas	Kentucky	Missouri				Mfg charcoal [illegible]	0		yes	yes	yes				
96	19	19	Bilyew David M	Head	w	m	Mar	1838	62	m	39			Missouri	Missouri	unknown				Mfg charcoal	0		yes	yes	yes	O		H	
97			—— Nicinda [illegible]	wife	w	F	Oct	1843	56	m	39	13	10	Missouri	unknown	unknown							yes	yes	yes				
98			—— Nettie	daughter	w	F	May	1871	19	S				Texas	Missouri	Missouri							yes	yes	yes				
99			—— Stephen	Son	w	m	Oct	1883	16	S				Texas	Missouri	Missouri				wood Hauling	0		yes	no	yes				
100	20	20	Bates Roy	Head	w	m	Jan	1877	23	m	4			Texas	Texas	Tennessee				farmer	0		yes	yes	yes	R		F	9

Census page for northwest Travis County, 1900. United States Federal Census, Ancestry.com, uploaded March 19, 2014.

Alfred Wesley Teague, 1936. Photo from a public member tree on Ancestry.com, attached to Alfred Wesley Teague in the Haverfield Family Tree on September 7, 2012.

cutting cedar in 1940. What A. C. Green said was true—working in cedar was a trade that was passed down to sons and sons-in-law, and it began with cutting ties and burning charcoal around the turn of the century.

Charcoal was made in a kiln with mostly green wood. The kids would strip the bark off the posts and pile them up like a teepee. Dick Boatright from Bull Creek would first dig out the dirt in a circle about a foot deep and drive a six-foot post in the center. Then he and his family would lean the shortest stripped posts against that, the posts in each circle getting progressively longer until the teepee was big—generally at least nine feet in diameter, but probably smaller than the one pictured on page 93. The mound would be covered with the cedar bark that had been stripped off and then with dirt. The center post was removed, some coals dropped in, and the hole covered up.[36]

The pile would smolder for days—the longer and slower, the better the charcoal. It had to be watched day and night, for if an opening allowed air to enter, the whole thing would catch fire and the

Charcoal kiln in Sussex, England, 1890. Photo courtesy of George Woods Collection, East Sussex County Council Library, U.K.

work would go to waste. Watchers had to be ready with dirt and water. After about five days the kiln was pulled apart with a long-handled rake. Kids, usually barefoot, would put out any coals still alive, and bag up the charcoal for sale after it cured.

It was a long, slow trip to Austin or San Antonio by wagon. Fred Teague remembers going into Austin with his dad Alfred Wesley (1869–1950), William and Sophia Teague's first child, when the streets were still paved with wooden blocks, and oil lamps were lit every night.[37] Like many other country folk coming to town from far away, the family would camp at Snyder's wagon yard, on Congress Avenue near the river, and sell their charcoal from cracker barrels. J. Frank Dobie recalls hearing the charcoal burners call out "Char-r-coal" as they drove their wagons through Austin in 1914.[38]

Keron Cantwell, born in 1913, would help her dad make the kiln, stripping off the bark and stacking the cedar. After it was cool she went with him from Spicewood to Austin, a three-day round trip, and stayed in the wagon yard. "It was such a thrill for me, seeing

Austin for the first time," she said. With the proceeds they bought flour, sugar, baking powder, oats, rice, tobacco, and medicine, and on one trip a pair of high-top button shoes for Keron.[39] Dick Boatright's kiln would make 100–120 bushels of charcoal, which he would peddle in town for $0.25 a bushel until late in the day, and then lower the price to $0.20. Alice Patterson went with her dad into Austin in the 1930s, through Zilker Park and down Congress Avenue, in an old Model-T Ford loaded with charcoal.

Burning charcoal was a hot, sweaty, dirty business. The green cedar left sap in your hair and on your clothes and skin, and black dust from the charcoal stuck to the sap and sweat. Frank Wilson said, "I've seen those old guys, and they'd bring that charcoal in tow sacks like they used to hold corn, and they'd just have that stuff all over, and they'd wipe it all over 'em."

Some people were embarrassed by the stigma. Pearl Pehl, a girl from a farm family on the Blanco River, said they sometimes had to burn charcoal to get by. Once an insurance man came to see them. "We didn't want him to know we were burning coal 'cause that was a disgrace, you know, so we told him that the people had left home and we was watching it so it wouldn't catch fire." When the kids from Boerne went to Center Point to play basketball, they were taunted with "'Hey, you charcoal burners.' Well, I can tell you, that made us mad," and it would often end up in a fight.[40] One farmer told his kid not to look down on them: "Those are charcoal burners son, but remember they are intelligent folks."[41]

The Depression

While the cedar people hunkered down in the hollows to cut cedar and burn charcoal, to hunt and fish and grow a little corn—for whiskey if for nothing else—the farmers to the east doubled down. As the price of cotton fell, they planted more: in 1920 Bertram ginned 5,000 bales of cotton; by 1928 production had more than doubled to 12,000 bales.[42] When cotton was $0.16 a pound in 1929, total production was 14.8 million bales; when the price fell to $0.05 two years later, production rose to 17 million bales.[43] By 1932 average farm income from cotton had fallen from $735 to $216.[44] A third of the farmers on the plains faced foreclosure.[45] The great exodus from the South began—the rural South lost more than two and a quarter million people from 1930 to 1940.[46]

The biggest losers were the tenants. They were already an unfortunate lot—the agricultural ladder had collapsed below them, and they became little more than wage hands, living in whatever ramshackle housing the landowner provided and giving him half of less and less. One third of all Texas tenants during the early 1920s moved when their lease expired, looking for a better deal on another piece of land.[47] They usually did not find it, and when the price of cotton fell they couldn't survive without government help.

But the help that came in the form of programs like those created by the Agricultural Adjustment Act (AAA) only benefited the landowners. Paid to take land out of production, they evicted their tenants and used the government money to put tractors on the acreage they still planted.[48] Cheap labor—slaves or sharecroppers—was no longer needed to grow cotton. Each tractor is estimated to have displaced three to five farm families. Between 1930 and 1940 the number of tractors in Texas tripled, and 83,000 farm operators—mostly tenants in Central Texas and the southern Panhandle—quit farming, fleeing to nearby cities and to California.[49] Williamson County's population fell each decade after 1930 despite the fact that the towns of Georgetown, Taylor, and Round Rock were all growing.

It was not just lowlands of the cotton South that were hit hard by economic change; the homelands of the cedar choppers—Appalachia and the Ozarks—had been transformed as well. Timber companies had moved in and created clear-cut wastelands, irreparably damaging the forests upon which the hill people depended. In Appalachia men worked in the mines to earn survival wages. In the Ozarks they went to the plains to pick cotton; when cotton collapsed, they had to leave their homes in the hills, for the land could no longer support so many people.[50]

But there was no grand exodus from the Hill Country like there was from almost everywhere else in the rural South. The famous anthropologist Oscar Lewis was a young man in 1945 when he wrote a report on Bell County for the Department of Agriculture. He called it "On the Edge of the Black Waxy," for like all the counties straddling the Balcones Fault, Bell County was divided into a fertile east and a hilly west. He noted that the farm families in the western parts "were apparently better able to weather the Depression of the thirties than were many of the farmers in the more prosperous areas."[51] They survived by hunting, fishing, trapping, charcoal burning, and growing a little corn.

Cedar was unlike any other product. The coal in West Virginia and the forests in Tennessee and Arkansas belonged to big companies, and work involved organizing teams of men and machines to get the product out of the hills. Cedar could be cut by a single man with a small axe and hauled out of the brakes in a Model T truck. In the early days you didn't even need a truck—there were local stores, like Engle's Store west of Boerne or those in the little communities west of Belton, that would trade cedar for groceries.[52] Oral interviews with the old-timers there show that cedar saved them. One said, "This was a cash crop, cedar posts was, 'cause you'd take them right to the grocery store and swap them for whatever you needed. And if you had some left over, you got a little money to bring home, or you just bought candy for the kids."[53] Another said, "I don't know of a community store that didn't buy posts . . . you didn't go without the essentials if you can get some posts. . . . Best resource we had for bad times."[54] Another likened a cedar brake to a bank where you could "cut a little post, take 'em to Sparta, and trade 'em for groceries."[55]

Not only was cedar a valuable product because of what you could do with it, but the government was starting to pay people to get rid of it. Ranchers had long realized that brush control was the only way to make money raising cattle, and those in some of the less populated western counties like Kerr and Blanco hired gangs of Mexicans to clear cedar in the 1920s, before the massive deportations to "repatriate" Mexicans began a decade later.

During the Depression the government would pay landowners by the acre to clear the cedar. County records show that 63,000 acres were cut and burned in Blanco County in 1938, most of it new growth sap cedar.[56] One source claims that 3.4 million acres in Texas were cleared, some of it in later years by dragging a huge chain between two dozers.[57] Independent ranchers who rarely had anything good to say about the government praised the AAA program for what it did for the rangeland in Texas. Don Simons remembers when the government paid five dollars an acre, and that groups of thirty to forty men would camp together and cut: "In a day's time those men could cut a lot of cedar."

The late 1930s were also the years when construction began on the huge Highland Lakes dams extending from north of Burnet down to Austin. The cedar had to be cut from the river valleys, and the cutters were paid either by the acre or by letting them keep the good posts to sell. The company would pay the chopper piece-rate by the post, rewarding those who could cut well. There was a big camp of these cedar choppers just west of Mansfield Dam, accessed from Austin by Bee Cave Road.

Nevertheless, just because the cedar people were able to stay on the land does not explain why they chose to do so. There were numerous reasons to move to the city—jobs for the men, conveniences for the women, and schools for the children. As the historian Thad Sitton wrote, "Persistence in the face of massive forces making for change is hard to explain—not just for historians, but for farm families themselves."[58]

Elsie Upton taught in one of the ten "mountain schools" in western Travis County during the late 1930s and got to know the cedar chopper families. She said they married young, had six to twelve

Clearing cedar with chain. Photo courtesy of Southwest Collection, Texas Tech University, Lubbock, Texas Sheep and Goat Raisers Association Collection, SWCPC 90(a).44.

children, owned a car to take cedar or charcoal into town, ate wild pigs and game, and canned wild fruit. They staged dances in the hills with local fiddlers. The school term lasted only five to six months, and kids attended irregularly because of the distance and the need to work. The ages of kids in the first three grades of her school ranged from six to sixteen, with a median age of eleven in the second grade. Sometimes a boy would show up after having trapped a skunk, and the school would applaud his obvious success. And, she said, they made moonshine.[59]

I wondered if the reason they stayed in the hills might have been answered by Jed Clampett of the *Beverly Hillbillies*. When he asked cousin Pearl if he should move from the hills, she wondered why he would even ask such a question—he lived miles from his nearest neighbor, cooked on a wood stove, got light from a kerosene lamp, had to use an outhouse, and drank homemade moonshine whiskey. He was overrun with skunks, possums, coons, and coyotes. She thought she made a strong case for leaving. Jed pondered all this and said, "Yeah, I reckon you're right. A man'd be a dang fool to leave all this."

But there was something about this way of life—about the hills in all their primitiveness—that had a hold on people. Its variety was always surprising, yielding nuts and fish and deer, as well as clear water and autumn colors and a dusting of winter snows. Perhaps such beauty helped to sustain the cedar people through hard times.

Mack Sutton was interviewed while taking a drive through the hills west of Austin. He pointed out a pool on Bull Creek: "This pool down here was fifteen feet deep and so clear." He said there were unwritten laws about taking care of the land—everybody cleaned out the springs and never threw glass or cans in them. "All of this should have been a state park," he declared. When he got close to Anderson Mill, he said, "I have always thought this was the most beautiful country."

But even when the land turned on you, and it didn't rain for months, and everything became dry and brittle in the heat, there was pride in being so strong and hard that you could take it standing. That was what Cactus Pryor meant when he said Charlie King was as much a part of the Hill Country as the cedar and limestone.[60]

John Graves put it another way: "The relationship between those people and this land had a kind of rightness to it that we who possess it later stand little chance of attaining."[61]

But one still has to wonder—was cash for cedar, independence, and a harsh but spectacular setting really enough to give up the comforts of the city? They had one other resource—a "raw white whiskey for solace and courage and cash"[62]—called moonshine.

Moonshine during the Thirties

Prohibition ended in 1933, but by then so had the stigma of drinking. The 1930s were hard drinking, rough, and violent times, and the sweet moonshine from the hills west of Austin was not only cheaper but stronger than store-bought liquor. Linda Vance discovered that almost all the fifty families in Eanes, "from high status down to cedar choppers," made their own whiskey, and some of them sold it. When wages were only $0.20 to $0.30 an hour, a batch of whiskey could fetch $100.[63] The famous bootlegger Earl Short said making whiskey kept him out of the soup line and that the only reason he ever burned charcoal "was 'cause we was waitin' for the mash to cook off and we had lots of time to spare."[64] Frank Spiller remembers that he would see smoke rising from all over the hills in the early mornings. One lawman estimated there were one hundred stills west of Austin during the 1930s, with remote Spicewood the leading area.[65]

The methods of transfer from seller to buyer without getting caught were ingenious. People from Bertram would drive down to the cattle guard at Cow Creek and honk their horns, leaving a quart or gallon jug with some money in it. They would drive away for a little while, and when they returned the bottle would be full of whiskey.[66] Dick Simons's wife Edith would listen for the train, its whistle signaling how much whiskey to send with her son to the tracks at Hooper's Switch.[67]

But the most ingenious method I heard of to avoid getting caught was used by Lee Simons, Dick's brother. Lee's son Don would go with his dad right into Austin on Sixth Street in broad daylight, the moonshine buried under a pile of cedar. They would load the liquor

"Cedar" trucks. Photo courtesy of Austin History Center, Austin Public Library.

in the center of the bed of the truck, stack cedar around the sides and on top, and put short pieces in the back. The whole bed would look as if it was stacked with posts. Since the revenuers didn't want to go into the hills without a big group, the real danger of being caught was being stopped on the road. Lee had rigged it up so that if he were being followed, he would pull a rope in the cab when they went around a curve that would release the entire right hand side of the bed. Don said, "They'd pull that slip knot and whip the steering wheel, all the whiskey and everything would go—cedar and the whisky and everything, down the holler."

One day in 1932 he pulled the rope and it didn't come untied. The load shifted, and the truck turned over, gasoline and whiskey mixing and catching fire. Dick and his two-year-old child were riding with Lee and escaped unhurt, but Lee was badly burned and spent a long time in the hospital.[68] He never recovered from the injury or from the morphine he was given for pain.

There were several big stories in the newspapers during the 1930s involving moonshine and the people in the clans. In two of them, liquor is ancillary to the larger story, of fighting in the first case and genuine viciousness in the second. The story of Ike Young, however, is mainly about liquor and the massive efforts by the feds to control moonshining in the hills.[69]

Ike Young had a sixty-gallon whiskey still up a draw across the lake from Mount Bonnell. He was a target of the feds not only because it was a fairly large-scale operation but because his family was already infamous for brother killing brother, not once but twice. Agent Wilford "Tommy" Thomasson was particularly eager to apprehend Young; the previous year he had busted Ernest Thurman and his wife Delia Mae Brust for operating a fifty-gallon still on Bee Cave Road.[70] Both Ern Thurman and Ike Young were well known outlaw bootleggers, Ike already having served time in Huntsville for burglary and Ern Thurman charged with intent to murder more than once. Thomasson, known as a particularly aggressive investigator, was determined to shut them down.

It was early evening on Valentine's Day 1937 when three agents rowed across the river from Kennelwood boat docks and worked their way north to the still. They had had it under surveillance for days, and were waiting for "the run" of the mash to begin before making the arrests. Although not originally a part of the arrest team, another lawman said, "Tommy was so eager to be in on the raid that he went along with Mitch last night."

Agent Marty Mitchell described the event: "Before we started down to the still site, Tommy, standing up on top of a ravine, held up two fingers to me and said 'two men.' When we moved on down the ravine to the still we found Ike Young and Hazel Hamilton there and arrested them, and I called up to Thomasson 'I've got 'em, Tommy.'" The agents were ready to leave with the two handcuffed subjects, but Thomasson said: "'You stay here, Mitch. I'm going down the trail a minute.' Shortly afterward I heard a burst of shots."

The shots were exchanged between Thomasson and Pete Martinez, who lived in the area and was working the still with Ike. Both died in the exchange, and except for the third agent seeing flashes of gunfire in the dark, there were no witnesses. That agent chased a second fleeing suspect through the thick brush and shot at him several times, but he escaped across the lake in a boat.

The fleeing suspect was fifteen-year old Hucel Hamilton. He and his sisters Hazel (eighteen) and Beulah (twenty-two) lived with Ike Young and other members of the Hamilton family in a two-room shack at Taylor Slough. Hucel had picked up the .38 revolver that

Martinez had used to kill Thomasson and had given it to a sister to bury.

The next morning dozens of agents from across the state descended on the area, ordering a roundup of all the residents between the dam and Mount Bonnell. They found young Hucel covered under a mound of blankets and charged him, his sister Beulah, and Ike Young with murder under a new law that made the death of an agent in the line of duty a federal offence. Another eleven people were charged with "conspiracy to defraud the United States of internal revenue taxes." The entire Hamilton family was put in jail, including three children under the age of nine; the sheriff said it was "to keep them from going hungry." Residents of the area were upset: a woman called Mitchell's wife and warned her to "keep her husband away from Taylor Slough."

It was a sensational case, occupying the front page of the *Austin Statesman* for days. More than fifty persons were called to the stand, including a storekeeper on 34th Street who said Young would frequently purchase fifty to a hundred pounds of sugar, rye and yeast. The paper called Ike Young an "unkempt Travis country hillman," eventually shortened to "hillbilly moonshiner." Once again, people in the cedar chopper clans were paraded through the news, and the fears of Austinites were confirmed.

The charges against Hucel and Beulah Hamilton were dropped, but the feds were determined to put Ike away for murder. They did not care that he was handcuffed at the time of the killing, that he was unarmed and had not resisted arrest in any way, or that the gun used to kill Thomasson had belonged to Martinez.

According to agent Mitchell, after Thomasson had gone down the trail he had asked Young if anyone else was around, and Young had said no. But Hazel had asked for a drink of water out of a barrel, and while leaning down she kept looking up the draw where Thomasson had gone. The charge was that Ike knew Thomasson was walking into a trap. Yet Martinez was not near the still and would have had no reason to shoot had someone approached in the dark, nor would Ike, already handcuffed, have gained anything by having Martinez kill the agent.

The star government witness for the theory that Ike had

orchestrated the killing was a convicted murderer who was beginning a ninety-nine-year sentence. His record at Huntsville shows him to have been an extremely unruly prisoner, receiving twenty lashes several times during one year for bad behavior. He resided in Fayette County and committed the murder in the Rio Grande Valley, so it is not clear why he was being held in the Travis County jail. He wanted a transfer, some say so that he could escape. Though he claimed he was not promised anything for his testimony, he was granted that transfer immediately after the trial.

The convict said Ike had told him he "knew when the officer left he was walking into a death trap," and that if it had been any other officer Ike would have warned him, but that Ike had said he didn't mind seeing that one go down. The convict admitted not liking Young but denied having written a note threatening to kill him because he wouldn't take a bath. But he added, "So we gave him one." One can only wonder how that came about: though not a large man, Ike was a cedar chopper and strong. It would have taken several men and the complicity of the jailers for a "bath" to have occurred.

Ike was sentenced to life in prison. A week before he was sent to Leavenworth, he formally married Beulah Hamilton in the jailhouse corridor. Two years later she was working in a Works Progress Administration (WPA) sewing room and supporting her mother, Hucel, two brothers, and son Alfred Carl Young. By then sister Hazel, who had pleaded guilty on the liquor tax charge, was married to Tom Short, brother of the famous bootlegger Earl Short (about whom more in chapter 7). Hucel went into the army in 1942. Ike died in Alcatraz prison in 1952. The murderer who put him away was stabbed to death in prison a year after his testimony.

It is no wonder that the cedar choppers mistrusted the law.

Fencing the West

But yeah, this used to be cedar country, cuttin' country, you know.

Stanley Allen, Interview

Free-roaming cattle caused huge problems. They had to be kept from where they were not supposed to be, like on neighbors' fields and railroad tracks. In Texas, an open-range state, they were fenced *out*, not in. Germans in the Hill Country solved the problem by using massive amounts of family labor to build stone walls around their fields. Had they been paying labor at the prevailing wage, the cost would have been prohibitive—$300 to $450 per mile.[1] To the east timber was used to make split-rail fences. But the open prairie offered no rocks and no wood. Bois d'arc trees could be planted, but they were expensive and took five years to grow together enough to be effective. One publication said it took $1.74 in fencing to keep $1.65 of stock from eating $2.45 of crops.[2]

Railroads had to pay for cattle killed by the trains. In 1877–78 the Texas and Pacific Railway paid cattlemen $65.84 for every mile of track.[3] During the next decade 94,000 miles of railway were fenced to keep the cattle off.[4]

But perhaps even more important than the costs of keeping cattle *out* were the benefits of keeping cattle *in*. Free-ranging cattle had to be rounded up and branded, a time-consuming activity requiring a group of men working together. A rancher would try to upgrade his herd, only to have it dragged down by a neighbor's inferior stock. Charles Goodnight was a pioneer in improved breeding and recognized these benefits, but he also opposed open range for another reason: "It simply means the use of the grass to the strongest arm. The six-shooter and free grass go hand in hand. . . . To monopolize free grass a man must have a tough set of hands, whom he has to keep around him all the time, and they will eat up the profits."[5]

The combination of the windmill and barbed wire transformed the cattle business by allowing cattle to be kept in fenced pastures with water. Joseph Glidden's patent for barbed wire– the "wire that fenced the west"—was granted in 1874. At first it was resisted: it came from a northern state, it competed with lumber for fencing, and cattlemen thought it cruel. But it worked. A dramatic demonstration was held in San Antonio the following year. A corral of barbed wire was erected in the main plaza, and the salesman invited ranchers to bring in their most unruly animals. He boasted, "This is the finest fence in the world. Light as air. Stronger than whiskey. Cheaper than dirt. All steel, and miles long. The cattle ain't born that can get through it. Bring on your steers, gentlemen!" Amazingly, it kept the wild longhorns in.[6]

What really sold the ranchers was its actual use in a cattle operation. In 1881 Glidden and wire salesman Henry Sanborn bought 250,000 acres in the Panhandle that they named the Frying Pan Ranch. The ranch was enclosed with 120 miles of fence, constructed with four evenly spaced barbed wires and strung on cedar posts from Palo Duro Canyon.[7] In 1882 Charles Goodnight fenced 240,000 acres of the T Anchor Ranch, and a year later he fenced the huge pastures of the Quitaque Ranch.[8] On the XIT, 3,000 cowboys built 1,500 miles of fence for 50,000 cattle.[9] There were no railroads in the Panhandle at that time, so the copious amounts of barbed wire had to be hauled out on the plains in wagons, which returned loaded with buffalo bones. Cattle had taken over the prairies, and now even the last traces of the bison they had displaced were erased.

It was after this initial fencing that Goodnight rescued Taos chief Standing Deer from a group of settlers who did not speak Spanish or know the difference between Comanches and tribes from the pueblos to the west. When Chief Standing Deer asked his friend Goodnight how to get back to Taos, Goodnight replied "You surely know the way back to Taos. Haven't you lived in this country all your life?" "Si señor," he said. "Pero alambre! alambre! alambre! Todas partes!"[10] Wire was everywhere.

While the mammoth cattle operations in the Panhandle initiated the use of barbed wire, the fencing of Texas was not completed until decades later. The smaller western ranches were fenced only when wire and posts could be hauled by rail to the towns. During the 1930s the cedar was cleared and the pastures were fenced on some of the bigger Hill Country ranches, like the 22,000-acre Sunset Ranch between Leander and the Colorado River.[11] When farming crashed during the Depression there was a massive conversion of field to pasture, all requiring fencing. This process was accelerated by shortages of labor during World War II. In 1940 most of the land in eastern Bell County was still planted in cotton; by 1945 only one-third was cultivated.[12] The rest was turned to pasture and had to be fenced. And about that time faster cars led to laws that made it a criminal offense even to have a cow on the road.

Practically all this fencing was hung on cedar posts from the Hill Country. There have been books written about "the wire that fenced the West," but little has been said about the posts that held these wires in place from South Texas to Montana. Good posts were equally vital to making a fence economical; if the posts rotted, new holes would have to be dug and the fence completely rebuilt. Only one species of wood—*Juniperus ashei* from the cedar brakes on the Edwards Plateau—was really rot-resistant: it would last longer than the wire that was strung on it.[13] There was simply no good alternative to what was called mountain cedar until cheap steel posts were manufactured during the 1960s.

The basic fence post was called a yard four—a 6½-foot post four inches in diameter at the top. It was set 1½ feet deep into hard soil or rock—deeper in sandy soil like in South Texas, requiring longer posts—and every so often a corner post with an 18-inch top would be set deep in the ground. With a post set every ten to twelve feet, it took about 500 posts to build a mile of fence. The thirty-mile stretch of Highway 29 between Burnet and Llano, site of the axe-cut posts shown on page 107, would have required 30,000 posts, or 250 days of cutting at a rate of 120 posts a day. This fence was probably built in the 1940s (there was only one mile of paved road in all

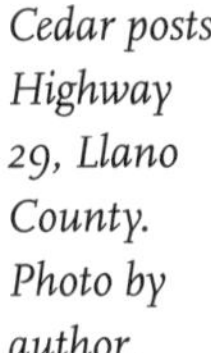

Cedar posts, Highway 29, Llano County. Photo by author.

of Llano County in 1937), yet these posts are still strong enough to stretch barbed wire seventy-five years later.

Several things came together to make it possible to meet this huge demand for cedar posts. The first was a really good axe, sometimes called the Kerrville cedar axe, because it was designed by the manager of a hardware store in Kerrville. He saw that the heavy, clumsy axes that he sold to ranchers employing Mexican laborers to clear their land during the 1920s were unsatisfactory. He designed an axe that was light and nimble, the balanced double-bladed head weighing only about three pounds. It quickly became the most indispensable tool of a cedar chopper. The Hartwell Company of Memphis is estimated to have sold 80,000 cedar axes before World War II, and companies like Collins and Kelly made cedar axes as well. [14]

A good axe was razor sharp. Simon Ratliff would sharpen his axe for an hour a day for several days with different files until it was so sharp that it would hold an edge for a long time. Olan Raley told me, "I guarantee you could shave with it. I mean, they'd file it and they'd take a whet rock and whet it down until it was thin and smooth. And, you know, you take a post that big around (four inches)—they'd cut it in two in two licks." Lee Cantrell said it took

Kelly cedar axe. Photo by Tina Patlyek.

only five or six licks with a 3½-pound Kelly axe (shown) to cut a post large enough to make a yard four. The hardwood handle, shaved smooth with a shard of glass so that it molded to the hand, was elastic so that it had some give when it hit the wood.

Because their axes were so finely honed and balanced, cedar choppers were protective of them. Olan Raley said, "I mean, one thing you didn't mess with—with the wood cutters—was their axe." A girl growing up in a cedar chopping family west of Belton said, "*Nobody* touched Daddy's axe!"[15] Moreover, they were contemptuous of anything less than this perfect tool. John Graves was trimming cedar near his house with a camping axe when the patriarch of a cedar chopper clan working nearby sidled up. "He watched me corneringly with long, shapely, slightly mad, pale-blue eyes as I hacked at twigs and branches, an alien amateur. He said finally, unable not to: 'Shame you got to work with a little old shitty play-toy axe like that. And 'hit not even sharp.'"[16]

The second essential component of the cedar business was a truck to haul the cedar from the brakes. Usually the choppers would take off the bed and place big posts crossways on the frame to support the stack of smaller posts. Cedar choppers would often convert a big sedan into what they called a "hoopie" by cutting off the back and leaving only the frame. Frank Boatright said Charlie Maynard had a 1938 Buick hoopie with a great radio: "He'd leave that thing on so all you could hear in the hills was chopping and that radio. And when he heard a song he liked he'd just take to dancin.' He cut a wing, just like an ol' rooster does."[17]

They took these trucks deep into the brakes. Good heart cedar grows best in the places that are hardest to get to, and they would often have to cut a road to get there. The terrain was especially hard on tires. Stoney Teague, Homer's son, told me, "There used to be

T. M. Pearson loading cedar, 1942. Photo courtesy of T.M. Pearson.

some of them old cedar choppers over there, they'd take them old truck tires, and they wouldn't—didn't throw nothing away. If you had an old tire that run over a staub [protruding root or stump] or something, and you couldn't fix it, they'd take a piece of a tire and cut it out with their knife, take stove bolts and put it in there, put two or three cubes in it, and pump it up with a hand pump. Put it back on one of them old trucks. Get out there and make a load with it." Al Ehrlich, owner of a big cedar yard, said, "Things that bother you and me don't faze them. Being always broke, they've got the poorest equipment of any workin' people I've ever seen. They'll load up one of their old trucks with cedar posts and have four or five flat tires before they get to the cedar yard. We would blow our lid. They take it in stride."[18]

That was still in the early days of hauling posts—during the Depression and early war years—when people were poor and tires were rationed. What was the point of putting more money than necessary into a truck that took such abuse? Sometimes a chopper would back up a hill to get to the cedar because there was more traction in reverse, especially if the bed was loaded with rocks. Mack

Long-haul truck. Photo courtesy of the Texas State Historical Commission, from documentation for the historical marker for Engle Store, Bergheim, Kendall County, Texas.

Long-haul truck. Photo courtesy of Southwest Collection, Texas Tech University, Lubbock, Texas Sheep and Goat Raisers Association Collection, SWCPC 90(a).174.

Modern long-haul truck. Photo by author.

Sutton said, "You'd be amazed and wonder how they could do it. They'd go up a really steep hill like that with an old Model T Ford truck with a Russell axle, and you just ch-ch-ch up there." Then they would unload the rocks, load the cedar, and chain a big tree to the back bumper to slow the descent. At the bottom they would cut up the tree and add it to their load. Sometimes they could stop only by running into a cedar tree at the bottom, giving the term "cedar brake" a whole new meaning.[19] Olan Raley from Junction said, "None of them trucks had brakes on 'em then, you know. So I'd stop up there on top of the hill and I'd fill that brake cylinder full of water. Damn brake fluid was too high, so we'd put water in it. And

Axe-cut cedar posts in Colorado (above) and West Texas (left). Photos by author.

I'd have brakes coming off that hill, you know. And if I was lucky I could get through town with a little bit of brake."

Because their trucks were always breaking down, they became some of the best backyard mechanics ever. Stoney said of Shorty Cantrell, "I'm not talking about a parts changer. I'm not talking about running up here and getting a water pump and putting it on. I'm talking about, if you broke it, he would take a cutting torch and welding machine and he'd set down there on the floor and put it back together." A cedar chopper rebuilt Hollis Baker's fuel pump with a pair of pliers and a Prince Albert tobacco can. Joe L. Roberts could put an engine back together on a tarp in his back yard even though he was blind.

Mountain cedar was trucked to places far from the Hill Country.

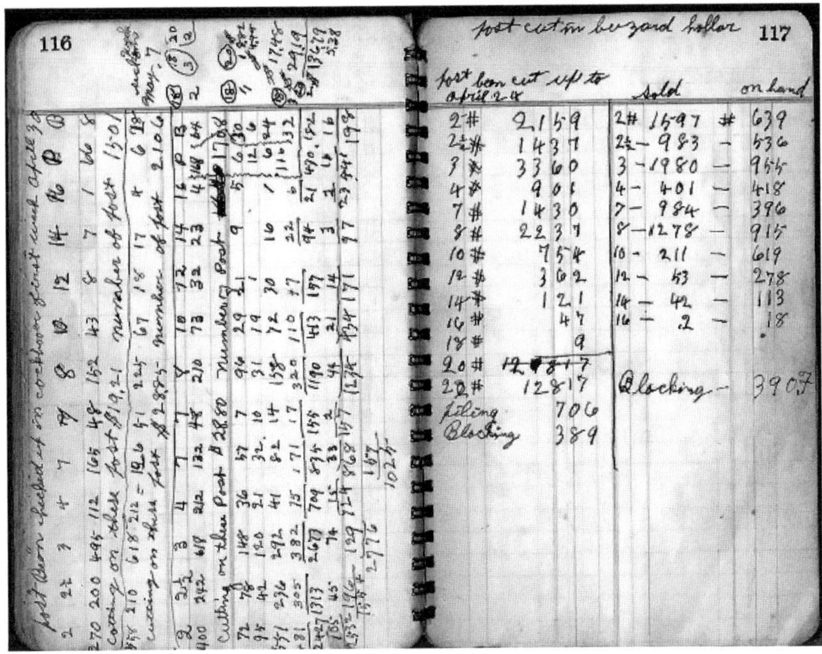

post cut on buzzard hollar 117

post been cut up to April 2-4		Sold	on land
2#	2159	2# 1597 #	639
2½#	1437	2½ – 983 –	536
3#	3360	3 – 1980 –	955
4#	901	4 – 401 –	418
7#	1430	7 – 984 –	396
8#	2237	8 – 1278 –	915
10#	754	10 – 211 –	619
12#	362	12 – 53 –	278
14#	121	14 – 42 –	113
16#	47	16 – 2 –	18
18#	9		
20#	~~12817~~		
22#	12817	Blocking –	3907
piling	706		
Blocking	389		

John Willess's cedar book. Book courtesy of Bob Willess.

I've talked to men who went with their fathers hauling cedar all over the Plains states and the West. Simon Ratliff remembered hauling a load to Montana with his dad in a straight-eight International that would get a vapor lock at high altitudes and stall; when they got to a pass, Simon would collect snow and hold it on the fuel pump as they slowly ascended. Ray Bertling went to Nebraska, South Dakota, and Wyoming; Dick Turner to Arizona, New Mexico, and South Dakota; Lee McKinnerney to Kansas and Nebraska; T. M. Pearson to Lubbock and Oklahoma; Arthur Lee Wallace to New Mexico, Louisiana, and Oklahoma. Even today you can find axe-cut posts made of Ashe juniper still standing all across the Southwest and Plains states.

Cedar Yards

At the hub of this industry was the cedar yard. The owner of the yard would contract with a rancher to cut the cedar on his land, paying him about 10 percent of the value of the cedar that was cut. The choppers would bring this cedar to the yard and unload it every day or two, being paid by the post. Dick Boatright's yard in Cedar Park received eight to twelve truckloads a day; each of the four yards in Ingram received ten. T. M. Pearson said, "Some weeks, I had forty, fifty cutters coming in." Joe Gillman said Cahill and Hickman had a twenty-acre yard at Jollyville, where three hundred cutters brought cedar from the canyons of what would become Lake Travis.

Shown on page 113 is a sample record from a 1938 cedar book of John Willess, the father of Bob Willess, one of my interviewees. Before Fort Hood took the land, John owned a cedar yard in the little community of Brookhaven, west of Belton. There are many pages in the book showing the loads of cedar he bought from various independent choppers. This page documents the cedar cut by four men he hired to cut in "buzzard holler"—from "deuces" (2-inch posts) all the way up to 16-inch posts, pilings, and blocking. The most common sizes from this brake are 3-inch and 8-inch posts.

The big semi trucks would line up at the yards to be loaded—a job Ronnie Roberts complained about having to do before school

Stephens yard. Photo by author.

as a kid. Charles Hagood remembers "trailer trucks loaded plum to the gills with cedar posts" rumbling through Junction, and three to five semis a day would roll out of Stephens yard in Ingram during the mid-1950s. C. R. Morrison was buying 20,000–40,000 posts a month in 1948 at his yard in Georgetown and shipping them as far as California. Just a few years earlier, he said, the business hardly even existed.[20]

Appendix 3 is a list of more than fifty cedar yards in Central Texas that have been mentioned to me or that have appeared in print. All the major roads leading out from Austin had cedar yards—Lamar Boulevard, South Congress Avenue, Fredericksburg Road, Bull Creek Road, Spicewood Springs Road. They were thick on what is now Highway 183 from Jollyville through Cedar Park and Leander and out to Bertram, Burnet, and Marble Falls. Margie Carlton told John Leffler that Cedar Park was "nothing but cedar yards—the whole town consisted of five or six cedar yards and one store, and there were other cedar yards in New Hope and Jollyville."[21] Myers Cedar Yard in Lampasas is still thriving today.

The yards listed that were in town, such as the Vaughn yard on South Congress Avenue, were from the early decades of the century. Cedar yards were not usually allowed in town because of the danger of fire, which was instant and intense. In the 1970s a fire started in a cedar yard in Camp Wood that jumped from one stack of cedar to the next. By the time the fire trucks arrived from Uvalde and Leakey, the heat had warped nearby mobile homes and caused the spontaneous combustion of a bird's nest in an oak tree across a wide street.[22] When F. W. King's cedar yard in Burnet burned to the ground in 1919, the city would not let him rebuild in town. He was a big businessman locally—one of the old limestone buildings on the Burnet square has his name on it—and his response was to close all his businesses in Burnet and move his biggest yard to Cedar Park.[23]

As the good cedar near Austin was cut, the cedar business moved west. The road built between Leakey and Camp Wood in 1947 opened up virgin timber, and there was plenty of heart cedar around Medina and Kerrville when Ronnie Roberts's dad had his yard there in the early 1950s. Mack Callahan closed his yard in Marble Falls and went to the Kerrville area, bringing a lot of cutters with him.[24] The names of many of the owners and managers of the yards in the western Hill Country are familiar—Roberts, Simons, Boatright, Cantrell—names from the big Austin clans. The clans who started in the hills near Austin dominated the cedar business as it moved farther west on the Edwards Plateau.

During the Depression the standard post, a yard four, sold for a nickel. In 1942 it cost a dime, and by 1950, with the surge in the demand for posts, it rose to a quarter. Men told me that that they could make good money cutting cedar during the 1940s and 1950s. Lee Cantrell would cut 150 posts—a full load for his three-quarter-ton truck—and would sell it for $23–$25. T. M. Pearson, known as one of the best cedar cutters in the Whitt-Maynard-Bonnet clan, said he could cut $21–$23 worth of posts in less than four hours. Even when cedar was bringing only fifteen to twenty cents a post, Henry Polk told Gary Cartwright, "I was strong as a bull. I could cut wood all day long. When the weather was good, it weren't nothing to make twenty dollars a day."[25]

Twenty dollars a day was a lot of money back in the 1940s and 1950s compared to what you could make doing something else. Picking cotton would pay about a dollar per hundred pounds, so a good picker would make four dollars a day. Working on the dam paid forty cents an hour during the late 1930s, and the quarry—the biggest employer northwest of Austin—paid less than a dollar an hour all through the 1940s. Artie Henry started working at the quarry when he returned from the war, but he gave it up for cedar. It was his wife Betty who first made me understand how lucrative cutting cedar was during the peak years between 1940 and 1960. She said Artie could make more cutting cedar in three hours than working a whole day in the quarry.

Artie wasn't even a "real" cedar chopper; that is, from one of the families whose major occupation had been burning charcoal or cutting cedar in the early decades of the century. The Henrys were an old farming family from western Williamson County, and Betty called the people living in the brakes to the west "hillbillies," although without any condescension. But Artie was ambitious enough to do what he could to make money, and for about ten years, from the mid-1940s to the mid-1950s, he cut cedar. He saved his money, worked for a while as a ranch foreman, and in 1968 opened a grocery store in Cedar Park.

Following that interview, I always asked something like this: *My understanding is that after World War II, a man could make more money cutting cedar than he could doing almost anything else—than he could in a waged job as a laborer. Is that right?* Everybody confirmed it. Alice Patterson told me, "At that time it was about the best thing you could do, it really was." Don Simons said, "That's right. Dick Simons [Don's uncle] got up every morning before daylight, and by daylight he was in the cedar brake. By eleven o'clock he was coming back with a load of cedar." Simon Ratliff also got up before daylight, sometimes building a bonfire so that he could start early. If he did that, he could make a load by nine o'clock and return to cut another.

I talked to several men from the last generation of cedar choppers who had tried other lines of work but came back to chopping cedar. Simon Ratliff worked for Brown and Root in Houston for a while but returned to Central Texas to cut. Charlie Maugham worked a while for the city of Marble Falls earning $35 a week. During the late 1950s, he claims, he could make more than that in a single day working in good timber.

Morris Bonnet told me, "When I got married—of course my wife was born and raised in Liberty Hill—she kind of frowned on me being a cedar cutter. And I said 'Hey, I make more money at this than I did—I was a Union sheet metal worker—and I could go out there and cut cedar and make more money than I was making as a Union sheet metal worker.'" Bob Willess said, "Oh, yeah, a cedar chopper wasn't nothing. But yet they made more money doing that than that guy trying to run that grocery store."

Yet I was still surprised when Stoney Teague told me that he had returned from the oil fields in West Texas to cut cedar. Somewhat incredulous—I grew up in Texas during a time when wages were rock bottom everywhere but the oil patch—I rephrased the question. *You could make as much in a day cutting cedar as you could roughnecking?* "Yeah, isn't that something." *Cause I always heard that roughnecking was the best paid job in Texas.* "It was, you know, it was."

It was hard for me to reconcile the kind of money they made with the shabby way they dressed and how they lived. Back in the early part of the century and during the Depression people living in the hills may have had to live like that, but during the 1940s and '50s the cedar choppers had money, more than most working-class folks. Frank Wilson, interviewed in 1978, said, "Well, you see now, those people, you wouldn't call them poor. They just liked to live that way. That's what I mean, they look like they were working for small wages or something, but they weren't. Bill [Farmer] might have had five hundred dollars in his pocket all the time. They weren't poor. They dressed that way because they were always working." Luther Pierce once went with his nephew Linwood to sell some pipe to Frank Boatright, who had moved from Bull Creek to near Luther's quarry outside Jarrell. When the time came to pay Linwood the $2,500 owed to him, "Ol' Frank pulled out a giant roll of hundred dollar bills."

The increased demand for cedar posts coincided with ranchers' need to clear the land for grazing. Barbed wire and the improvements in breeding had increased the value of cattle to the point where ranchers would pay someone to clear the cedar, especially when the cost was subsidized by the government. If it was good timber, the rancher might get a percentage of the value of the posts or get to keep some for fencing. If it was poor quality and wouldn't make good posts, the cutters would be paid by the acre for clear-cutting the cedar.

Either way—whether they sold the posts or were paid to cut them—the demand for their work soared. When they cut the cedar out of the canyons for Lake Buchanan, C. W. Wimberley said that cedar cutters moved into the houses vacated by farmers who had fled during the Depression. He wrote, "The cedarwhacker ate high on the hog. He moved into the sore-necked farmers' vacant houses, ate the biggest steaks, drank the most beer, and made more down payments on second-hand cars than anyone from that neck of the woods ever."[26] This was the heyday of the cedar choppers, the time when they emerged from the hills and became a part of the fabric of life in Central Texas.

7
The Life of a Cedar Chopper

Yeah, I can cut posts. I'm a cedar post cutter. That's what I do.

Arthur Lee Wallace, Interview

Working in the Brakes

During the summer cutting began early in the morning. The brakes would retain the cool of the night for a few hours, but by the afternoon, when the slightest breeze was blocked by the dense foliage, they turned into ovens. A few men worked alone, but most worked with a member of the family or a friend. Alice Patterson went with her father Ross when she was a kid: "Dad would take us to the cedar brake early in the morning. We'd go as early as we could before the sun got up. And then he would put us to carrying out the cedar posts that he cut, or cutting some by ourselves. We did a whole lot of that ourselves."

C. W. Wimberley described a family of cedar choppers headed by a man named Honest John, who said he and his family could cut forty dollars' worth of posts a day.

> Over in the pasture I found John's tribe scattered like a bunch of Spanish goats in a peach orchard. Two of the biggest girls were spotting the best post timber and taking care of any underbrush in the way. Five or six licks from John's four-pound Kelly felled the tree, and by the time it hit the ground John's

> wife or one of the big boys was on it, trimming and cutting off the top. Then two of the little ones would grab the post by its end and go kiting it out to where the Ford was being loaded. . . . By 9:30 or 10:00, a couple of the younger boys would pull onto the cedar yard with piles of poles riding the front fenders, posts sticking from both back windows and a four-foot stack racked atop the rear bumper. Sometimes they would make a second or third of such loads before the Tudor came in on its final run for the day, with kids and cedar posts in and all over it, and John's head hanging out to see where he was headed.[1]

Cedar posts had to be cut correctly or the yard wouldn't buy them. A 6½-foot 4-inch post—the standard yard four—had to be round and straight, knots and limbs trimmed smooth, and four to five inches in diameter at the top. Cedar men at yards were exacting in their measurement: one yard man would fit horseshoes around the posts to determine their different sizes. Doug Lavender, owner of two of the few remaining yards in Texas, takes the circumference of the post about six inches from the end and divides it by three to calculate the diameter.[2]

A tree might have several different sizes of posts. Usually the limbs were at least good enough for a deuce—a two-inch post—or a stay, a smaller limb that was attached to the wire between posts to keep it from sagging. An average tree might have about a dozen of these branches, which would be cut first, leaving the trunk. Some of the larger old growth trees had limbs big enough to make a yard four, and the main trunk could then make blocking or very valuable posts that could be used as beams or corner posts. In 2015 a yard four at Doug Lavender's yard in Lampasas sold for about three dollars; a twelve-foot post the diameter of the ones pictured on page 121 was ten times as much. A really good cedar cutter could tell the grade of the posts as he cut and plan the work to make the most money during his time in the brake. One of Morris Bonnet's friends could tell within a dollar the value of all the different sizes of posts on his truck.

A good cedar chopper could chop down a small tree for a yard four with four swings of a sharp axe. Albert Boatright Jr. said of

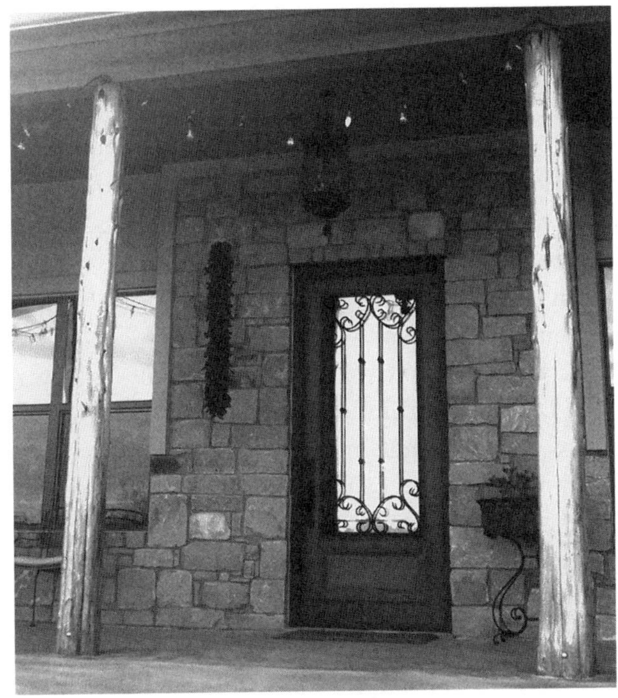

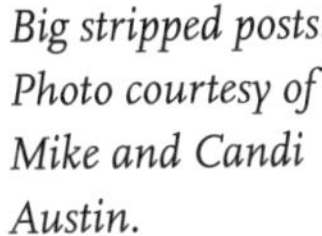

Big stripped posts. Photo courtesy of Mike and Candi Austin.

his uncle Raymond Shannon, "Boy, he was a cedar chopper! Man, about two licks on each side of that tree and it would be cut in two. Yeah! He was unbelievable, he was good." Olan Raley said the best choppers would cut from one side and switch hands for the other, but he admitted, "I'd have to crawfish around it."

At the beginning of the day they could cut fast. Frank Boatright said, "I timed my dad one day. It took him 17 seconds to cut and trim one neat as a pencil."[3] Richard Ringstaff, whose sister married a Williams of the Roberts-Teague clan, could cut a post a minute. "He did, I timed him," said his wife Minnie. "I was getting breakfast, and he says, 'I'm going across the creek and chop a few,' and then he looked at the clock and told me what time it was. When he come back he told me what time it was, and he had cut thirty posts, and it was half an hour." Simon Ratliff said he could cut a post a minute for the first hour, and then he would slow down. But still, including staves, he said he could cut over two hundred posts in a day with an axe, more than he ever could with a chainsaw.

Milton Lentz told me that his older brother Buford and Dick Simons could each cut two hundred posts a day. Dick Simons, like all the Simonses, was a big man. “He had big ol’ long arms, and man, he could take that axe, and he just went through it—*whop, whop, whop*—downed about twenty of ’em. He and my brother were the most magnificent thing I could see with an axe. You’d be amazed. It looked like a bulldozer going, pushing things out, with them cutting side by side.”

You can hear a lot of pride in these voices—the cedar brake was a real equalizer, and a measure of a man was how much cedar he could cut. Lee McKinnerney claimed his dad could cut 300 posts a day, while the men around him might cut 200 to 250. That is more than the men west of Austin, but perhaps it was because McKinnerney was working in virgin brakes in the hills north of Uvalde. Don Hibbitts, a resident of Camp Wood, told me, “We had some people here that were excellent cedar choppers, I mean, they were strong men. Toby Weaver was one of the best in the country—everybody always said he could go out and cut a truckload of cedar and a road to it in a day! He was just good. He was a very strong person. Course he had a lot of stamina too; he’d just keep going.”

Chopping cedar all day would make you strong. Charlie Maugham from Mable Falls was not a tall man, but even at eighty he was stout: “I was husky—I could lay that cedar down.” Emmett Shelton said of the Shorts of the Roberts-Teague clan, “All these Short boys, they’d look at an object and walk around it, and if it weren’t growed to the ground, they’d lift it.” Homer Teague was only five foot eight and weighed 165 pounds, but his son Stoney said, “He was all muscle. Well, them ol’ boys, all they done was swing an axe all day long, you know. And they stayed in shape.”

When you combined this strength with size, you had a very powerful man. Stanley Allen said of his son, “That big boy of mine, he’s a monster. His hands are three times bigger than me. He, that kid, God—he got big! And my youngest boy, of course they worked every day of their lives, you know. They all muscle. They ain’t no fat to these boys.” Lee McKinnerney’s dad was another powerful man: “They were afraid of him because he’d hurt ’em. And he didn’t care how many there were.” *He was pretty big, right?* “He was six foot one, weighed two-twenty." *And probably was very strong from cutting cedar.* "Oh shit! There wasn't nobody close. The police were afraid of him because they knew he was so strong. They couldn't handle him. They would have had to shoot him."

Ronnie Roberts showed me a picture of Rex Simons—big like all the Simons men—with a huge log on his shoulders, probably twelve inches in diameter and eight to ten feet long. The picture was from a 1999 interview with Rex in a collection of stories from the Medina area. He said, "Some of the canyons and hills around here are too rough and deep to get a truck into the cutting area. You have to carry every log out on your shoulders. You find a balance point and start packing. Some big long posts can weigh a couple of hundred pounds or more. I remember my grandfather's grip was like steel. All my uncles who followed the cedar trade were the strongest men around."[4] Rex's dad Willie had followed the cedar west to the Medina area from the Simons's home on Bull Creek.

Arthur Lee Wallace was one of the men I interviewed in Junction, along with Olan Raley and Charles Hagood. Arthur Lee was born in 1966 and so had never cut with an axe, but he was a cedar chopper, tall and lanky. He said, "I've cut some ten foot posts, you know, about sixteen-inch big around. Have 'em in the yard, and big men—six-five, big wide-shouldered men—come in there and grab the end and just shake, you know. It'd be that heavy. I'd just grab hold of it, pull it out there, throw it up on that truck. And 'Boy,' they'd say, 'How in the hell did you do that?' I'd say, it's all in the balance, you know. You're letting the post do the work. You don't do the work because, you know, it'd be a hundred forty, a hundred sixty, seventy pounds."

It was in the same interview that we started talking about women cutting. Arthur Lee said his grandmother, a Cantwell from the Roberts-Teague clan, would go with the men and cut stays. Olan Raley chimed in, "Little Amy Pell—y'all remember her? I guarantee, she cut five hundred heart stays every day. With an axe!" Charlie Maugham said, "Man they were stout! They could chop more cedar, some of 'em can, than the man."

Ozelle Maynard of the Whitt-Maynard-Bonnet clan was interviewed in 1961; she first said her age was 45 but corrected it to 52, saying, "Well, I don't feel but 45, and I can still chop and pack out 150 cedar a day. That's not bad."[5] Ed Pierce, Luther's oldest brother, is buried in Tucker Cemetery next to his wife Lorraine. Above their graves is a plaque that reads, "The Best Cedar Choppers." It was probably true, because Joe Gillman remembers that they would cut a big load together every day, and that Lorraine could cut almost as much as Ed. "She cut just about as much as anybody," Joe said.

Dangers

You not only had to be strong to cut cedar—you had to be tough. You would sweat until your shirt was stiff when it dried, and you would have cedar wax all over your hands and face. And there were lots of dangers in the cedar hills, things that bit you and stung you—scorpions and wasps and prickly pear and poison oak. Big diamondback rattlesnakes were common, but their bites were infrequent because they usually warned you; copperheads would blend in and strike when you were working down low. In the western Hill Country where Willie Simons worked resides a species called a rock rattler: "Mean little rascals that lays up in the forks of cedar trees; have to be careful you don't get one down your collar."[6]

By far the most serious danger was getting cut, and it happened to every cedar cutter I talked to. Their axes were so sharp that just a touch would cut you. Charlie Maugham showed me a scar where he cut his arm when the file slipped while he was sharpening his axe. Alice Patterson's sister and brother were chasing each other through the brakes when the boy ran into the axe Alice's husband was carrying. "It cut him, right here. Man, the blood went straight up to the sky! I didn't know if they was gonna make it with him or not. But they did, they got him to the doctor and he sewed him up and he was all right."

Simon Ratliff said one time he was cutting long posts for telephone lines. "I grabbed one and throwed it on an axe and that axe come at me. And I grabbed it as it cut my face in two." *Oh, my gosh. How deep did it go?* "It went pretty deep (laugh). The doctor said 'Ratliff, you just lacked an eighth of an inch of killing yourself.' I said, 'No, the devil lacked a mile of killing me.'" He showed me the scar that took seventy-seven stitches.

Willie Simons was fifteen and cutting cedar with his eleven-year-old brother Ben. "Ben yelled at me, 'Bubba! Come here! I think I've cut my foot off!' I ran to him to help, pulled off his shoe, and sure enough, he'd split his foot in half. I ran for Dad who was some distance away. I yelled, 'Ben's been cut bad.' Dad came running, took a look, and did the only first aid he knew. He poured table salt all over the cut, then poured coal oil on it. Using his shirt to bind the wound, he took Ben to the nearest doctor. The doctor sewed the foot back together and saved it, but Ben's foot never grew to a normal size."[7]

Getting cut was not the only serious danger. Morris Bonnet had to quit cutting cedar because a log fell on his foot and crushed the bones. Alice Patterson got hit by a falling log: "One time we were in the canyon over there off of Bee Cave down near the river, and he was throwing posts off of the hill, from the top, and I was down by the bottom. And he says 'Are you out of the way?' and I said 'Yep.' And he throwed that post down and it hit me. Hit me right there. I didn't know any more after that (laughter). Took me off to the hospital. I woke up in the hospital—I didn't know what happened to me."

Driving worn-out trucks carrying heavy loads with bad brakes was also dangerous. Floyd Cantwell's father was killed and his brother critically injured by a train at Hooper's Switch in 1937; his truck had stopped on the tracks and had the hood up. Milton Lentz's dad died hauling cedar in 1947, though his loss of control of the truck was probably due to a stroke. In 1951 Lee McKinnerney's younger brother and uncle died in an accident hauling cedar.

Cedar choppers were fearless in the face of such dangers. Alice Patterson told me of three serious injuries requiring a doctor or hospitalization, yet she laughed about it. That same fearlessness shows up in their attitude toward fighting and, for some, the physical damage resulting from drinking too much. Their Scots-Irish heritage undoubtedly played a role: Jim Webb said, "The measure of a man was . . . whether he was bold—often to the point of recklessness."[8]

Emmett Shelton tells a story about Earl Short, who worked for him dynamiting roads. Another worker for Shelton named Pete Torres came in one day to complain about Earl. "Mr. Emmett, I can't work with that man. I've got four daughters I've got to live and support, and you know what he does? He goes out there, and he takes these dynamite caps and he pins them on the dynamite with his teeth. He's biting them with his teeth, and one of these days he's going to make a misjudgment and he's going to bite into that dynamite. And it's not only going to kill him, it's going to kill me. And I can't live that way."[9]

Housing

Nothing about cedar choppers was more baffling to city folks than the way they lived. When Benton Beard built his store on Bee Cave Road in 1932, he said, "I remember the cedar choppers. They lived in tents and shacks with dirt floors, and they couldn't read or write. I couldn't believe people lived like that. Some camped by the Marshall's spring and some just squatted on land in the area."[10] Della Edwards drove the Eanes school bus for years. She wrote, "The poor people as they were called back then were cedar choppers and coal burners. They lived down Walsh Tarlton in little ol' bitty—some of them lived in tents, some of them lived in huts—like they'd just throw up pieces of tin and cardboard and maybe they didn't even have a wood floor. Some of them were just dirt floors. . . . And there was just absolutely a village of them down there."[11] Charlie Dellana, who had a ranch in the hills, joked that you couldn't put up any metal signs on roads out there because the cedar choppers would steal them to use for siding on their houses.[12]

Alice Patterson married Bill Oestrick in 1945, when she was fifteen years old. For a while they rented a house, but to save money they moved into a place Bill's brother had built on Lake Austin across from what is now Emma Long Park. She laughed when she told me, "Actually, it was a shack. We papered the walls with real thick wallpaper so that the wind wouldn't come through. We lived in it for twelve years. Yeah—it was a two-room shack."

Of course Alice did not have electricity or running water, so she either had to haul water from the lake or get it from the spigot that the city provided on Bee Cave Road. *So you raised your children in that—what you called "the shack"?* "Yes, we did. We raised 'em in the shack. Bill picked me up one day and I went right through the floor, both of us" (laughter). Alice was a delightful woman who laughed all the time, especially at the hardships she had faced. The only time I saw her sad was when she talked about Bill, who had died just a few years earlier. "I miss him like crazy," she said.

I wondered if the conditions in Eanes were unique, so I asked Don Simons if they had had electricity in the Bull Creek area. He responded that even in the 1940s, "none of them choppers had electricity." The wife of Don's cousin Clarence Simons said, "I can remember Clarence talking about living in a house and you could—they would be playing poker or whatever, eating—and there were

Alice and Bill, 1945 (right) and the "Shack" (below). Photos courtesy of Alice Patterson Oestrick.

holes in the floor where you could see the hogs underneath."[13] Sam Kindrick tells a similar story in his *Secret Life and Hard Times of a Cedar Chopper.* Johnnie Pale—the same legendary cedar chopper who claimed he could rope an armadillo from a running horse—was living in a shack on Governor Coke Stevenson's ranch outside Junction with his wife, whose skin was so dark from the sun that she was called "Black Mama." Their pet pig Winchie lived under the bed, and chickens roosted on the bed posts, so they had to put a tarp over the top of the bed posts at night to protect themselves.[14]

Even if they had a regular place to live, cedar choppers might camp in the brakes to be close to where they were working. Floyd Cantwell said, "We'd go somewhere, take an old mattress or something, and take some kind of old tarp, hang that over it, didn't have no sides or nothing you know. Rain, or whatever." Floyd was single then, but the whole family of Eli Simons from Bull Creek was working and camping up on Sandy Creek. It was there that his son W. B. Simons met and married Margie Carlton, whose father owned the land. Marriages between ranchers' daughters and cedar choppers did not happen very often.

John Hoover said a lot of cedar choppers would stay in the hills rather than come back to Burnet every night. There was good cedar up around Morgan Creek, west of Burnet, but no place to live. Four cedar chopper tents were on the South Morgan and several more on the North Morgan during WWII. Some had wooden floors but most did not.[15]

There were no outhouses for these tents. Oscar Lewis found that almost a third of the dwellings in the western part of Bell County had no indoor or outdoor toilet in 1948, compared to only 3 percent of the houses of the Czech farmers to the east.[16] Princeton Simons said the big soft leaves of mullein weed were often used for toilet paper.

Zeke Bonnet and his wife Katy Whitt lived in a tent in the hills near Round Mountain school. She told Genny Kercheville, "Sometimes we didn't even have a tent—we would just sleep under the truck, or if somebody's chicken house was not in use." She told of a time the boys in the family were playing with a tire when it rolled into the tent and knocked over the stove. "It caught everything on fire and mother got the kids out, and pulled the mattresses out because that was real important. And mother said for us to get up against the cedar tree and we sat up—put our backs against the tree and we waited for daddy to get home. And he didn't get home all that night."

The Hill Country can get cold and raw in the winter. I asked Don Simons of Bull Creek, *Did you ever visit anybody that lived in a tent in the winter?* He said, "*I* lived in a tent in the winter. Yeah, all over these damn hills. When I was born we moved back to the cedar brakes, and I probably spent the first five, six years of my life in the cedar brakes living in a tent. And I slept on the ground with a pallet with a quilt. When it rained you'd get wet, and in the winter time, boy that was miserable. Very miserable." *You did not have a floor, a wood floor in that tent?* "Not nothing like that. It might be a tent for mom and dad and maybe they, a couple of girls slept there, we might sleep under the truck or something. I tell you, it was ragged."

Ronnie Roberts (pictured) lived in a tent when he was a young child. So did Katie Maples, the sister-in-law of his aunt Ruby. She is the older woman standing in the middle of the group in front of the

Ronnie Roberts in tent, 1953. Photo courtesy of Gail Roberts Gonzales.

The Gumberts, 1941. Photo from a public member tree on Ancestry.com, attached to Herman Henry Gumbert in the Gumbert Family Tree on May 10, 2012, consent Earl Gumbert.

tent. Next to her is her husband, Herman Gumbert, and to the far left are their son Willie Gumbert (1922–2014) and his wife Minnie (1925–2013). This picture was taken near Lake Victor (between Burnet and Lampasas) about 1941, so Minnie would have been sixteen years old.

The story of the Gumberts was told to the Ingram newspaper in 2013 and is worth recounting because it illustrates several important themes regarding the lives of cedar choppers during their heyday in the mid-twentieth century.[17]

First, their family illustrates just how interrelated everyone was. The Maples were closely related to the Robertses and the Pattersons: Katie Maples's younger brother Fred married Ruby Roberts, the daughter of Joe L. Roberts; her younger sister Ola Bell married Carl Roberts. Her youngest sister Nora was married to Ellis Patterson, the brother of Mary Patterson, Ronnie's grandmother. Nora's twin sister Dora Maples (pictured on page 131) was fifteen when she lived with her uncle Alex Cox, the grandson of Texas Ranger Hugh Cox of the Indian fight in chapter 3, and then married the son of a Hutson of the Roberts-Teague clan. The young couple on the right of the picture on page 130 are Willie's seventeen-year-old sister Vinie Mae Gumbert and her husband George Moore, the uncle of one of my interviewees, Raymond Moore of Ingram. The conclusion drawn from this complex web of interrelationships is simple: over time the clans mostly continued to marry into other families in the clans, so that by the time of the last generations—those born in the 1920s and 30s—everyone was related to everyone else.

The second theme illustrated by the Gumbert family relates to their move to Kerr County in the western Hill Country. Willie Gumbert was born in a wagon on the way to the hospital in Travis County; he cut cedar near Burnet, and had a child born in 1942 in a tent near Marble Falls. His wife Minnie said, "We were happy there. We didn't know the difference, and many people back then were the same way. Later, when we got a porcelain refrigerator and put it in the girls' bedroom, we thought we were really living uptown." Willie and a lot of other choppers followed Mack Callahan from Marble Falls to Mountain Home in Kerr County, and he later opened a cedar yard in Ingram. George Moore and Vinie Mae also moved from Burnet County to Ingram. Even Fred Maples and his wife Ruby, who ran a yard on South Lamar, ended up in Kerr County with his sister Katie Maples and other siblings. The good cedar

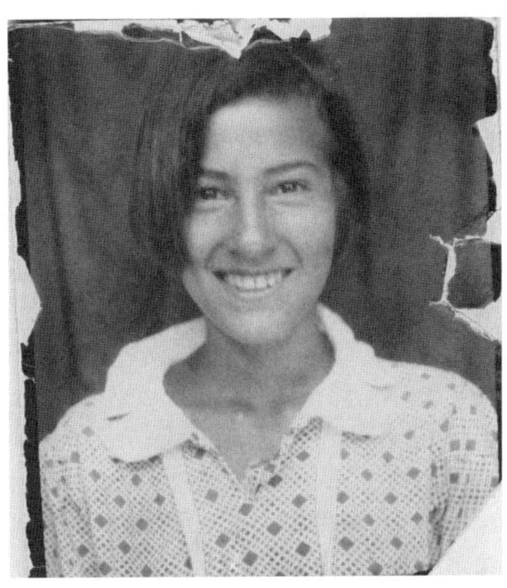

Dora Maples. Photo from a public member tree on Ancestry.com, attached to Dora Inez Maples in the Marsha Dry Family Tree on February 19, 2011, consent Earl Gumbert.

was getting scarce in the hills near Austin, so branches of the clans moved west.

Another theme repeated in the Gumberts' story is the risk of serious injury. Willie's son Earl was cutting with an axe at thirteen when he "hacked his leg down to the bone. Willie said he tied the leg off with a cord and rushed Earl to the hospital in Kerrville, and despite many stitches, he recovered with his leg intact."

A last theme illustrated by the case of the Gumberts—one that should be told to counterbalance some of the more dramatic stories of violence—is that of a loving and successful family. Willie and Minnie married when they were teenagers and raised eleven children. When they were interviewed, they had been married for sixty-eight years. After a hard life built around the cedar business, Minnie looked fondly at Willie and said, "Our kids all adore and respect him, and we're still very much in love. There's been a few scares — and a lot of happiness." Minnie died that year, and Willie joined her the next.

Food

Cedar choppers ate simple food. There was not much in the way of vegetables; they didn't have big gardens like farm families because they were so mobile. When they were working in the brakes they might be able to supplement beans and cornbread with something wild, a squirrel or armadillo or maybe some rattlesnake meat. Once Floyd Cantwell was cutting with friends near Wimberley, and coming back to camp they found a big soft-shelled turtle in the creek. "So we jumped out, grabbed him, put him on back in that truck, got up there and we skint that son-of-a-bitch . . . cut him up in pieces, and gave everybody, everybody in the camp up there turtle meat. We had some flour, you know, we'd salt and pepper it and put it in a skillet. Man, you talk about good eating."

That was memorable because game had gotten scarce by the middle decades of the twentieth century. By then the cedar choppers were buying most of what they ate. Hollis Baker's father owned a store in Burnet where they went to buy flour, cornmeal, bacon, pinto beans, and canned vegetables. Luther Pierce remembers eating a lot of macaroni and tomatoes, pinto beans, and fried potatoes. Frank Wilson said, "They had adequate food. There weren't none of 'em undernourished. They weren't none of 'em unhealthy or anything. They were strong and tough."

Like many farm families in the South, they had cornbread as a daily staple. Albert Boatright told me a story illustrating the importance of cornbread; it happened when he was visiting his uncle Floyd Boatright for Christmas. Floyd was another transplant from Bull Creek living in the western Hill Country and running a cedar yard in Leakey. He had a big blended family—seven kids from his first wife Elsie Shannon, who had died in her mid-thirties, seven more that his second wife had brought into the marriage, and two of their own. Albert said,

> We was out there eating one day and had my brother-in-law that one of my sisters met at Bergstrom Air Force Base. I know there was fifteen of us out there or twenty eating, and this brother-in-law of mine from Washington state. Well, they cooked up a nice big bunch of cornbread. Oh, it was beautiful—it looked like cake, you know. And they was passing it around, and it got to him, and he said, "No, I don't think I want any cornbread." And everybody in the room stopped—just stopped and stared at him—because he wouldn't take a piece of that cornbread. They stopped and stared. Boy, he looked around and said, "Well, I think I will" (laughter). So he took a piece of it. So everybody went back to eating. I'll never forget that. That was so funny. We grew up on cornbread and beans.

Most of the cedar choppers did not own land. Many of the early families had started out with land but lost it over the years for a variety of reasons. Dick Boatright lost his land on Bull Creek in a poker game.[18] The Browns and others lost theirs because they didn't pay property taxes.[19] Emmett Shelton got a lot of land from the cedar choppers in payment for legal services. John Teague used land to pay for food. About once a week his son Homer would walk the

Homer Teague with Bill Dog. Photo from a public member tree on Ancestry.com, attached to Homer Teague in the Jamison Family Tree on July 3, 2007, consent Stoney Teague.

nine miles into town to Charley Wolf's Grocery Store on East Fifth and carry groceries back in an old tow sack. Emmett Shelton said, "At the end of the year Charley would figure out how much Homer owed him, and old man Teague would deed him a piece of land on Bee Cave Road."[20]

Homer Teague (1898–1965) was the youngest of John Teague's children. We have already met brothers John and Tom and sisters Mamie and Myrtle at John's 1911 murder trial. Homer's life spanned the heyday of the cedar choppers during the mid-twentieth century, and he was one of the most colorful men in the clans.

Homer stopped driving after he ran his Model T into the only grocery store in South Austin, wrecking the car and scattering groceries all over the floor.[21] After that, when everyone else had cars and trucks, he used a wagon and mule team to haul the cedar into Austin. He stopped that in 1937 only because the county would not let his mules on the newly paved Bee Cave Road; after that he would use the mules to haul the cedar out of the brakes to the road, where he met a friend like Ed Pierce, Luther's oldest brother, who would haul it in his truck.

Homer lived with his father across the creek from the Roberts-Teague Cemetery near Bee Cave Road and Patterson Lane. For a while in the 1930s a WPA gang was working on Bee Cave Road, chopping cedar and widening the road, and Homer's older brother Tom was working on the road gang. Homer was his father's favorite son—it was apparent that whatever land he still had would go to Homer, not to John or Tom—causing resentment between the brothers. When Homer went into town he would have to walk past the WPA gang, and there would be Tom with his axe. Homer took to carrying his axe as well. Emmett Shelton said, "Every time Homer'd come by, they'd wind around like two old tomcats and cuss each other, and then Tom (in his fifties by then) would back off." There were too many people around for it to have "gotten close to a chopping contest."

Robert E. Lee and Stonewall Jackson Teague, about 1948. Photo from a public member tree on Ancestry.com, attached to Robert Lee Teague in the Teague Family Tree on December 26, 2014, consent Jerry King, Stoney Teague.

Homer had two sons: Robert E. Lee Teague was born in 1939 and Stonewall Jackson Teague in 1941. Stoney, as he is known, says his mother Mary Marx left them the year after he was born. Stoney showed me her handwritten note dated June 28, 1942: "I am the wife of Homer Teague and I am leaving home giving my rights of my 2 children Robert E. Lee Teague Stonewall Jackson Teague to their father Homer Teague also the home and ever thang and I have taken one dollar and don't claim any thang at all any more."

Homer never remarried, and he raised the boys under rough conditions. They lived in the old Brewton Springs schoolhouse, abandoned on Homer's land when classes moved to the new school at Eanes. Homer cooked their meals outside on an open fire until Stoney was eleven or twelve. They ate beans and potatoes, and what Stoney called "pone bread—just a big old biscuit in a frying pan. Take a knife and cut it up, pour a little bacon grease on it and that was a meal." The boys would have to walk about a quarter of a mile to a well near Barton Creek to get water for the mules, making three or four trips carrying a five-gallon bucket on a cedar pole between them. Linda Vance writes, "Neighbors remember that Homer taught those two sons of his to curse a blue streak. It seems that when they were only six or seven years old they could 'let fly with a string of cusswords that would make a sailor blush.'"[22]

Despite the fact that Homer drank a lot and was a friend to all the moonshiners, not only those in Westlake but people from Bull Creek, like the Simonses and the Boatrights, he was made a deputy constable under Deputy Sheriff Jim McCoy. Homer would help the sheriff by talking to some of the more violent families, to avoid the risks of their having a confrontation with the law. Stoney said, "When them boys would get into something, you know, they wouldn't—it was impossible to go out there and arrest 'em. They'd send my daddy out there" to talk them into coming in. Because of that, for a while, he was allowed to carry a gun.

Homer was described during those years as having a long beard and a big black floppy hat. He wore old clothes, seldom bathed, and talked with a sing-song Elizabethan cadence. People saw him walking down Bee Cave Road all the way into Austin once a week, always with his dog and sometimes carrying an axe or a gun; it was no wonder that he became a legend in Westlake. Ronnie Roberts remembers Homer coming into Ronnie's grandfather's yard with his friends. "I mean, these guys looked like they were right out of fucking Appalachia. I mean, they're rough (laughter). Like Homer Teague, shit, he used to walk around with a pistol. He considered hisself like the self-appointed sheriff of that area. He lived in this old schoolhouse that sat right on the corner of Patterson Lane and Bee Cave Road. He was crusty—shit, man, I mean, you know, nobody jacked with him."

Property

Did Homer Teague choose to live the way he did, or was it forced on him by poverty? His lifestyle and attitude toward land—so different from that of the Hill Country Germans—was fairly representative, though more extreme than it was for most of the married men in the clans. Those familiar with cedar chopper life all agree that the accumulation of land and material goods was not important. Frank Wilson said they did not build anything of value or even dig a well because they moved around so much. Perhaps this attitude was a reflection of their Celtic heritage, which had taught their ancestors not to invest much in fixed property that could so easily be destroyed or lost in war. Jim Webb wrote of the Scots-Irish, "They were destitute but did not measure themselves by wealth; their properties were frequently attacked and they did not risk their slim assets in fancifying an abode. . . . They concerned themselves more with personal ties than with the ownership of a specific piece of land."[23] I asked Bob Willess, whose dad had a cedar yard in western Bell Country and who hauled cedar most of his life, *So it doesn't sound like most of them owned their land?* He replied, "They didn't own the land. They didn't own nothing."

But they did buy things that more frugal people would call frivolous. Bob Willess said that when television came into being, "those cedar cutters was the only ones that had a TV." *So they'd spend it not just on—they'd spend it on luxuries too?* "Yeah, oh yeah! Yeah, anything you see, they'd buy it. It didn't make any matter what it was if they wanted it. And it would go through the whole tribe of the cedar choppers—if one bought something or other, every one of 'em had it." Harold Preece, the son of the couple who sang Elizabethan ballads for Alan Lomax, wrote, "The merchants of East Sixth Street in Austin always get out their most showy goods when dealing with customers from Bull Creek, Travis Peak, or any of the other mountain communities."[24]

Stoney Teague told a funny story about Baldy and Charlie Brown, sons of Buddy Brown's marriage to Mattie Tucker, and his cousin Earl Short, all of the Roberts-Teague clan. There was a liquor store close to the river on South Congress where Baldy and Charlie would buy their wine.

> They had a cardboard display sitting up on the counter, you know, and had all them old watches on that display. Charlie and Baldy and all of 'em, and Earl Short, they all stopped in there and Earl seen them watches. Well, wadn't none of 'em could read, write, tell time, but Earl just had to have one of them. Well, him and Tom (his brother) was cutting cedar out there on Barton Creek. Well, it got along up in the morning the next morning, Tom hollered at him, said, "Say there Bud, what time are it?" He took out that old watch and he said, "Thar she be," and he said," Damn if it ain't, let's eat!' They didn't know what time it was—they couldn't tell time (laughter).

Al Ehrlich was a businessman who bought and sold cedar for decades and owned a successful lumber company on the road to Fredericksburg. He said, "A man from Fort Worth once asked me, 'Are cedar cutters happy people?' and I told him, 'I don't know. Their idea of happiness is a heck of a lot different from our idea of it. Happiness to them might mean spending their last five bucks on a soda pop and wine and marble machines. I've seen 'em work like fiends all day in the hot cedar brakes, then goof off all the money they've made before they get home for supper."[25]

Buck Simpson, the war hero buried in the Roberts-Teague Cemetery, would stay out in the brakes for two or three weeks at a time and get paid a bunch of money when he came in. His little brother Leonard recalls a friend suggesting that he put some of it away for when he would really need it. "Buck looked thoughtful and nodded, and peeled off a fifty. 'You're right,' he said, 'Hold this for me, I'm going to spend the rest.'" Leonard added, "He didn't look ahead, he didn't look back. He just lived in the present."[26]

Even their big purchases were seldom anything of lasting value. Lee McKinnerney's dad, the big man from Uvalde who could cut so much cedar, bought Lee a new Mustang and his other son a new Corvair. Lee said, "They always had nice cars, I mean, you know, they paid their money. That's one thing about cedar chopping back in the day was it was fruitful, because nobody else wanted to do it. And so, you got paid well for your wear."

Not only did the cedar choppers not own property; they didn't have any respect for it. Jim Webb says of the Scots-Irish in Appalachia, "One of the culture's great strengths is that it persistently refuses to recognize human worth in terms of personal income and assets."[27] When property rights came up against the way people felt about their rights as individuals, property rights lost. The story of Harve Roberts and Jesse Lee Teague's goat is a perfect illustration of this conflict and its resolution. It is one of the best stories told by Emmett Shelton in his remarkable "Cedar Chopper Tapes," available at the Austin History Center, because it says a lot about why the cedar choppers trusted him.

Jesse Lee Teague (1914–54), along with brothers Charlie, Raymond, and Bert, were called the "Fightin' Teagues." His sister was Tiney Teague, the old woman who had the confrontation with the county health woman recounted in chapter 1. Jesse fought in WWII, first in Europe and then, when that ended, in the Pacific. Shelton said, "Poor little fellow, he didn't know where he was any of the time he was fighting." He came home with PTSD (then called battle fatigue) and moved out to his father's place near Bee Cave Road and St. Stephens School Road to rest and recuperate. He bought a goat for a pet.

Next door to Jesse's father's place was a little rock house built by Harve Roberts, the son of Henry Roberts and brother to others mentioned in the narrative, such as Joe L., Ollie, and Lonnie. Harve had a job doing mechanical work at the University of Texas, unusual because most of his brothers and brothers-in-law were cedar choppers. Like them, he was handy at rock work and had built the house himself. But it still did not have doors or windows.

There were not any fences, so pretty soon Jesse's goat "made a habit of going over to Harvey's house and going in the kitchen, and eating everything he could get his mouth ahold of. And generally when Harvey come home in the afternoon from work, Jesse's goat would be over on his kitchen table." Harve just shooed him off the first couple of times, but finally he hit him with a broom and ran him all the way back to Jesse's place.

"Jesse said to Harvey he didn't appreciate him beating on his goat that way. And Harvey said, 'Well, Jesse, you keep your goat at home. He's over here on my kitchen table and eats everything I've got up, and I just don't want that to go on.' 'Well, Harvey,' he said, 'I don't see no harm in my goat being over here on your kitchen table, and I don't want you beating on him no more.'"

The goat was on the table the next afternoon when Harve came home, and Jesse was next door waiting with his rifle to see what Harve would do. When Harve hit the goat with the broom, Jesse fired a warning shot into the house. It was enough to scare Harve into hiding until it got dark; even then he was afraid to start up his car, and so walked all the way to Emmett Shelton's house in South Austin. He arrived about 9:00 p.m. and told his story, asking Emmett what he could do about it. This was Emmett's reply:

> "Well," I said, "Harvey, you are kin to him—you know him better than I do," I said. "Now you don't have a lot of choice. You can go back out there, and I believe if you will work it just right, you can catch old Jesse when he's not looking, and you can probably kill him—if you get the first shot at him." But I said, "Now, of course, you know that old man Teague, he likes little Jesse. He's been off to the war, and he's been a hero so far as the family is concerned. And the old man, he won't like that very well, and you're gonna have to kill him. You know that for

> sure. And, of course, his mother; she loves little Jesse. You'll have to kill her." And then I said, "And how many brothers and sisters has Jesse got? I know there's Raymond, and there's Bert and two or three sisters, and all of them are pretty good shots. Now you know as well as I know, Harve, that you're gonna have to kill every one of them. Or, you can do this. You can either do that, or you can just pick up and leave." And Harvey left. He went back out there and got his clothes, and he didn't go back out there, I don't believe, as long as Jesse lived.

Frank Wilson was convinced that this way of life—a lack of adherence to conventions concerning property, appearances, or middle-class values—was a choice. He said, "They were very able to take care of themselves, and they lived like they wanted to. They wanted to live that way . . . a very unique bunch of people." They lived day-to-day, and when the cedar was paying they could count on making enough money to pay for whatever came up. I was talking to Floyd Cantwell at his wrecking yard in Leander when one of his stepsons interjected that his dad went out and cut forty dollars of cedar on the day he was born to pay the hospital bill.

Living in town was too confining for most of the choppers. Lola Peterson, a county welfare worker, told of a cedar chopper family with six or seven kids living in a tent during the winter out on Bee Cave Road. The county paid for them to move into a house in town. "A few days later they came trooping in here to me and said, 'We'll die if we don't get out where there's some air. We just can't breathe in that house. We want to go back where we came from.'"[28] Even Ronnie Roberts, who had worked in Austin his whole life, couldn't live in town. When he retired he and his wife wanted to get away from Austin and moved out to a historic house in the town of Mason. When I told him that I thought Mason was a pretty little town, he replied, "It was great and I couldn't stomach it. It's like, it's like people next door to me, you know. I mean, I was almost like ready to go to a mental institution." Ronnie moved back to the hills outside Dripping Springs.

Women and Family

Historian of the Scots-Irish Jim Webb described the women in Ulster who were transplanted from Scotland by the British in the 1600s—the core of the Scots-Irish who later migrated to Appalachia—as women who married at young ages, bore many children, worked beside their men, and ran things when the men were away. This applies equally to women from the cedar chopper clans. Most of the women from the families I talked with married young and had big families. Sisters Edna and Mary Patterson, as well as their niece Alice, all married by age fifteen. A few of the women married even younger, and most were married by seventeen.

Edna Patterson had ten children, one of whom died at birth and one more from an illness when she was eight. Edna said, "I had lota young, good days raisin' all my family. I'm proud of it. I took good care of them children. I enjoyed raisin' children. I never did get to go nowhere, just stayed at home all the time." Alice Patterson agreed about the confinement: "I felt, I felt left out in the cold there, from my sisters because they were all having a good time and there I was tending to babies. But, I got over that (laughter). Decided I wasn't so bad off after all."

Because Edna had so many children, she had to work and mind the young ones at the same time. "I had a hard time getting the clothes washed, packin' laundry outta them hollers. I'd have to set my baby down some way—if he couldn't set up, I had to have an ol' horse collar . . . and set him in it so he wouldn't fall over while I cut my wood out. . . . But I'd finally get that wood loaded and get that young 'un on my hip—come on in and have that meal ready when it had to be ready."

Some women had even more children than Edna. Jake and Minnie Stark had six living with them at the time of the 1940 census and could by then have had one or two more who had already left home. They were having a child about every two years, and she was only thirty-two at the time of the census. Stoney Teague heard they eventually had twenty-one—though this is likely an exaggeration—compared to fourteen for Tom Teague and Etta Williams.

Stoney said, "Tom told me that he'd of beat ol' Jake if Etta hadn't run off and left him (laughter). I said, 'Man, after that many kids, I believe it would be time to go.'"

As we have seen, women also cut cedar. Sometimes they did it with their men—their fathers or husbands or brothers. Frequently they would go to the brakes and cook for the cutters—Charlie Maugham remembers his aunt fixing brown beans, fried potatoes, and corn on the cob.

At other times they did the work *instead* of their men; when their husbands were injured—such as by a serious cut—they might take their men's place in the brakes. Connie Simons of Liberty Hill drove a truck for Stoney Teague, but when Connie was unable to work for six months, his wife Betty took over and drove for him.

When something like this did happen—anything that injured the breadwinner and interrupted the day-to-day flow of cash—the extended family and clan were the support system. Stoney Teague said, "If a man got cut with an axe or got burnt out, you know, anything that happened to him—everybody jumped in, you know, and they'd bail him out. They'd cut a load of cedar and buy his groceries, pay his bills, and get him back up, you know, where he could take care of hisself." *So, everybody out there stuck together?* "Oh, yeah, they stuck together." If a family didn't have enough to eat, Stoney's father Homer would kill a deer and butcher it for them to eat.

These kin relationships extended far from the immediate family. Luther Pierce's aunt, Mary Patterson, married Joe L. Roberts. Joe L. Roberts is the nephew of Tiney Teague's husband, Charlie Roberts. That makes Tiney Teague the sister-in-law of the father-in law of the aunt of Luther Pierce, a distant and complicated relationship by marriage between the Patterson-Pierce and the Roberts-Teague clans. Yet Luther was close to Tiney while she was still alive, and Tiney's son was Luther's best friend. We were talking about the Roberts-Teague Cemetery when Luther said:

> That's where we put Tiney. Tiney always used to call me. She called every day. She was lonesome. She said, "Lufer"—she never could say my name, she said it like Lufer. "Uh, Lufer,

> you gonna dig my grave when I die?" I said, "I sure am." She said, "Well, I want to be buried right there next to Sonny Boy and the Old Man." "Well, that's where we're going." But, anyway, I went on out there one evening to bow hunt and got to talking to her. And you know, and I didn't even go hunting that night. I sat right there and talked to her until dark. She was a good ol' woman.

The support system of extended family and kin was particularly important when some family matter impaired people's ability to take care of children.[29] We already know about Ronnie Roberts and his three sisters, who were taken in and raised by their grandparents. Floyd Cantwell was five years old when his father was killed by the train and his older brother seriously injured. I asked him if his mama raised him—he said she did, "and all my aunts and uncles and wherever I could stay at. Yeah. My grandfather mainly, you know. He always had food, you know, whatever, when I was hungry." Stoney and his brother Robert would stay with their father's first cousin Jesse Teague and his wife Lizzie when Homer made one of his regular trips to Austin and stayed a few days.

Don Simons's family is an example of what happened when the parents were unable to take care of their children. The behavior of his father forced his mother to leave home for a few years. Don's two sisters and younger brother went to live with his aunt Nell and her husband Tom Cantrell, a big family in the Bull Creek clan who later resettled in Liberty Hill. Don was eight and his brother Fritz was ten, and their father was supposed to take care of them. But he often let the boys fend for themselves, once for two months. Different people, like the Boatrights or his uncle Harve Simons, would check on them and bring them food to supplement what they scrounged from the woods.

The man who had the most positive influence on Don's life was his uncle, Dick Simons. He said, "Dick Simons made so damn much money because he was sober." He would go to the brake early and be home early. He "took a shower, ate up, got Edith, and went to the movies. They went to the movies every day. I know—they used to stop by our tent and say, 'Come on Don, let's go to the movies.'" Once he took Don to the airport to watch the planes, and there was a man there giving plane rides. Dick paid the man five dollars to take Don up. This had a big influence on the course of his life—he became a paratrooper and continues to fly even now.

Another person I talked to in the same family was Clarence Simons's wife Earleen. Clarence was the youngest child of Dick Simons (1904–60) and Edith Simpson (1909–87), Buck Simpson's niece. He was born prematurely in 1933, weighing only two and a half pounds, and was kept on a pillow in a chest of drawers. He was not expected to live and was called "Baby Simons" for the rest of his life, despite the fact that like most Simons men he was big—six foot three and 240 pounds. Earleen married Clarence in 1985 and was not related to other families in the clans, so she brought an outsider's perspective to the stories she heard. She said, "A lot of 'em, if things were not good at home, they'd move in with just a friend or whoever. Family, friend, it didn't make much difference." And by this time, most of their friends *were* family.

Edith Simpson had two sources of stress in her life that could have contributed to the premature birth of her baby. Her three-year-old child was in the hospital with pneumonia, and her nineteen-year-old sister Eva Mae had left her husband, Berry Pierce. Berry was born in Bandera and cut cedar in San Saba, but his family was unrelated to the Pierces of the Patterson-Pierce clan.

Eva Mae had come to Austin and was staying with her father Charley Simpson. After a couple of weeks, Berry came to town to try to get her back. He actually stayed for a while with his wife's grandmother, Lucy Hutson, and then with Edith and Dick at their house in East Austin.

Eva Mae came to the Simons house one morning with a friend to fix breakfast for Edith, still recovering from the premature birth. Berry was there, and again tried to talk Eva Mae into coming back to him. She told him to leave her alone and to leave Austin, and it turned into a quarrel. Dick had already left to take a load of cedar to Camp Mabry, and Eva Mae begged her friend to run for help because she was scared of what Berry might do. After the friend left there was gunfire—Berry Pierce had shot Eva Mae twice with a shotgun. She died in the hospital. Berry then tried to kill himself—he said that was his plan, and there were powder burns on his face. He was apprehended without resistance. The jury took less than two hours to reach a verdict of guilty.

I can tell this story because it is a matter of public record.[30] In the course of my interviews I heard other stories of domestic violence—not many, but enough to make me aware that it was a fact of life for some women. One was resolved by the woman presenting her husband with a credible threat of incarceration; another through a standoff with a baseball bat. In both these cases alcohol was a major factor, and the memories of these encounters are still fresh in the minds of their children.

Alcohol was not the problem with Berry and Eva Mae—it was about insane jealousy and rapid recourse to violence with a firearm. Three years earlier there was another case in the newspaper of a man—not from the clans—murdering a granddaughter of William Riley Teague with a pistol after she had left him, again sober, and again after a long talk between the estranged spouses.[31] The early 1930s were incredibly violent and gun-happy times in America, and quarrels in the hills among some of the rougher individuals sometimes turned deadly. With few exceptions, all the killings in the clans occurred during the 1930s.

Domestic violence was not accepted among the clans, but neither was interference with other people's business. These two values came head-to-head in the case of Buck Duval and Fred Stark. According to Emmett Shelton,[32] Buck Duval (1900–66) was not an exceptionally large man, weighing only two hundred pounds, but he had the "strength of an ox." His mother was Sallie Burleson—it was her husband Dempsey Brown who was killed in the 1896 gun duel in Colorado River (chapter 3)—and Buck was a child of her second marriage.

Buck was married to Ollie Young, the sister of the "hillbilly moonshiner" Ike Young, and Ollie's sister Effie Young was married to Fred Stark. The two couples shared a small house. One day when Buck came home from work his wife told him that her brother-in-law Fred had been hitting her sister Effie. Shelton said, "She thought Buck ought to go over there and admonish him to leave this woman alone; it wasn't right to whip a woman." A request from a man as strong as Buck probably would seem more like a command,

and Buck preferred not to get mixed up in it, but his wife persisted.

Fred Stark was a small man; Shelton said Buck "could'a throwed him over the house if he'd taken the notion." When Fred saw Buck he knew what was coming, and as soon as Buck started talking, Fred grabbed his axe and attacked. Buck ran out of the house and through the picket fence that surrounded it. His truck was parked by the back gate, and there was a shovel sticking out. The first time Buck passed the truck he saw the opportunity, and the second time he grabbed the shovel and whirled around. Stark ran up on him too fast, the swing of his axe coming down over Buck's shoulder and just cutting his leather jacket. The impact of the blow knocked Buck off his feet, but he was able to swing the shovel and hit Stark in the head, flipping him completely over the picket fence.

Stark went into town and filed a complaint against Buck for assault. Buck, like so many of the cedar choppers, turned to Emmett Shelton for representation. It was an easy case—the defense was the slashed leather coat.

This incident probably happened sometime in the 1930s. In the 1940 census Fred and Effie are shown living together in the Eanes precinct of Travis County with their two teenage children and his father, who had come to Travis County from New York in his twenties. In 1952 Fred was still married but serving time in Huntsville for robbery and assault. He was pardoned in 1961, and in 1969 Effie and Fred divorced. They remarried in 1980, and divorced again in 1982. It was obviously a tumultuous relationship.

The Kids

When I began this project several years ago, I visited with people on the historical commissions of the Hill Country counties. A local historian of Kimble County was like several of the older women I talked with—reticent to say anything bad about anybody—and there was not too much good that they had to say about cedar choppers. She admitted, "We felt like they were ignorant, uneducated." She called the children's education a "tragedy" and said they only went to elementary school, if that.

It did not take me long to figure out why they dropped out of school so young. Kids were needed to work—to help their fathers in the brakes or their mothers with the younger children, though girls tended to stay in school longer than boys. Some of the boys started working very young. Milton Lentz said his dad made a two-foot axe handle so that he could begin working around age six. Floyd Cantwell, born in 1932, went with his grandfather to the brakes at about the same age, after his father was killed by the train, taking an old gray mare down into the canyons and hooking her up to drag out timber. He said, "I didn't dare come up unless I had a post on my back." Charlie Maugham started cutting at nine and T. M. Pearson at ten. Lee McKinnerney claims he began at four years old cutting staves off the posts his dad had cut, using a single-bladed axe so that it wouldn't bounce back and cut him.

Using the 1940 census of Travis County, I looked at the number of years of education of 141 persons whose occupation was listed as cedar chopping, rock masonry, or working on the dam or in the quarry. Within the clans, these occupations appeared interchangeable in the censuses, with some men in the household doing one and others another at different times. Stoney Teague validated this merging of occupations, saying, "Yeah, they cut cedar, drove truck, laid rock, whatever it took to make a living." In this sample, the median number of years of education was five for boys between fourteen and twenty years old; that is, half the boys had dropped out before or during the fifth grade.

This was a lot less education than was the norm in 1940, even for Hill Country kids. In the fifteen Hill Country counties that are the focus of this book, one-third of the adult males in 1940 had attended high school for at least some period, and only 23 percent had four years or less of schooling. Among the cedar choppers I reviewed, only 11 percent had attended high school and 44 percent—almost double the Hill Country average—had not gone past the fourth grade. This was even worse than the 1940 educational level in nine poor Appalachian counties (four from Kentucky, two each from Tennessee and West Virginia, and one from North Carolina), where 16 percent went to high school and 30 percent hadn't gone past the fourth grade.[33]

When looking at information on families in the 1940 census, I noticed that the educational level of children who had completed their schooling was frequently less than that of their parents. Even if the average level of education was low, one would hope that it was at least improving over the generations. In fact, what I noticed was confirmed by the Travis County sample, where the median level of education for men born between 1900 and 1920 was one full year more than that of the boys born after 1920 who had already finished going to school. In fact, it had risen from four to six years from the oldest cohort (born before 1900) to the middle cohort, only to fall to five years for the youngest. There had been educational progress from the end of the nineteenth century to the early twentieth century, but it was reversed from 1920 to 1940.

A variety of factors worked against cedar chopper kids going to school. The most important for boys was their value in the brakes. When Dick Boatright moved his family from Bull Creek up to Cedar Park, he told his son John, "You ain't going to go to school here. You're going to work. Right now!" John T. was twelve, and was given his own 3½-pound double-bit Kelly axe, the same size his dad used.

A second factor discouraging attendance at school was that cedar chopper kids moved around a lot and would have to start in a new class without preparation. Don Simons said, "When you get there you don't know anything and the teacher gives you a report card; it's straight F's." You may have missed so much that you were held

Kids at Brewton Springs school. Photo courtesy of Eanes History Center.

Schoolchildren at Eanes. Photo courtesy of Eanes History Center.

back—Kenneth Bertling went to sixth grade with an eighteen-year-old cedar chopper, and had no cedar chopper classmates in his high school though there were many living in Marble Falls. Jerry Hawes, who grew up on a ranch near the San Gabriel River, said a cedar chopper kid came to his elementary school. On the first day of school the teacher told them all to write their names on a sheet of paper and turn it in. When his was turned in blank, he explained, "I can't write—that's what I'm here for!"

Another impediment was that school could be far from home and hard to reach. Floyd Cantwell's mother Ethel Rogers, born in 1912, was about six years old when she was living in an log house up a hollow off Spicewood Springs Road. Floyd said, "When she went to school, it used to be over on RM 2222. And she had her an old donkey, and in the morning, at six years old, before daylight, she had a trail. Would you let a little six-year-old girl go about five, six miles over the mountains, on a jackass to go to school? I mean, back in the old days, there were mountain lions and everything else." Frank Wilson grew up in Hyde Park and went to Baker Elementary. The cedar chopper kids from Shoal Creek could get there relatively easily, but it was a five- or six-mile walk for the kids from Bull Creek, who were only eight or nine years old. He said,

"They'd go to school until they were too old to go to Baker, and that was it. I never saw one of them in junior high school."

Going to school with city kids could be humiliating for a cedar chopper. You would probably be dirty: Lee McKinnerney remembers having so much wax on his hands that it would not come off—"you smell like a cedar chopper," he said. Don Simons said, "Of course you hated it. They made fun of you. And no shoes, you know." Earleen Simons, the wife of Don's cousin, captured this humiliation: "You know, sometimes you don't feel worthy. The kids, they pretty much put a deal on you, you know, if you were poor. I didn't know anything about deodorant and stuff like that. I didn't know. I had Brogan shoes. I don't think I got out of them until after Daddy died. That's all I had was a dollar ninety-eight Brogan shoes, you know. People make fun of you. Shoot, I was lucky to have shoes."

Teasing was not a problem at Eanes school, where most of the kids were children of cedar choppers. Built in 1937, it had a shower, and the teachers started providing towels and soap for the hillbilly kids to take a bath. Linda Vance wrote, "It wasn't long before the kids enjoyed it and a lot more of them began to come to school just so they could take a bath."[34]

Children not fitting in where they went to school received a lot of attention in California, where so many "Okies" from the Dust Bowl migration ended up. There, writes historian James Gregory, "The social pressure and ridicule of classmates and the insensitivity of many teachers made it hard for some children to face going to school . . . almost barefoot, with ragged or ill-fitting clothing. . . . If you were a little child, how would you feel going to school that way?"[35] Their response was a cult of toughness: one boy said, "About the time they'd say 'Okie,' I'd put a fist in their mouth."[36]

The Okies in California were a minority in a middle-class society. West of Austin, the hillbilly kids had the advantage. Frank Wilson said there were fifteen to twenty families living along Shoal Creek in West Austin: "Well now, if you weren't one of 'em you'd better have pretty good sized rocks in your pockets and be able to run pretty fast, or you couldn't go down in there." At Eanes, Linda Vance writes, "The hillbilly children made life pretty difficult for 'the city-slicker kids' by chunking rocks, chasing and spitting on the new students, especially if the newcomers were unfortunate enough to wear clean, prim clothes and shiny new shoes to school. Most children in the hills still wore coveralls and shoes only in the coldest weather. . . . Apparently it was not unusual for new shoes to disappear, only to reappear later on a cedar chopper child."[37] Note that the majority of the children pictured on page 150 are not wearing shoes.

One teacher who taught at Eanes during the early 1930s was thought by some of her students to be "the meanest woman to ever walk the earth," because she freely used a cedar switch on the kids. Cecil Johnson, interviewed in 1976, said, "One day she made one of the biggest mistakes of her career by taking her switch to a sizable hillbilly girl. When assaulted by the stick, the enraged girl retaliated by unloading her desk on the terrified woman. She threw with great force every book and heavy object that she could lay her hands on. As the old woman retreated from the room for aid, the girl helped her along with a good boot in the hindquarters. That was the last time she ever made an attempt to discipline that girl."[38] It did not take long for outsiders to learn that a defining characteristic of cedar choppers was an instinctive resort to extreme aggression in response to injury, without regard for authority or age or power.

Despite all these impediments, education was valued by many of the cedar choppers. The Teagues had given the land for Eanes

Eanes school "bus." Photo courtesy of Eanes History Center.

school, and Mart Maynard was a trustee for the school at Nameless. The anthropologist Oscar Lewis wrote of an illiterate charcoal burner in western Bell County who paid for boarding his daughter in town so that she could attend high school.[39] T. M Pearson quit school to work with his oldest brother to make enough money to put his ten younger siblings through school, and later he took correspondence courses and earned his GED. Alice Patterson dropped out of school after Eanes to marry young, but both of her younger sisters went all the way into Austin on the "bus"—a two-ton flatbed cedar truck—and graduated from high school. One of her sons became a lawyer. Luther Pierce, Edna Patterson's youngest child, studied by the light of a kerosene lamp until 1957, the same year he started junior high at O. Henry, and he graduated from Austin High.

If humiliation and fortitude and hard work were the price of being a kid from the cedar hills, the rewards may have made it worthwhile. Boys had the run of the countryside—not flat farmland but creeks and hollows and hills and caves. They could fish and swim and hunt squirrels and rabbits. Kerry Russell spent a stage of his life running with the chopper kids who lived west of Liberty Hill. He told me, "We were all kids and sort of the last generation of the real cedar choppers. We loved to hunt and fish, so we'd just head to the woods and stay out for a few days at a time."

With this as the alternative—helping dad but with plenty of time to roam freely—lots of boys chose to quit school. A young cedar chopper interviewed in 1965 near Johnson City said, "Daddy can't write his name, but he used to keep us clean. We could'a gone to school all the way but we were just hard-headed."[40] Buddy Brown, the iconic cedar chopper with the rattlesnake hatband who reigned in Westlake before Homer Teague, said of school, "I went in the front door and went out the back window."[41] One is reminded of how quickly German farm boys captured by the Comanches would adopt the free lifestyle of Comanche youth.[42]

I have fond memories of Bull Creek, before Loop 360 was build and development moved west. A little road turned off RM 2222 and crossed the creek several times. It was a paradise: streams ran crystal clear over a serrated limestone bottom and pooled into deep holes, waterfalls cascading over rock ledges. Cliffs on one side were fun to climb, and there were little meadows on the other side to explore. Even as late as the 1960s you could find beauty and privacy in a world removed from development.

This lifestyle left vivid impressions with the people who grew up there. Frank Boatright told Mark Lisheron, "When I was growing up I had the whole run of this country. When you once lived like we did, in the 1940s and '50s, you never forgot that. That stays with you."[43] His cousin Albert lived in town but spent the summers on Bull Creek. "Oh, yeah, ol' Bull Creek. We'd swim in that thing, especially me and the boys, my cousins and all the Simonses, and there was some Faglies that lived out there. And we'd go down there, us guys, and we didn't have a bathing suit. We'd just swim in the nude, you know. And, uh, we'd just walk. You know, where we went we walked. Of course, we were barefooted. And I remember it, you know, the bottom of your feet get so tough that you get out in grass burrs, you'd get some grass burrs in your foot, and you'd just stop and rake 'em out."

When it was warm enough, Floyd Cantwell went swimming every day as a kid. Once when Floyd was older, he and his brother were cutting with their stepdad near Georgetown and were stranded there for a few days when their truck broke down. The boys cut a few more loads of posts, but they were missing home-cooked meals. So they walked all the way home—down the old Austin road to Round Rock and then across to Spicewood Springs Road. He said, "Mama had a big pot of ribs, we ate them, and that night we went coon hunting. We made about forty miles then went coon hunting" (laughter). It must have been incredibly empowering to have that kind of stamina and the freedom to exercise it in whatever way you choose.

Leisure

People had plenty of time then. From three o'clock on, they had time.

Joe Gillman, Interview

The cedar chopper sense of humor was intended to mess with people's minds—to scare them or startle them or make them do something foolish. Kerry Russell was a rural mail carrier on Spicewood

Springs Road, and one of the tricks people played on him was this: "They'd kill a snake, rattlesnake or whatever kind of snake, makes no difference, and they'd tie a string around its head, put it in the box, and tie a string to that lid so when the mailman comes up and flips that lid, he just pulls that snake out like that." Mark Lisheron tells how Frank Boatright would nail a wallet to the asphalt on Spicewood Springs Road, just so he and his daughter Marie could laugh when some city boy driving a nice car would come to a screeching halt to pick it up.[44]

I talked to Mark Lisheron soon after reading his *Sundown of the Cedar Choppers*. He told me I really needed to talk with Junie Plummer, who met Frank Boatright when she was working for the City of Austin in the real estate division in the late 1980s. She was then in her thirties, and her job was to purchase land along Bull Creek for the city—land that is now St. Edward's Park. Frank Boatright owned some of that land, and his daughter Marie still does.

Over the years Junie got to know Frank and Marie—they always called her "Juno"—and they finally told her the backstory of one of their first meetings. Animals were and still are welcome in the sprawling rock house on a knoll above the creek. They had a goat named "Shadow" because he was like your shadow, always behind you. One of the first times that Junie came to talk with Frank and Marie about selling their land (Marie was not happy about this, telling Mark Lisheron that she too deserved a chance to live off the land the way her father and grandfather and great-grandfather did), they set her up. Shadow was behind Junie. "The goat was being bad," she said. "He was nudging, shoving his nose where it shouldn't be. Frank was so mean. He acted like nothing was happening. I would push the goat away and it would come back." Frank and Marie were straight-faced throughout the meeting. Later, they told her they had both "rolled on the floor" after she left. She knew them well enough to tell them, "That was bad."[45]

Mack Sutton told a story about a Jess Clawson (there are three persons in the family tree during the twentieth century with that name) "who could just charm a bird right out of a tree, you know. He was a huge man . . . and he never was much of a workin' man. If he got mad, though, it would take six guys to even slow him down. When he got mad, which was pretty rare, thankfully (laughter).

But ol' Jess made and sold whiskey, and he came in there one day and says, 'Well, there's no sense in me wastin' this mash' that was left over after he had cooked the whiskey, so he fed it to the chickens and pigs. The chickens started 'rammernecking' all over the yard, and the sow ran over a bluff, with all the piglets following her to their death. So he says that he's got some fresh pork . . . and he'd just grin and grin about it. Another time he got drunk and bought a saddle for fifty dollars. That was a lot of money in those days. Well, everybody would hoo-rah him and say, 'Jess, you bought that saddle and you don't even have a horse—ha, ha, ha.' All these hillbillies made it a point to come over and rib him. They said, 'Well, what 'er ya gonna *dooo* with it?' And he threw it up on the fence and he hopped up on it and said, 'I'm gonna practice!'"

For more organized fun they had coon hunts and cock fights and parties. Ronnie Roberts's grandfather "loved his fox hounds." Even after he was blind he kept six or eight of them. He would have twelve-year-old Ronnie drive him over to the Rob Roy Ranch and let them run just to hear them bay. In the 1920s there were cock fights on the Dellana Ranch that would attract two hundred spectators, always with an eye out for Jim McCoy and the law. Olan Raley's father raised fighting roosters in Junction.

During Prohibition, before the time of dance halls, dances were held at people's houses. Harold Preece, whose parents Dave and Hallie May were recorded by Alan Lomax, wrote an article in 1932 for the *Dallas Morning News* titled, "Where a Dance Still Means the Virginia Reel."[46] He wrote:

> Generally the dances are performed by the light of one or two flickering kerosene lamps. An old fiddler, with a tobacco-stained white beard, saws out traditional tunes in one corner of the cabin; and equally venerable character calls out figures from the other. Lank mountaineers in clacking boots swing calico-clad women and girls. Everyone participates, small children joining hands with gray-bearded grandfathers. There is a succession of dances until midnight, when they adjourn to the

> kitchen for molasses cake and strong black coffee, boiled in a washpot. After supper the dancing generally continues until daylight.

Mack Sutton, the nephew of Dave and Hallie May Preece, was probably thinking of these same dances when he described them doing the "chicken scratch" in their cowboy boots—they'd "reach out with one leg and scratch like a chicken scratchin' and jumpin' up and down on the other one." The kids would sleep on pallets in the other room. But, he said, "There were very few of them that didn't end up havin' a fight before the night was over. I'll tell you, they worked hard and they played hard, and they played pretty rough too." It probably wasn't coffee that fueled this dance.

Out on Morgan Creek north of Burnet, Hollis Baker's aunt would have dances for the cedar choppers camping and cutting on her land. There would be a fiddle but no refreshments; the men would sneak off with a bottle so that their wives wouldn't know.[47] Rush and Will Riley played the fiddle at dances in Westlake and made their own instruments out of beautiful heart cedar.[48] Since Rush Riley was a bootlegger, it is highly likely liquor was involved there as well. In later years, when drinking became legal, honkytonks became common and the dances became rougher.

Of course, for those who did not indulge in such earthly pleasures, there were church events such as revival meetings and baptizings. Keron Cantwell would go to church every Sunday with her parents, ten long miles by wagon, and during the summer they would have a week-long meeting under a brush arbor.[49] Don Simons said his aunt Nell and uncle Tom—the family who took care of his sisters when his mother was gone—were very "churchy," going two or three times a week. So were George and Lizzie Farmer, who lived on Shoal Creek and went to Wednesday prayer meetings across town.[50] Alice Patterson said her family regularly went to the Baptist church in Westlake.

But it doesn't appear that organized religion was a big part of the lives of most cedar choppers. One woman remembered the cedar choppers near Nameless being a very religious people but said they didn't attend church regularly.[51] Another man likewise said they seldom attended church but were "intensely religious."[52]

Their religion manifested itself in times of crisis. Morris Bonnet was cutting with his family on the Sunset Ranch near Round Mountain school when his older brother sustained an injury: "He cut his right foot here, right behind his little toe, cut it plumb off. The little toe bone was the only bone he didn't cut in two." They wrapped it and drove all the way into Brackenridge Hospital in a 1946 Ford truck, stopping to pick up his mother at Cedar Park on the way. He said, "Now, this is where I'm gonna give you a little religion (laughter). My mom was a prayer warrior. She grabbed his foot and rode in that truck. Oh yeah, she believed totally in God. She prayed all the way to that hospital." They sewed his foot back on and he recovered enough to where he could serve in WWII, though not in the infantry. "My mama believed in God healing his foot," Morris said. Simon Ratliff said the same thing about a bad cut he had on his foot: "I'm a Pentecost and I went to church and they prayed for me . . . the Lord healed that foot."

Probably the biggest source of family entertainment was to go to town. Depending on how long it took to get there, they would go once every week or two. Olan Raley lived far out and would go into Junction only every other Saturday, as would some of the choppers living west of Liberty Hill. The Teague boys would go in every Saturday, but First or Second Street "was as far 'uptown' as these mountain boys ever got," according to Emmett Shelton.

Charles Hagood remembers Junction in the 1950s: "The shops were all full, and on Saturdays all those wood cutters came to town. All the ranchers came to town. Saturday was the day of the week everybody gathered in town. And Preston has told me that (in earlier days) there'd be wagon loads of people coming in. Folks on horseback. There'd be old trucks. And said people'd come down early in the morning. The old men get drunk—so damn drunk—by the time they went home, half the men were hanging out the back of the wagon and the old lady's taking things home loaded down with groceries and stuff."

Carol Goble remembers Bertram during the 1930s, when it

would get so crowded on a Saturday that there was no place to park. There were lots of Model As, and the cedar choppers would come in on trucks and wagons, play cards, and get rowdy. She was a kid and didn't care—fifteen cents would buy her a movie, popcorn, and a coke.[53] Milton Lentz's dad was a mason working on the Capitol building, and the kids would walk six miles into town on Saturdays to meet him at Lammes Candy for ice cream sherbet.

Several people mentioned Charlie and Baldy Brown's weekly trip to town. Linda Vance said they would load their families onto an old flatbed truck on Friday afternoon and go to Austin, sometimes with their relatives the Simpsons. There they would buy a few staples, a stick of peppermint for the kids, and a jug of California wine for the men at the liquor store near the river on South Congress. "Usually by the time they had reached Bee Cave Road the women would have had to make a stop or two to pick up one of the men who had fallen off the truck."[54] Stoney Teague offered a correction to this story: "They didn't just go in there and buy a bottle. They'd go in there and buy a case each."

Fighting

And it's bad, bad Leroy Brown, the baddest man in the whole damned town.
Badder than old King Kong, and meaner than a junkyard dog.

Jim Croce, "Bad Bad Leroy Brown"

Fighting was a class of fun all by itself. Not all fighting was for fun—fighting could be about pride or insult or retribution—but a lot of it was simply about having fun. This was something I always had a hard time understanding; even when I was a kid I didn't get the part in the John Wayne movies when the men would all start pounding on each other. Fighting for fun became another topic that I would probe for understanding.

I asked Stoney Teague, *I mean, did you as a kid, like, enjoy it?* He replied, "Yeah, we used to, you know, see if a man could spank me or not. . . . Shoot, we'd just do it for fun. Get about half drunk, get out there and just skin each other up for the fun of it." *And then be buddies the next day?* "Oh yeah. We'd never get mad at anybody. You never heard of anybody getting mad." He said his father and Brucie Young were best friends. "They'd go down there on Sixth Street and fight in them old beer joints." *Did they like to fight?* "Oh, yeah, man, they loved it. Yeah, my daddy—hell, he'd get on a mule and ride ten miles to get in a fist fight." Albert Boatright said of his uncle Raymond Shannon, "Him and one of his cousins, Forest Shannon, they'd go down on Sixth Street and they'd drink and fight—oh, they loved to fight! (laughter). Anybody that come upon them."

Luther Pierce said Sonny Short, the grandson of Duff Short and Lula Tucker, stole a deer rifle from Luther's oldest brother Ed and pawned it. Ed confronted him at a Westlake beer joint, and they fought for an hour or more. They were both young and strong. "They'd stop and rest, and drink a beer, and then get back. Ed said, 'I couldn't whup him but he quit, so I guess that means I won.' Because he said he asked Sonny, 'You ready to go again?' He said, 'No, I think I've had enough.'" This fight appears to have been almost ritualistic, a necessary retribution for stealing from a friend. He got his rifle back, and the Pierces and Shorts remained friends.

Olan Raley told a story about his father and a friend named Willis Holden who were cutting cedar on Coke Stevenson's ranch.

> They got to playing poker, and they got drunk and they got in a fight. And I don't know who won the fight, but they both laid up in bed for a week (laughter). I think Daddy had some busted ribs and stuff. But anyway, as soon as Willis got to where he could get up and move around, why, he came to the house and he talked to Daddy, and then when they got healed up they went back to work again. Still partners.

Olan said that on those Saturdays when everyone would come to Junction, "It was nothing to stand there in the middle of town and see two or three fights going on, and Daddy might be right in the middle of it."

Olan Raley, Arthur Lee Wallace, and Charles Hagood lit up when the talk turned to fighting. Charles was a banker from an old ranching family; Olan was his friend and protector growing up in Junction. When I talked with them Olan and Charles were in their sixties (Arthur Lee was younger), and although they teased Olan, saying "Raley is a shadow of his former self," he was still a hard-muscled, compact man. Charles said, "I'd drink beer with him, whatever, nobody give me any crap, nobody bothered with me. Cause he kinda had a reputation. He'd never got in many fights. Hell, he was the good guy, always. But everybody knew if you did, shit, he'd just break 'em in two. He was a stout son-of-a-gun and quick, all that. Now, Arthur's uncle Jerry, this fella that Raley's talking about, now there was a different case for ya. Now, Jerry'd whup your ass and make you like it. He was good at it, and he liked it."

Arthur Lee looked at a picture of his father, Arthur Dee. "Meanness," he said. "That was a mean bastard (laughter all round). Well, that's what they tell me—he was mean!" *Well, you should know,* I said. "He wasn't ever mean to me," Arthur Lee objected. Charles said, "I don't know of any fights Arthur Dee ever lost. He just quit fighting after a while." Arthur Lee agreed, "Yeah, I think he just got tired of fighting."

I later realized that I was interpreting the word "mean" to indicate motivation, such as malice, or disposition, as in Taylor Swift's lyrics, "Someday I'll be living in a big ol' city/And all you're ever gonna be is mean." But they weren't using it this way; instead it was more like "bad, bad Leroy Brown"—simply signifying really, really good in a fight.

This use of the word is illustrated in a story told about Buck Simpson (1895–1969), a cedar chopper from Westlake who became the second most decorated soldier in WWI for singlehandedly capturing a machine gun and turning it on the Germans. His captain wrote to the family, "I told him to run, but he told me 'Hell, I come from Texas, and I don't run from nobody.'"[55] Buck was a genuine hero, and the city tried to reward him by teaching him to read and giving him a job as a night guard at the Capitol. But none of it really took; he quit school because "I got tired of a bunch of little bitty kids smarter than me."[56] Then he lost his job at the Capitol because he couldn't tell time and punch the clocks at the stations. Instead, he would walk down Congress Avenue to the Dixie Cafe and spend the evening telling stories.

One afternoon when Emmett Shelton was a boy, his father and brother were facing the consequences of having taken on the Ku Klux Klan: his brother was going on trial in the district courthouse at Eleventh and Congress. Buck was there, and they were looking out of the second story window at a small crowd of Klansmen who had gathered below. A big South Austin man nicknamed Country Day bragged to the crowd about what he was going to do to the Shelton brothers. Emmett's father said, "Now Buck, you've been wanting to whip a Ku Klux. There's old Country down there trying to get himself in trouble." He offered to pay Buck's fine if he would take care of Country.

Buck bounded down the stairs four at a time. The courtroom emptied, and everybody came over to the windows to watch the excitement. Buck worked his way through the crowd to Country Day, grabbed his shirt, and said, "Country, you talk like you're the meanest sonofabitch in Austin. You're gonna admit that I'm the meanest sonofabitch in Texas, and I'm meaner than you, or I'm gonna kick your ass all the way from the bottom of these steps to the foot of the river bridge."

"Mean" meant that like a junkyard dog, you came on hard and never quit—and that it would take someone even meaner than that to beat you. Lee McKinnerney was talking about his dad and Irish fighters in general when he said, "They're just, you know, they don't never give up. They keep on, keep on. You hit 'em, knock 'em down, they get up. You hit 'em, knock 'em down again, they're still gonna get back up. Till they just can't get up no more. That's just the nature of the beast."

They used the word "bad" differently also. Bad can mean naughty, as with Junie's description of the incident with Shadow the goat. Or it can mean criminal, as in "bad boys"—outlaws with an attitude. We'll meet some of them in the next chapter. Floyd Cantwell started talking about his uncle Ruf Young fighting on Sixth Street. He said, "He absolutely was the meanest man in the world." Thinking he was in the immediate family of Ike Young and his brothers—those that "hadn't had a natural death among male members for three generations"—I said, *Yeah, the Youngs were bad, weren't they?* He replied:

> He wasn't bad. He was the best guy, big red-headed guy, weighed about two hundred fifty, maybe two eighty, all muscle, man. He'd go down to the beer joints on Sixth Street. I'd go in, ten–twelve years old, they'd serve me a beer just like they served him one, no questions asked. And he'd go in there and he'd get drunk and when he was drinking, unless you had something kind to say to him, don't say nothing, you know. I've seen him take a bar stool and just pick it up and wham, just like that. And old Jim McCoy is the only guy that could come in there and arrest him. He'd come in there and he'd say, "Now Ruf, you know, you've done wrong, you've got to go to jail." He said, "Well, you gonna damn sure have a beer with me or I ain't going nowheres with you." He'd make Jim McCoy sit there and drink a beer and they'd get that drank and he'd get up and go with him.

Liquor was the fuel for fights—it turned parties raucous and turned some people into a version of themselves that they wouldn't recognize when sober. Lee McKinnerney said his dad "was the nicest guy in the world as long as he was not drinking. But if he got to drinking beer and you pissed him off, you gonna get hurt. I mean, he would knock you down. When you got up, he'd knock you down again. And he didn't care how many there were."

Parties during the early decades of the twentieth century—those described earlier by Harold Preece and Mack Sutton—were held at houses with the whole family participating. There might have been alcohol around, but it wasn't the main event. But as Prohibition wore on and was increasingly ignored, the alcohol flowed freely and the parties got wilder. Frank Wilson said, "They had dances . . . drunken, whiskey, drunken dances. Kill each other, end cuttin' one another up with knives. That was the party they had, yeah." Frank once took some lawyers and judges up to Rip Farmer's place in the hills to buy liquor. After they bought a gallon Rip said, "Now you all clear out, don't hang around here. There's fixin' to be a dance startin' up over at my place,' and he said all hell would break loose in about an hour, 'I don't want you all in here where you'd get hurt.'"

After Prohibition, beer joints and dance halls sprang up everywhere that wasn't dry. Coming in from Cedar Park in dry Williamson County, at the top of the hill overlooking the state hog farm (now Twin Lakes Park), was the Hilltop Inn. T. M. Pearson said he didn't like to go there:

> No. That was a rough place. Whew! You go in there and turn around and you looked at someone wrong, and he's ready to fight. Yeah. I was in there one time when I went over there to pick up my uncle. He'd gotten in a fight with six or seven Spanish guys. He had 'em all backed up in the corner. *Just that one man did?* Uh-huh. He, he wasn't but five foot eight and weighed about one hundred and sixty pounds. That's all he wanted to do, was drink and fight.

The uncle he was talking about was Harve Pearson, who was married to Alpha Whitt of the Whitt-Maynard-Bonnet clan. In 1953 Harve was serving a two-year sentence in Huntsville for a second DWI offense; the prison record shows him only five-foot eight and 140 pounds.[57]

After the Hilltop Inn was the Silver Top Inn, and once you got to Jollyville there were taverns on both sides of the road about every half mile all the way into Austin. The last one on the north side of town was Landrum's at Hooper's Switch. On the other side of town, Beard's Store in Westlake had moved, and the building became a place for the cedar choppers to stop for a beer on weekdays and for dances on weekends. There was a tavern in Oak Hill where fights were so common that it was known as "The Bloody Bucket." When the Cedar Crest nightclub opened on Bee Cave Road, Emmett Shelton asked the proprietor, "How're you gonna keep those hillbillies from coming up here and taking you over? If you do, these townspeople are not going to come out here and gamble with you, and stay around here." "Well," he said, "the best way to do that is to put a napkin on the table with a tablecloth."

Going west from Cedar Park toward Anderson Mill there were several more honkytonks in an area called Dodd City (now Volente), including the Vagabond Club, Tommy's Place, and the Anchor Inn. Lee Cantrell said, "There used to be a lot of beer joints, but they was a lot of cedar choppers and old hillbillies back in there. Boy, they'd just wreck them places, you know." Morris Bonnet remembered the same area:

> All of them guys in that area over there, they were all cedar cutters. And, I guess, they did want to prove what kind of man they was, and they fought. I mean, they'd have fights every night. This a story I heard. There were two college boys come out there from UT one time, they've heard about these bad cedar choppers. And they thought they were mean. And they come out there to Four Points or Dodd City, they were gonna see how tough these cedar boys were. And they found out. They whupped them boys and sent 'em back to Austin like you never . . .

I asked Stoney Teague if he even got into fights with city kids. He replied, "Oh, yeah. Yeah. Them little ol' kids down on Sixth Street, you know, why there wasn't no contest. They never got out and done any work, and at the time I was big enough to carry a post out for my daddy." Lee McKinnerney's mother ran a café in Uvalde, and he and his brother Lee were helping her cook and wait tables. He said one of the toughest football players, one who worked out all the time, came in half-drunk with his buddies. "I had both hands full of food and was walking over to the table and this little short son-of-a-bitch stood up and hit me as hard as he could. Before I could get to him my brother was on him, and he whupped his ass so bad it took him a week to get the nerve to come see my mother [to apologize—it was one of the few cafés around] because he was so black and blue."

The best story of the cedar choppers taking on outsiders concerns Earl and Charlie Short, two of the sons of Duff Short and Lula Tucker, one of Mattie Teague's daughters. The Shorts were always on the edge of the law. Earl was a bootlegger; they were cousins to some of the really bad boys like the Youngs as well as some other rough families like the Browns and Jesse Teague's bunch, the Fightin' Teagues; brother Tom Short was married for a while to Hazel Hamilton, the girl apprehended when the federal agent was killed on the raid at Ike Young's still; and a few years later brother Walter would drown under the Congress Avenue bridge trying to escape after assaulting a cop.[58]

This 1932 incident started when a young fighter from Austin named J. T. Reese—not a cedar chopper—came out to a party in the hills looking for a fight. Mack Sutton said, "He would insult every woman that came along, tryin' to get into a fight with one of the husbands, you know. . . . He said, 'Some old man's gonna get excited and get mad and jump me and then I'm gonna whip him. I'll whip his tail.' . . . I says, 'Now J. T., you know that they know that you're gonna be out there and one boy's not gonna be out there by himself. He's gonna have reinforcements, and you're gonna get yourself killed.' He says, 'Naw, I'm too tough to die.'"

So he went ahead, according to Frank Wilson, and "whipped one of those boys with his fists and beat him up pretty bad. I imagine it was a pretty bloody fight, and they told him not to come over there anymore. And those people's name was Short. . . . They weren't mean people, they just didn't like to be pushed around, kind of like the rest of us. Well, they told him not to come back over there, and he did, he went back to another dance and they killed him."

The incident made headlines for days, and Emmett Shelton got involved, so there are lots of witnesses and stories.[59] It happened on a Thursday night in December at a dance at Landrum's, the little two-room beer joint at Hooper's Switch. J. T. got there first, and later Earl and Charlie Short came in with a woman. She danced with Reese, and he told her loudly enough for the Shorts to hear that he had "come out there to get the Short boys and was a fighting son-of-a-bitch."

From here the stories diverge. The newspapers say Earl Short was seen with a pistol in his hand from the beginning. The witnesses, most of whom were friends of the Shorts, tell another version. They said Reese was "a dangerous and violent man." Ruby Williams, whose husband was a grandson of Evan Williams of the Patterson-Pierce clan, said several months earlier Reese had come into her house, torn it up, and assaulted her and her husband. Lade

Young, a sister of Ike Young, said Reese had recently threatened to get the Short boys, and they had been told of his threat.

Ivey Allen, whose sister was going out with Charlie Short, gave this version of events in his sworn testimony on file at the District Court of Travis County:

> He saw several folks around Earl Short in the dance room talking to him as if they were trying to keep him from fighting; that J.T. Reese was in the kitchen, and some women were trying to keep him out of the dance room where Earl was, but he pushed them aside and said he was twenty-one and would do his own fighting; that he then rushed into the room and started toward Earl Short and struck Earl, when Charlie Short stepped in and knocked him down; that Earl then retreated toward the door and Reese got up and ran after him, but Charlie Short knocked him down again before he got to Earl, and he caught Earl just before Earl reached the door; that he struck at Earl again, and as Earl threw up his guard, Reese staggered over into the corner; that as he came up toward Earl, he reached in his pocket, and witness heard a shot, though he did not see a gun, nor does he know who fired, but he heard Reese say, "You have killed me now."[60]

It was one of Emmett Shelton's first cases as a lawyer. He said of Earl, "Among that class of people at that time, whenever a man survived an altercation of that kind he became a sort of hero, and he was looked up to."[61] Because nobody would testify against him, Earl Short was acquitted on self-defense.

Over the years both Earl and his brother Charlie became good friends with Emmett and worked for him regularly. Emmett's version of the story, told in the "Cedar Chopper Tapes," is that Earl didn't even draw his pistol when he shot J. T. He had it in his pants: "He just reached inside his belt band and without even taking the pistol out to where anybody could see it, he just aimed it and shot. It's a wonder he didn't shoot his outfit off."

8

So Close, Yet So Far Away

He turned his back and walked away, sayin' Little Miss, you'll rue the day. You'll rue the day that you were born, for givin' me the devil cause I wouldn't hoe corn.

Alison Krauss and Union Station, "The Boy Who Wouldn't Hoe Corn"

Fierce Independence

Cedar choppers and all those who knew them emphasize one of their characteristics above all others: that they were fiercely independent. It did not take much equipment to become one, just an axe and an old truck. They made good money, more per day than for any other type of manual labor. And they faced little competition from others wanting to enter the field.

The reason, of course, was that no one else wanted to do it. An article on cedar in the rough country of Leakey and Camp Wood says the ranchers got along with the cedar choppers because they needed them. "No one wants to do the hard work of cutting cedar—not in the pioneer days and not today."[1] As a result, said Olan Raley, "None of 'em that I knew of ever worried about finding a place to go to work. I mean, they wasn't worried about their job being gone."

Not only could they always find a place to cut cedar; there were plenty of yards where they could sell it. Contrast this to the situation in Appalachia: there, big mining and timber companies were the only source of employment, turning the workers into wage slaves, exploited and surly. But cedar choppers, Olan Raley told me, "They'd cut wherever. They was the most independent people in the world. They'd tell you to take it and shove it and not a dime in their pocket, you know. If you made 'em mad, they just walked off."

C. W. Wimberley, the author who knew them better than any other, described the choppers' attitude toward their work.

> The cedarcutter chopped for himself. The post[s] he cut belonged to him until they had been hauled to the yard, checked, entered into ledgers, and he had been paid his full fair share of their value. He was his own man, his earnings determined only by his skill and effort. The cedarman could determine the grade and price he would receive for his post, and the brake boss could set rules for running the brake, but nobody, nobody, could tell the cedarcutter anything he had to do. No anchors held him in place, and he drifted with the first restless wind. He was among the last of an independent breed.[2]

A cedar chopper rarely worked for wages. A few show up in the 1940 census working for the WPA or in the quarry, but most, if they were not cutting or hauling or buying cedar, were doing something like driving a truck or laying rock, where each was his own boss. Frank Wilson said, "Now you wouldn't find one of 'em in town working for the city as a day laborer. Hell, no! They wouldn't do that. They'd do hard work for themselves or for each other, because they weren't lazy, but they just didn't draw wages."

Bob Willess was seventy-five and still hauling cedar when I interviewed him. He said he had probably drawn wages only a few years in his entire life. For the past several years a younger woman had gone on the road with him after quitting her job as a professional nurse. Five years previously she had told him, "I want to do the same thing that you're doing. . . . I will not ever go back to work for nobody." I asked him, *Well, do you think most of the cutters were like that?* "No, *all* of 'em," he replied.

He later told me a story about that woman that I didn't record. She was attractive and enjoyed going to honkytonks and having a few beers. When she would meet a man, inevitably she would be asked the question, "So, what do you do?" She was ready for it, and would say, "I haul cedar posts," all the while watching their eyes. If they squirmed or glanced away, that was it—it was over between them.

I shared Bob's stories with Alice Patterson, and summarized my impression: *You're free. You're your own boss.* She replied, "Yes, yes, that's what dad always said. He said 'Yep, I don't have to do anything for anybody else. I can do what I want and when, and I don't have to do it if I don't want to.'"

The cedar choppers didn't particularly like to farm either. They might have a couple of acres of corn for meal and whiskey and mules, but as Frank Wilson observed, "They're not farmers." Elmer Kelton wrote about a cedar chopper in his novel *Barbed Wire.* A rancher named Doug had offered him a job building fence. He declined, saying "Sounds like hard work. That's the main reason I quit farmin' back in East Texas, wanted to git away from all that hard work." Kelton wrote, "Doug grinned. There wasn't any harder work in the world than cedar cutting."[3]

It was probably the regularity required by both wage labor and farming that they found most distasteful. In these occupations you have to work at a specified time, when the boss or the agricultural cycle requires it. You have to be responsible—you can't work a day or two, get some money, and then quit. Al Ehrlich, who owned a big lumber company and cedar yard in Austin, said, "I get along with them as an employer, but I don't understand them. Never will . . . I don't think they know what they want. . . . I know they don't want responsibility. They only work when they feel like it."[4] Barbara Langham captured this attitude in the title of her article in *Texas Highways*—"A Man's Got a Right to His Own Mind." It came from a quote from an old cedar chopper explaining why another had just picked up and left in the middle of the night: "Hell, a man's got the rights to his own mind without havin' to have a reason. Ain't he? He just went; that's all there is to it. Nothin' else."[5]

A second defining characteristic of the cedar chopper mentality—a corollary of their independence—is that they demanded respect. The rancher Troy Joseph said, "Every cedar chopper considered himself the full equal of the Governor of Texas, and they all expected to be treated with respect."[6] They were proud of their fortitude—that they could cut cedar all day and go coon hunting at night; that they could survive in the hills without electricity or running water or much else; that they could get cut or bit or beat up and be back at it. Willie Gephart lived out in northwest Travis County where weekend property owners came to cut firewood. He said, "Nothing disturbs me more than when people come out here representing themselves as cedar choppers. They haven't got the right to call themselves that because they haven't been out in the woods, freezing. They haven't been hungry, or sick out there. They haven't paid their dues."[7] Troy Joseph summarized cedar choppers' attitude perfectly, "They lived a tough life and they honored it."[8]

They certainly did not want any favors. When cedar choppers dealt with the outside world, it was direct and as an equal. During the Depression Frank Wilson would go up into the hills to buy coon hides from boys who would trap them for money. He would holler to the man of the house, "'Any of your boys got any hides they'd like to get rid of?' And he'd say, 'I don't know,' and he'd call one of them's name and he'd ask 'em if they had any, but he knowed whether they did or not. And one of them would say, 'Yeah, I've got a few,' and they'd be hangin' around the back of the house, and we'd go back there and look. That was about it. He wasn't selling them to me, I was buying them from him, and that's the way it was." Frank got along fine with them, but said, "If you went out there and try to indicate in any way you were going to show them how to do something or help them do something, you'd best get out of there fast. They wouldn't put up with it."

They were very resistant to accepting any form of welfare, which usually required submission to authority. At one mountain school the free lunch program had to be abandoned for a while because it was perceived as charity.[9] Willie Gephart, a stonemason with a wife and four children to support, hurt his shoulder and couldn't work. He said, "My wife went in there to get the food stamps, and they spoke to her like she was a child. I went back to work with my shoulder busted so we wouldn't have to deal with that again."[10]

The Outside World

Secret cedar places from whence you could peer out at the far world of other men, without having to feel yourself a part of it.

John Graves, *Hard Scrabble*

How are we to understand this attitude? A Scots-Irish background was certainly an important factor. Jim Webb, describing the influence of the Scots-Irish on the American working class, said they combined "a simple, sometimes combative directness when dealing with authority, an unbending demand for personal respect and a complete lack of fear"—phrases familiar to anyone who knew the cedar choppers.[11]

But there was something more. They had a self-awareness in assuming this attitude, as if they were deliberately choosing to emphasize it, perhaps as a response to their position in society. John Hoover said, "They developed it. When they come to town they were a little bit like the cattle drive guys, all gun smoke, you know." The Ozark hillbilly in Daniel Woodrell's *Tomato Red* put it this way: "This Scary face is all them such as me has to show this other world, the world in charge of our world that musters any authority, gets any reluctant respect at all."[12]

During the early decades of the twentieth century, as others were moving in droves from the farms to the cities, the clans in the hills had turned to a strategy of subsistence survival supplemented by cutting cedar and burning charcoal. They became more and more removed from the larger society. C. W. Wimberley said they "withdrew further from the society of other people and became more clannish. They developed habits, mannerisms and philosophies of their own."[13] John Graves speculated that the old Scots family bonds "sometimes grow crazily tight against a hostile and incomprehensible outside world."[14]

During these early decades they lived in places practically impossible to reach. A deputy sheriff who had to deliver an occasional summons said, "There was nothing but paths up there, little rutty things, and it used to take you all day to get there and back."[15] When Frank Wilson first went into the hills to buy hides, he would come to the end of a road and go on up the top of a hill and shout. Pretty soon somebody would come out and ask, "'What do you want?' And maybe he'd know me and say you can bring your truck in here. So that's the way it was, you wouldn't think that anybody at all lived in there."

Cedar choppers used to camp near Monkey Springs on the Marshall Ranch in Eanes. When Bruce Marshall was a boy he would go to the creek to get a bucket of water. Once he saw a girl about his age drawing water from the other side. "She was wearing what they called a gunny sack, had no shoes—bare feet, hair all tangled up, looking much like a creature of the forest—and she saw me and she dropped the bucket and just ran, she ran just like a deer, you know, back into the woods."[16] The Eanes census taker always had to identify herself as she approached the cedar choppers' shacks, or they would run off before she could talk to them.[17]

Cedar choppers were reclusive and wary of strangers during this period, because anyone who chose to come out into the rough hills usually wanted to do something that was not in the choppers' interest—to collect taxes or serve a warrant or kill a deer. They were suspicious of the townspeople, and the townspeople feared the cedar choppers. They had a bad reputation. It didn't take many front-page stories like those of Dempsey Brown or John Teague or Ike Young to make a lasting impression about violent mountaineers and hillbilly moonshiners.

Some of the cedar choppers whom people regularly encountered actually were wild and became legends. Buddy Brown, who married one of the Tucker girls, lived on Tucker Lane, now Walsh-Tarlton Lane. With his big white horse, rifle, and rattlesnake hatband, he cut quite a figure. "People steered clear of him. . . . You know, he look just like one of those latter day hippies, but he was for real!"[18]

Charles Hagood from Junction met the legendary armadillo-roping cedar chopper, Johnnie Pale.

> We went over to Lacy Flemings—my cousin was gonna buy a bull from Lacy Flemings in Rock Springs—and John Pale was working for him. And we kids were standing in the pen looking at his bull and we heard a scream—a blood-curdling-ass-scream. And here comes John Pale. He was riding as fast as

> he could bareback and he came running up there and jumped off that horse. He was barefoot. Had on a pair of old slacks that looked like they'd been worn for about two months. No shoes on and no shirt on and an Indian feather braided into his hair, and jumped off and came running up there and started talking about half-gibberish.

The cedar choppers emerged from their seclusion in the hills during the 1940s and 1950s, the heyday of the cedar choppers, when the demand for posts was high and they had trucks to haul them in. They could be seen in places like Austin and Marble Falls and Burnet hauling cedar and buying supplies. It is ironic that it was during this period of relative prosperity that they became the most disparaged.

You knew a cedar chopper when you saw one. Hollis Baker's father ran a store in Burnet and sold groceries to a bunch of cedar choppers. Hollis said they would come in covered with cedar wax, their long-sleeved denim shirts encrusted with salt rings. Usually they had not taken a bath and they smelled. Margie Carlton remembers that one of the Maynards brought a load of cedar to Dick Boatright's yard when somebody was there peddling goods. That man "kind of turned up his nose and said, 'You stink. When was the last time you took a bath?' And that guy went, 'I don't know, I guess a month or two ago.' And he says, 'Well, I take a bath every day.' And he says, 'You must be a stinking blackity-black if you take one every day!'"[19] Luther Pierce said, "I'll even admit this—that in O. Henry and Austin High, they could probably smell me, the stench. We took baths 'cause mama made us. But we didn't take that many."

It might seem that in the Hill Country, where almost everybody was white and poor, society would be relatively classless. But there was a clear social hierarchy. At the top were the ranchers, whose status in Williamson County "towered above the German Lutherans and Czech Catholics," who were farmers. The ranchers were "a masculine society of tight-lipped individuals who attended Methodist and Baptist churches in town where drink was forbidden." Farmers with good land and merchants in towns like Liberty Hill were in between. And at the bottom were the cedar choppers.

Jerry Hawes's father had a ranch on the San Gabriel River. Jerry told me he rode the school bus to Georgetown with a few cedar choppers; they smelled of cedar smoke and the other kids made fun of them. Hollis Baker's family had a ranch on Morgan Creek outside Burnet, where several families of cedar choppers lived in tents. His aunt would hire a fiddler and hold dances for them. There was a girl there who "was pretty nice-looking after sundown," but Hollis said, "I didn't want to eventually get tied up with her. These folks were pretty earthy. They didn't read. We felt we were here and they were here socially" (puts one hand below the other).[20] I asked Marble Falls rancher Guthrie O'Donnell if he had any cedar choppers as friends. "Not really," he said. "Most of 'em were, well they were, were more trashy-type people." But like most ranchers who worked close to cedar choppers, he respected their hard work. He added, "Man, their old hands showed it, and they were really brown and they worked hard for what they got. . . . People respected them because they were doing something to try to make their own way." Comal County farmer Lorenz Bading looked back with this same mixture of superiority and respect: "I shouldn't say this, but I guess we sort of looked down our nose at 'em. They seemed to be well, not inferior, but—why, that's the way they had of makin' their livin,' I guess."

The rancher attitude was grudging respect combined with social distance. John Hoover, a rancher with a hardware store in Burnet, knew them well and had nothing bad to say other than that they could be pretty wild, living on the fringe of society. I asked him, *So, everybody was living poor. I mean all over the Hill Country it was just dirt poor. But would it have been OK for, you know, your daughter to marry a cedar chopper. I mean, was that kind of mixing going on?* He replied, "Let's say I had a daughter, and she's got her eye on this cedar chopper boy that's been out there chopping cedar and never went to school, he's got no education. I'm probably gonna grit my teeth on that one."

This attitude contrasts sharply with that of people in the small towns, who would see the cedar choppers regularly when they came in. The kids in Liberty Hill avoided them. Kerry Russell said, "Yeah, they were afraid of the cedar chopper kids 'cause they were pretty rough. I mean knife fights and stuff like that, that was just commonplace." For a while in the 1950s Charles Hagood's father worked nights at the drive-in movie in Junction, and Charles and his mother would go often because they could get in free. Sometimes little Charles would see Arthur Lee Wallace's teenage uncles and their friends at the concession stand and restroom. He said, "Now you want to talk about somebody that'd scare a young boy. They were pretty tough, and they were not opposed to giving you a little grief. You know, they'd pull your pants down and whip your ass or something and send you back up to the car just for meanness. They were mischievous. They never, they never hurt me, but they scared the *shit* out of me."

For the adults the strategy seems to have been denial of their existence, at least in retrospect. A respected historian of Kimble County had hardly anything to say about them, a reflection of the common practice among rural women of a certain generation that if you have nothing good to say, it is better to say nothing at all. C. W. Wimberley remembers the scathing disapproval of a churchgoing lady when she saw him fishing on a Sunday: "She'd give me a look like she was seeing one of the devil's imps sitting there on that log."[21]

Real County, with its biggest towns Leakey and Camp Wood (with a combined population of just over a thousand in 2014), was not good for much but goats and cedar. Yet because of the stigma attached to cedar chopping, the only book on the history of Real County "almost went to press without a chapter on cedar." The reason was that "cedar is at the base of whatever fragile social hierarchy developed over the years," so that "until this very day in Real County, Cedar Choppers 'don't get no respect.'"[22]

When I first started researching the topic I was excited to discover a book with the title *Culture of the Shin Oak Ridge Folk*.[23] Shin Oak Ridge is the area of high plains cotton farms astride the Burnet-Williamson county line, on the edge of the cedar country, and the area includes the towns of Leander, Liberty Hill, Bertram, Florence, and Briggs. The book was written in 1964, which would be ideal for a twenty-year retrospective on the place of cedar choppers in local society.

But they were not even mentioned. All the stories were about men who grew up poor but persevered and became successful doctors, lawyers, and businessmen. The author spoke of a reunion of the important families and emphasized that nobody there drank. Again and again he said things like, "Shin Oak Ridge still has a high curve of cultural achievement and morality." And, he continued, "It also has a low occurrence of violence. Sober, happy people do not fight and kill."[24] I was puzzled about who this "other" was to whom he kept alluding—the people who drank and fought and never achieved anything—until I finally realized he was talking about the cedar choppers!

The cedar choppers emerged from the hills only to step right in to a cultural stereotype that had begun sweeping the country in the 1930s. It was the beginning of the age of the hillbilly. The degenerate characters in Erskine Caldwell's 1932 novel *Tobacco Road* became household names in the 1930s, and the play ran on Broadway for eight years. Tucker Lane became known as "Tobacco Road" because of the large cedar chopper community there.[25] *Esquire* began to publish the Mountain Boys cartoons in the 1930s, highlighting "standard tropes that defined hillbilly culture: social isolation, physical torpor and laziness, unrefined sexuality, filth and animality, comical violence, and utter ignorance of modernity."[26]

These images had first emerged immediately after the Civil War, when the North stereotyped southern whites as a hard-working but degraded group.[27] The term "white trash" was first used in 1860 to describe a family with "a half-dozen dirty, squalling, white-headed little brats," a family who subsist on game, "pretend to cultivate" their small plot, and who lie around and get drunk.[28]

By the late nineteenth century the stories would paint a different picture. "Color writers" in magazines like *Harpers* and *The Atlantic* described the people of Appalachia and the Ozarks as relics of an earlier era stopped in time, who preserved some of the best of American values—rugged individualism, a pioneer spirit, strong family bonds. These images of a bucolic past resonated with America's increasingly urban and industrial society.[29] When Harold Preece described life in the hills west of Austin in the 1930s, he wrote, "Here exists a certain flavor of life, a pastoral freshness and innocence not to be found in those mechanized incongruities we call cities."[30] These contradictory images of squalor and primitive beauty allowed a middle-class audience to imagine a romanticized past, while distancing themselves from the hillbilly lifestyle and recommitting to the benefits of modernity.[31] Or as Larry King wrote, the middle class should give thanks to the "poor tacky peckerwoods who did us the favor of having somebody to look down on."[32]

Popular characterization of hillbillies began in earnest with the massive migration from the farms, beginning with Okies from the Dust Bowl to California in the 1930s and continuing with poor whites from coal country to midwestern cities.[33] Readers could only take so much of the luridly graphic descriptions portrayed in *Tobacco Road*, but "the deviance of white, Anglo-Saxon, Protestant, native-born Americans living in the present and within miles of the older centers of American civilization" needed explanation.[34] This was material that was better served by humor. During the 1940s and 1950s comic strips like *Snuffy Smith* and *Li'l Abner* ran in newspapers across the county, bringing all the hillbilly stereotypes to life—including the corn-licker-drinking Snuffy from Hootin' Holler, the voluptuous Daisy Mae, and the mountain vixen, Moonbeam McSwine.

During the 1950s and 1960s these images moved to television and included shows like *The Real McCoys*, the *Andy Griffith Show*, the *Beverly Hillbillies*, *Gomer Pyle*, *Mayberry RFD*, and *Hee-Haw*. In the late 1960s an average of six "southern" shows were airing per season.[35] *This* was the social stage, defined by derisive images of their distant cousins in Appalachia and the Ozarks, onto which the cedar choppers of Central Texas emerged in the late 1940s and 1950s.

The generation who felt this discrimination most acutely were those born in the 1930s and 1940s. Milton Lentz said the school kids called him names, "They'd all run you down. . . . I had to get used to it, you know." He recalls one time when his family—all eight kids and their parents—went to a hamburger place on Highway 183. "But the people asked us to leave because, you know—I guess we were tattered and barefooted and stuff, so the people asked us to leave." I asked Don Simons, *And how did you guys feel when you came into town and you saw these nice green lawns, and these guys walking around with their white golf shoes on. What did you think about that?* He replied, "Terrible. When you didn't have no shoes. And the end of your toes were bloody because you stubbed them on the rocks. You felt, you felt terrible because people looked at you. They don't know how to deal with you. Very degrading."

Like all the Simonses, Don is a big man—six foot six and built like an athlete. He loved to play football and was good at it. When he was going to junior high school in New Braunfels, the coach wanted him to play quarterback. But he had to load posts at his dad's yard from daylight until the school bus picked him up (meaning he was always filthy) and again after school. He told the coach he couldn't play—that he had to work. "So he gets all the cheerleaders and the football players and puts them in a hay truck, you know, a hay-ride deal, and he come to our house. It wasn't a house, it was a tent when we lived out there at Sattler (northwest of New Braunfels). But anyway, they come out there, the cedar truck and everything, and all them kids started hollering at me and everything, saying 'We want to talk to your daddy, your mama and daddy. We want to talk to them. We want you to play football!' He wouldn't come out of the house, drunk on his ass. And I couldn't stop thinking about it."

Luther Pierce, my classmate at O. Henry, simply said, "I knew I wasn't as good as y'all."

Their Response

For those who did the work and made the money, there was no shame. Lee McKinnerney's dad—the Uvalde cedar chopper who bought new cars for his kids—was a fighter but didn't consider being called a cedar chopper an insult. I asked Lee, *What about people are gonna call him a cedar chopper, or do something like that?* He replied, "That wouldn't bother him in the least. He was proud of what he did."

So was Alice Patterson. I asked, *Did y'all ever feel, when you went into Austin, that some of the people in Austin kind of looked down at you as country folk?* "You know what? It didn't bother me. They do. They did." *They did?* "Yeah, they did. And I didn't know it. But I found out later when my kids started growing up, and some of 'em was ashamed of it. My sister wouldn't even tell anybody about it at all. She wouldn't tell anybody where they come from. It didn't bother me that bad. I said it was an honest living. We did well by it. It was dirty living, but it was a good living." She went on to say that they stayed dirty working in cedar and that maybe that was why people looked down on them. Other than that, she said she didn't really understand.

Luther Pierce is another success story, his rock hauling business eventually growing into ownership of a quarry that served the growing Central Texas economy. While his father Litten could be a bit of a problem when he took to drink later in life, his mother Edna Patterson was the strong matriarch of the family, and Luther had great relationships with others in the clan, from his oldest brother Ed to his best friend Charlie Roberts and Charlie's mother, Tiney Teague. Luther is a humble man but was realistic about how he was perceived by others in the rapidly changing Eanes community, which by 1956 had an estimated population of three thousand. The little rock house he grew up in stood alone on the road that led from the low-water bridge to Bee Cave Road, and I remember marveling when as a kid I heard how many people were living there. Luther said he wanted to join the Future Farmers of America, but would have had to raise an animal and bring the class out to his house to see it. He said, "I didn't want to do that and take 'em out there to my house. To look at where I lived." Luther had a girlfriend in the fifth grade who usually rode home with her parents. Once she rode the school bus: "When she seen where I got off the bus at, she never—just never spoke to me again."

Some sought distance or escape. I promised not to reveal the names in this story, but it concerns a woman who married into one of the families in the Bull Creek clan. I was told, "She did not like the lifestyle of his parents. And so she didn't go to the reunions and things and the girls don't know any of their kin folks. I don't know if she was ashamed of 'em or what." *By the lifestyle, do you mean, the physical appearance of their house?* "No, I think the education. I mean, most of the people that chopped cedar did a lot of drinking and smoking and chewing, you know. I don't know if she was embarrassed or she just didn't want to associate."

Don Simons had another means of distancing himself. I asked him, *You as a kid coming into town, someone looks down on you—didn't it make you mad?* "Course it did. It also screwed you up. But we had something that would fix it, called alcohol. I started drinking early. Those few days I did go to school I would meet up with a couple guys. I always had money and we'd go pick up a six-pack, ride around in the truck, drink."

But for the older generations, those who had survived the hard years and were making good money, the very characteristics that most defined them—fierce independence and a demand for respect—predetermined the results of their encounters with an outside world that generally defined them as hillbilly trash. Never mind that they did not fit the stereotype—they worked hard, made good money, distained welfare, and were not common criminals. They wore old clothes because they were always working, and working in cedar was hot and dirty. Many of them would clean up when they went to town. Lee McKinnerney's father would take a bath and put on his new hat: "He was quite a lady's man. The women just swooned over him, 'cause I mean he was six foot one, two-twenty."

But it didn't matter—their occupation defined them. "Cedar chopper" joined the lexicon of regional terms, like "cracker" in Georgia, "linthead" in the Carolinas, and "Okie" in California, that put them at the lower end of a scale of whiteness, somewhere above white trash because they worked hard, but not anywhere close to genteel, white middle-class society of American cities during the middle of the twentieth century.

This was a formula designed to trigger aggression. Frank Wilson said, "They were very independent and very proud people, and aggressive, very aggressive." A man who cut cedar with an chainsaw spoke of the earlier generation: "They was hard people. . . . People thought of them as white trash with their apple-cart houses and beat up trucks. But I tell you, this is hard work with a chainsaw. And these folks went out and cut cedar with an axe. Now, those were some touchy hombres."[36] Milton Lentz said, "All those people, you didn't mess with 'em up there. When they're tired and they're aggravated and stuff, you just didn't mess with them." Charlie Maugham, himself a cedar chopper, said of some of the cedar cutters, "You would say one word to 'em and boy, if they didn't like it, they'd put you down. *So they got insulted pretty easily?* "Oh, yeah. You had to talk nice to 'em." *What kind of thing would make them mad?* "That I was gonna spend the night with them, or something like that. . . . Drinking too much and flirting with his wife. Just bat an eye at one of 'em, you'd be on the ground."

Whether it was bred into their culture, a result of their treatment by the larger society, or simply their physical prowess, their immediate response to perceived insult was aggression. Linda Vance did many interviews for her history of Eanes, and she told Mark Lisheron, "Every source I ever interviewed told me the only way they knew to settle a score was violence."[37] The historian Thad Sitton, who has written about marginalized white Texans, met with me several times over the course of this project. He concluded that the cedar choppers were "an attack culture"—in any confrontation, the stakes were raised so quickly that the opposition was just overwhelmed.

Sometimes this aggression was verbal but just as effective. Stanley Allen was burning brush during a burn ban, and firemen came to put out the fire even though the ban should have been lifted because it was raining. He said,

> They drove back there in the pasture and got stuck! And then they asked me to pull them out. And I said, "No, sonny boy." And I said, "You need to learn the code of the country. I told you not to go back there. If you ain't man enough to listen to me," I said, "you better get your tail out of here and do not come through that gate again. You might be a fireman, but I'm gonna tell you something. I'm a type of man—I'm still the old school. I don't put up with any bullshit off of you or anybody like that. The law respects me because I've got common sense to know what I'm doing. I ain't no damn quack. You get that truck out of here and don't bring it back."

When unsuspecting suburbanites pull over in front of Marie Boatright's land on Spicewood Springs Road to rid themselves of an unwanted pet, she tells them, "If you drop off that dog, I'm gonna shoot it before it hits the ground."[38]

Even if somebody did succeed in winning a confrontation with a cedar chopper, it wasn't over. Troy Joseph said, "If an outsider messed with one of them, he messed with them all; and news that a cedar chopper had somehow been insulted spread amazingly quickly across cedar-chopper country."[39] Lee McKinnerney agreed, "If one had a problem the others would be right there to cover their defense." And if the law was called in, Stoney Teague said, "Everybody'd go to the courthouse to make sure, you know, that it was told right."

Their reputation for violence was greatly enhanced by the actions of just a few families, and of these none was more notorious than the Youngs. Ol Young married Kate Tucker, one of the daughters of Henry Tucker and Mattie Teague. We have already met two of the Youngs: Ol's brother Tom, the last man hanged in Williamson County, and Ol's son Ike, the moonshiner sent to Alcatraz for conspiracy to murder a federal agent. Ol Young himself was killed in 1917 in an argument over some lumber.[40] Two of his daughters, Effie and Ollie, were married to Fred Stark and Buck Duval, who were in the fight over spousal abuse. This story is about two sets of his sons, Ellis and Buster, and Bruce and Pete.

On September 29, 1931, Ellis Young, aged twenty-two, killed his brother Buster, twenty-four. Ellis lived on 26th Street in a rough area running along Shoal Creek. According to a twenty-year-old female witness, Buster drove up to the house one Tuesday afternoon, stepped out with his rifle, and threatened to shoot Ellis. She grabbed the rifle as he raised it to fire, and the shot went wild, but that gave Ellis time to reach for his shotgun and shoot Buster from only ten feet away. He was found by officers lying in a pool of blood, the rifle nearby. Ellis said, "I hated to do it but it was his life or mine." He would not say what their argument was about. The verdict was self-defense, supported by the fact that Ellis was in his own home.[41]

On April 15, 1935, the *Austin Statesman* ran another story: "Violence, for the second time in less than two years [it was actually more than three], caused the death of a member of the Young family, Travis county hill folk."[42] Bruce Young, twenty-one, had killed his oldest brother Pete, fifty, with a shotgun. Their brother Ike (the incident at the still that sent Ike to Alcatraz was a couple of years in the future) was jailed for attempting to kill Bruce, probably in retaliation for the murder of Pete. The story was short and ran on page two, next to a story about the robbery of thirty-eight dollars from a café; the antics of these ruffians did not merit much attention any more. According to Emmett Shelton, the sheriff said, "It's a shame they didn't kill each other. But half a loaf is better than none."

Brucie, as he was called, was undoubtedly one bad hombre, as were his brothers and friends. Emmett Shelton, who represented him, said Brucie had one eye that looked back over his shoulder, the result of a fight with one of the Stark boys. The story Emmett told was that it was accidental homicide. He claimed that during an argument, Pete "picked up his chopping ax and made a pass at Bruce, and Bruce run out the door and run off down through the brush to get away from his brother. He heard the door open, and Bruce just fired his gun back over his shoulder and, without knowing it, he shot his brother and killed him." They took Pete to the hospital—"They didn't report it to the police or sheriff, because that was the last place they ever went for justice"—and he died at 5:00 a.m.. Stoney Teague told me what happened next, when the law heard about the killing.

> Jim McCoy told my daddy, he said, "We're gonna take five or six of these deputies and we're gonna go out there and straighten them Youngs out." The old man said "Alright, y'all go ahead." "Well, you're going with us." My daddy said, "No, I'm not going with you. You want to go out there and straighten them out, y'all go out there and straighten 'em out" (laughter). The old man said they talked about it a little bit, and said they finally decided well, better send Homer out there and let him get Brucie Young. My daddy said he got on his mule and went out there, and he said, "Now Brucie, I'll come by

> here in the morning and you be ready to go." And the old man said he went by there the next morning and got him and took him to the courthouse. I think Daddy said he stayed in jail two or three days and they got him out of it.

We've already heard the names of some of the pallbearers at Pete Young's funeral: Buck Duval, married to Ollie Young, Fred Stark, married to Effie Young, and Rudolph Gephart, Willie's Gephart's uncle. Another was James Ellis "Pude" Plumley, whose father Jim was married to another of the Tucker girls. Jim Plumley was found on the day of Pete's funeral in his car out by Oak Hill, the top of his head blown off by a shotgun.[43] The report ruled death by suicide. He had $13.50 in his pocket that he had collected for the burial of his nephew.

One can only wonder about the underlying causes of this violence between brothers. One thing is certain—even in the most egregious of cases, no cedar chopper would ever tell a story to the police that would land another in prison. Joe Gillman said, "They didn't need no law. If somebody done something wrong, they took care of it." Elsie Upton, the teacher in the hills west of Austin in the 1930s, said there might be a few outlaws among them, and even though people might not like someone they would never appear in court against the person, exhibiting "a clannish spirit that makes it impossible to get information in court."[44] Of all the stories told in this book so far, only a few led to convictions—John Teague, Ike Young, Rush Riley. Most players walked away—Earl Short, Paul Waechter, Dick Boatright, the Youngs, and, as we will see, Jesse Teague and Ernest Thurman.

The case of Paul Waechter, the Bull Creek native charged in the "Travis County Dog Wars," is a good example of the effectiveness of this code of honor. A reward of $250 was posted for information leading to an arrest, and though everybody knew the persons involved, and the reward amount was significant—over $6,000 in today's dollars—nobody responded. The sheriff at the time said, "Sure, me and Constable King may be able to serve the subpoenas on those hillbillies, and like as not most of 'em will show up.

But getting one to testify against his neighbor—well, that may be another story. I'll bet a five-dollar gold piece that those mountain folks will stick together like flies in a spoon of molasses."[45] More than one hundred witnesses were summoned to the Waechter trial, but when the constable went out "with an armload of subpoenas, he found himself accompanied on his rounds by a grizzled, erect mountaineer. The mountain man, unbeknownst to the constable, was the leader of the hill folk—and his very presence at the lawman's side meant to every hillbilly: 'Keep your mouth shut before the grand jury.'"[46]

Buster Toungate of the Bull Creek clan was arrested in 1937 at a whiskey still near Anderson Mill. He was only twenty-one years old and was clearly working for others. But he wouldn't tell who the owners were and took a fine of a thousand dollars and seven months at the prison farm for his silence. Brothers D. L. and Gladden Turner were boys at the time, and they remembered the case. D. L. said, "I know one of them went to jail. He took the whole rap, served some time for the group together there." Gladden added, "Well, he didn't have no family or children, he wasn't married or nothin,' so I guess he felt he could do it easier than some of the others who had families, you know."[47]

Sometimes the intimidation was more direct. Jesse Teague, who had returned from WWII with PTSD and lived with his goat next to Harve Roberts, became a "wino" and hung out with others under the Congress Avenue bridge. In 1948 one of these men, Santiago Vargas, was found dead with a fractured skull, probably from a blow with a wine bottle. Based upon the statement of a witness, Jesse Teague was charged. [48]

The next month, the witness showed up at the district attorney's office and said that Jesse Teague and Leslie Young—the youngest of the troublesome Young brothers—had threatened to kill him if he planned to testify.[49] Emmett Shelton and his son Polk represented them and once again got an acquittal. The following year Leslie Young himself was murdered, stabbed by Ivey Allen—the same Ivey Allen who had testified for Earl Short seventeen years earlier (in the case where Shelton claimed Earl had shot without even removing the pistol from his pocket).[50] The reasons for all this violence remain a mystery.

It is clear that their code of honor sanctioned violence along with some other criminal activities, such as moonshining and hunting out of season. Frank Wilson said, "They weren't criminal types, they were just rough people. Very few of them ever got put in jail or went to the penitentiary or anything like that. The only reason any of them got in trouble was for killing or for bootlegging. But petty thievery and burglary, no. They looked down on that sort of thing. They were as much against that sort of thing as I would be." Milton Lentz agreed, saying, "The biggest thing that aggravated my family with others—thieves, stealing and stuff like that, more so than anything else."

I wondered what they thought about some of the wilder and more violent men in the clans. Ronnie Roberts said it was "kinda scary" to know he was related to some of the people Linda Vance wrote about in her history of Eanes. I asked Milton Lentz, *How did they handle those folks? I mean, you ever have any sense of people talking, your dad or something, talking about "Well, ol' so-and-so, he's a good worker, but, you know—got an alcohol problem, or spent some time in the pen," or something like that?* "Well, I'll tell you what they thought about some of that. They was scared to and they was scared not to. They had an everyday battle over that, you know. But these people were neighbors and stuff like that, and didn't pay attention to that stuff." (He gave the example of liquor run out of Bull Creek.) *Because it might get you in trouble?* "That's right. If it didn't get you in trouble with the law it would get you in trouble with them. And they did honor that thing. Some of them were fighters." Before I had made the big family tree, I asked John T. Boatright about Frank Boatright, the cedar chopper in Mark Lisheron's article and John T.'s first cousin. *What relation is Frank to you?* "None!" *Why? Don't you claim him?* His daughter-in-law Mary replied, "Oh, he's just a rounder. A wild one."

Emmett Shelton played no small role in the life of the wilder cedar choppers. He represented them in legal scrapes, and they deeded him land in return. Ronnie Roberts said, "I'm not saying that there is anything wrong with that, but he ended up with a lot of land." That land became very valuable when the bridge that he promoted—the one I have been calling the low-water bridge—gave easy access from West Austin. It was later renamed the Emmett Shelton Bridge.

Luther Pierce tells the story of his brother Ed, and how Emmett protected him in a confrontation with the law.

> What caused it was somebody had cut cedar posts in the wrong place, on Emmett 's side. And Ed followed their muddy tracks out of there. And Emmett had a double-barrel shotgun. Well, he took it with him, him and Ed went over there. Have you heard of John Lloyd? John Lloyd was real rich. He had built all kinds of mansions over there in West Lake Hills. John Lloyd's son-in-law was there and he was talking real, real smart. And the sheriff was there too. And John Lloyd's son-in-law walked up to Ed and shaking his finger at him, right in his face, said, "What are you doing over here anyway? You're the son-of-a-bitch that probably cut these posts." So Ed hit him and knocked him down on the ground. And that sheriff told John Lloyd's son-in-law, said, "You can file on him for that." He said, "Well, then, that's just what I'll do." So the sheriff was handcuffing Ed. Ed said Emmett scared him more than the sheriff—he got one handcuff on him before Emmett knocked 'em. "You leave that man alone. You get them handcuffs off of him. I am his attorney." And then he turned to that man and said, "You file on him and I'll charge you five thousand dollars a tree for every cedar that you cut on my place and we'll go through there and count the stumps." So they unlocked the handcuffs and let him go.

Emmett Shelton was a very effective lawyer. If the cedar choppers couldn't win a confrontation one-on-one, the whole clan would jump in. And if that didn't work, they called Emmett Shelton.

While the Youngs might have been the most notorious family of cedar choppers, the most notorious individual was Ernest Thurman. He was born in 1904 to Pearl Tracy, the daughter of Mattie Teague's second marriage and the sister of Bud Tracy, the man who had survived six months hiding in the woods. After the birth of Ernest she left her husband and married wood hauler Albert Brust. Ern stayed with his grandmother and uncle Bud. By the time he was sixteen he was back with his mother and her new husband Albert, and by twenty-six he was married to Delia Mae Brust, the much younger sister of Albert. Thus Albert Brust was both Ern Thurman's stepfather and his brother-in-law. They had a volatile relationship, always fraught with danger.

In 1927, when Ern was only twenty-three, he was charged with the attempted murder of Albert Brust.[51] Ern and a man named Jim Young, an uncle of the notorious Young brothers, went to Albert's house in South Austin to collect some money. Ern was in the passenger seat of the car facing away from the house. He said he was going to kill Albert, and Albert fired at the car. Ern wasn't hit, but Jim Young died in the exchange. No charges were filed against Brust.

These years were filled with criminal indictments against Ernest Thurman—intent to murder with a knife in 1926 (dismissed), intent to murder Ed Fisher in 1927 (dismissed), moonshining in 1936 (dismissed), aggravated assault with a knife in 1931 (60 days in jail).[52]

The most egregious case, one that captured the attention of the entire city of Austin, involved the shooting of a UT student.[53] Ern and some friends were camping out by Onion Creek and saw two hunters about three hundred yards away. One of his friends said, "I'll bet you can't hit that ol' boy down there." Ern prided himself on being a good shot, and replied. "I'll bet I can."

And he did. Gilbert Smith was shot in the back and almost died. The boys all ran and hid their rifles, but the law knew that Ern had his camp nearby and was capable of doing something like that, so they arrested him. He told Emmett Shelton that if either of his friends turned state's evidence, he would kill them. They kept him in jail a long time without bond in case the boy died, and it appears that he was tortured to get a confession, but Smith recovered, and Ern Thurman was released for lack of evidence.

If anybody deserved killing, it was Ernest Thurman. It finally happened in 1936.[54] Ernest was running a little beer joint on Bee Cave Road and, having made up, Albert and Pearl Brust were helping him. But Ern got mad at Albert; Emmett Shelton said, "Every time he'd go to drinking a little bit, he'd get mad at Albert." He told people he was going to give Albert a good cutting before the night was over. When Albert heard about this he slipped out and started walking to Austin, thinking he would hide until Ern sobered up. He took his rifle just in case.

When Ern noticed that Albert was missing, he went to Albert's tent to look for him and found the rifle was gone. He prevailed on a friend to drive him to Austin. He saw Albert walking on the road, got out of the car, and shot him in the groin. Albert fell—and started rapidly shooting his gun at the car. The driver, petrified he would be hit, quickly backed up the car, and his lights fell on Ernest Thurman. Brust used the opportunity to shoot Ernest through the neck and kill him.

Despite the fact that Ernest Thurman was the most violent man during the most violent period, there was a big funeral. Pallbearers were Litten Pierce, Charlie Short, Claude Cooper, Buck Duval, and Jasper Simpson, among the best known men in the clans. Pearl Brust later divorced Albert, the husband who had killed her baby boy.

THE DEMISE OF THE CEDAR CHOPPERS

Remembering lingers in the cedar. . . . Maybe it never amounted to a hell of a much, what happened around these hills. But it happened to us. Here.

John Graves, *Hard Scrabble*

Technology—barbed wire and trucks—had created the era of the cedar choppers, and it was technology—T-posts and chainsaws—that were the final nails in its coffin. By 1960 ranchers across the West were using cheap steel posts imported from Japan instead of the standard yard four. They lasted a long time (except in salty coastal soil, where cedar is still preferred), but more important, they could be pounded into the soil, eliminating the backbreaking labor of digging holes.

About the same time, chainsaws were becoming lighter and easier to handle. Compared to today's light-weight, high-performance saws, the early saws were monsters, but in the 1960s McCulloch began making saws that weighed under twenty pounds. Cutting this way was quicker than cutting with an axe, but at that weight it wore you out just the same. Raymond Moore's father Robert would have been in his early sixties when photographed with a McCulloch chainsaw after a long day.

These chainsaws were not only heavy; they were very dangerous. Modern saws have a brake that stops the chain if the saw kicks back toward the operator's head and a centrifugal clutch that prevents

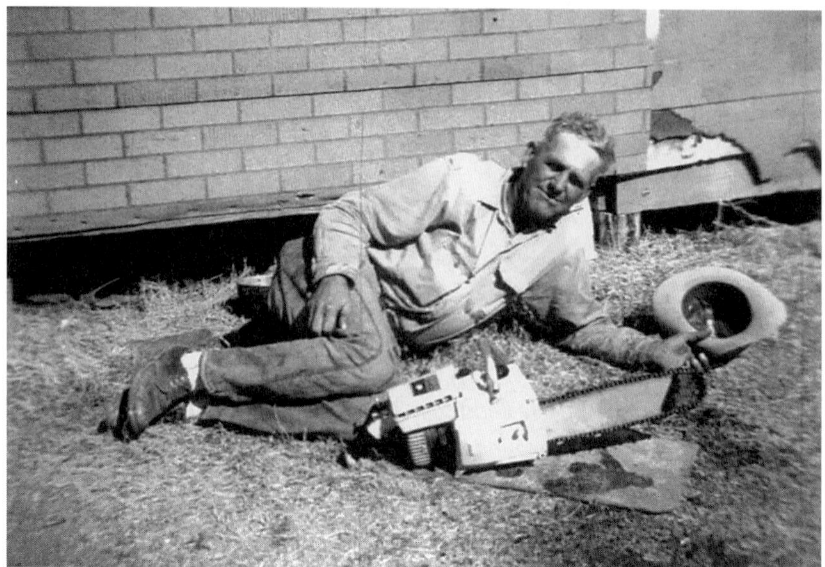

Robert Moore and McCulloch chainsaw. Photo courtesy of Raymond Moore.

the chain from moving at idle, and if the chain breaks or is derailed, there is a device to catch it. Old saws had none of this; in fact they sometimes just flew apart. Jesse Faglie, Frank Boatright's uncle, died in 1957 at age twenty-three when struck in the head by a piece of a broken flywheel.[1]

But even before the impact of technology, the cedar business was over as an industry. The heart cedar in the brakes west of Austin was gone; some families in the clans had left a decade or more before this for Ingram or Leakey or Junction, where there still was good cedar. Most of the land that qualified for government money in the eradication program had already been cut. An article in the *Brownwood Bulletin* said that at one time there were cedar yards at every crossroad in the southern part of San Saba County on the edge of the Lampasas brakes. By 1961 there was only one.[2]

The other huge economic force affecting the cedar choppers was the expansion of Austin and other cities along the Balcones Fault west into the scenic hills. In Austin the low-water bridge connecting the city to West Lake Hills was completed in 1949, and by the mid-1950s land the cedar choppers lived on was being divided into one-acre lots selling for $2,000 to $3,000.[3] Frank Wilson said, "Of course they didn't pay any taxes or anything like that, they just lived there. And when people came in and started buying land and building homes, well then, they had to leave." Sometimes this required force: when a deputy from Pflugerville "was called on to do some of the evicting, he did it with a shotgun because the squatters didn't take kindly to being moved. And most of them had guns, and practically all of 'em wouldn't pay to fool with."[4] This was only the beginning of the gentrification of the hills: today the top ten richest zip codes in Austin are all straddling the cedar hills west of the Balcones Fault.[5]

The final factor that ended the independent life of the cedar chopper was not a human one—it was the weather. Texas experienced the worst drought in recorded history during the 1950s: the years from 1950 until 1957 were "The Time It Never Rained," the title of one of Elmer Kelton's most famous books. The cedar choppers lost the precious resource that that they had followed from Appalachia to the Texas hills, the one resource that had allowed them to survive well into the twentieth century with hardly any connections to modern society—clean spring water. The springs dried up, and then the rivers, stranding the fish in brackish pools until these, too, disappeared. Then the shallow wells dried up. The only water in the hills came from the Trinity Sands formation a thousand feet below. When Andrew Zilker gave land to the city of Austin for a park at Barton Springs, he stipulated that the hill people should always have access to water from a deep well on Bee Cave Road. During the drought, they would haul water home from there in wooden barrels.

By 1960 most of the choppers had left the hills, moving reluctantly into town and working as truckers or masons or at any job where they could maintain some semblance of independence. Keron Cantwell's dad moved into Austin and became a mason, but she wrote, "He was never satisfied. He had been in the country most of his life and he missed the freedom that he no longer enjoyed."[6] At the end of the era, in the early 1960s, a young cedar chopper from Johnson City went with his father to Arizona to look for work. "But we got homesick. Daddy said he could just see the cedar trees a-growin' in the hills."[7]

Some of them, especially the boys who had grown to men during the heyday of the cedar choppers, were just too old to work that hard. Stanley Allen, in his sixties, said, "I can't get out there and fight it like I used to. You know, I'll still go do a hell of a day's work, but I can't cut them ol' big posts and throw 'em on my back and carry 'em out like we did years ago, you know." Still, some cut until they couldn't do it any longer. Pete Kaufman told me that Punk Cantrell of Liberty Hill "cut cedar damn near till he died." Stoney Teague added, "It kinda got where Punk couldn't get out there and work by hisself because, you know, he just, he'd give plumb out. And they were afraid that he'd get out there and he'd give out and he couldn't get back. So Shorty (his older brother) finally just cut with him until both of 'em got to where they just couldn't cut anymore." It was the first decade of the twenty-first century, and the Cantrell brothers, in their upper seventies, were still cutting cedar.

But these men were the exceptions, like old Comanches participating in a buffalo hunt in the last decades of the nineteenth century. Some had to quit young because of an injury. Milton Lentz's brother Buford quit at thirty because he almost cut off his foot. His father had a heart attack and died at fifty. Milton said, "Your physical thing takes its toll. . . . My dad, he worked himself to death." Luther Pierce's best friend Charlie Roberts died in the cedar brakes at forty-five. Kenneth Bertling of Marble Falls observed, "They didn't live that long. They died very young." Yet I knew men like Simon Ratliff, born in 1931, who had cut cedar all his life and was still alive (he passed away in 2016 at eighty-five), and the old man Roy Bedichek encountered cutting in the hills west of Austin was eighty-six. Working that hard would make you stronger if it didn't kill you first.[8]

The last generation—those who cut cedar as boys—were not so fond of having to work that hard. Morris Bonnet said, "I made better money cutting cedar than any construction job I was ever on. But, like I said, it was *harrrd* work. I mean . . . we would be driving to Goodrich [a ranch near Lampasas]. We'd leave our house four o'clock in the morning, and we'd be in the cedar brake by daylight." Willie Simons said, "These younger generations don't want to do the brutal work it calls for. I taught my four sons, Sam, Rex, Dutch and Tony, just like my Dad taught me, but only a couple of them are now cutting, and just for extra money."[9] Don Hibbitts remembered a young man who was cutting with his father during a hot summer in Camp Wood: "He was out there chopping one day and he was saying, 'The longer I cut, the madder I got.' He said he sunk his axe into a cedar tree. He took his gloves off, sat 'em on the handle and went and told his daddy, he says, 'I ain't cuttin' no more cedar.' And he came into town and went to Uvalde and joined the navy."

A few of the men I interviewed ended up in working in the cedar business all their lives. Simon Ratliff, Charlie Maugham, Stanley Allen, and Lee Cantrell cut until they retired; Bob Willess hauled cedar; and Olan Raley owned a chainsaw shop. Others, like Alice Patterson's husband Bill, Albert Boatright, and Don Simons, worked in construction. Stoney Teague was a trucker, and Luther Pierce owned a quarry. The Farmers got into the grass business and expanded into a nursery, and Floyd Cantwell had a wrecking yard on Spicewood Springs Road that made him rich when he sold the land. But all that money didn't change him much, and he still runs a yard in Leander that sits on prime real estate.

Others weren't so lucky. In 1961 Ozelle Maynard was living with her second husband and uncle in a broken-down house trailer in North Austin without running water or electricity and thinking that life was better back in the brakes.[10] Gary Cartwright's 1977 *Texas Monthly* article told the story of one-time cedar chopper Henry Polk to illustrate the struggle of poor whites on welfare. In 1954 alcohol claimed Jesse Teague, the WWII veteran with the goat who drank under the bridge, and a few served time in prison for crimes like DWI and forgery. But the violent days were mostly over.

An exception occurred in a 1951 event that was reminiscent of the jealous, alcohol-fueled violence that had run through the clans during the 1930s. Harrell King, the nephew of cedar chopper Charlie King (profiled by author Cactus Pryor) and the great-grandson of Ranger Jim King (mentioned in chapter 3 by Don Simons) killed his wife Peggy Freitag, grand-niece of patriarch Joseph Almar Roberts. It was a nasty, modern crime—he had been forcing her to go with other men for money; the district attorney said "he was the lowest form of pimp, one which would be found under a rock." Harrell stabbed Peggy in a bar on Sixth Street.[11] Those who testified at the trial were familiar names in the clans—Simpson, Farmer, and Shannon—and the murder must have been a tragic reminder of a

Harrell King and Peggy Freitag. Photo from a public member tree on Ancestry.com, attached to Harrell King in the St. John, Monday, Hogan 2009 Family Tree on April 13, 2012, consent Shirley King.

part of their past they would have preferred to forget. Harrell King was sentenced to death, but received a stay of execution three days before he was to die; the following year his sentence was commuted to life imprisonment.[12]

Epilogue

Three Questions

At campsites near water they stopped to . . . chop select timber into posts so long as the brake suited their whim, to follow hounds at night, to dance barefoot to fiddles on grounds cleared among the cedar, to curse and fight and drink raw whiskey, to take their women and raise their children—all done in strange ways foreign to other eyes.

C. W. Wimberley, *Cedar Whacker*

The Balcones Fault

This book began with a story about my confrontation with cedar chopper kids over some fish. It took place at the bridge connecting Austin to the Hill Country, right on the Balcones Fault, a fundamental division of place and time. People of Scots-Irish descent had migrated from the hills of Appalachia to the Hill Country of Texas, and their subsistence livelihood enabled them to hang on there while the farmers across the South left in droves during the early decades of the twentieth century. Ironically, the key to their survival was cedar, the same plant that had spread from the hills and deep ravines to consume a land already degraded by overgrazing and cotton.

In addition to their woodland subsistence livelihood, these Scots-Irish also brought from Appalachia and replicated in the Hill Country an interconnected family support system. Families were large and intermarried with those nearby, so that within a few generations there were kin networks along the major creeks in the hills west of Austin. Families in these clans, as I call them, helped one another and enforced a rigid code of honor. They didn't want or need the law or political interference, and the rugged hills provided sanctuary from intrusion by outsiders.

Yet they were close enough to the cities along the Balcones Fault to haul their cedar and charcoal and sell it there. These trips were long and infrequent, so that the hill people were rarely seen during the first four decades of the century. In 1941, at the end of this period, an Austinite could still marvel that "within sight of the capitol dome" live mountaineers who spoke a dialect and got their water from springs.[1] I remember my sister's boyfriend telling me in 1957 that once a week a flatbed truck would roll into Spicewood from the rough hills to the west with a big load of cedar, the people riding on top speaking to one another with "Thee and Thou" and buying supplies for another week in the brakes.

But the hill people were not entirely invisible to Austinites. During these early decades there had been plenty of stories spread across the front pages of the local newspaper about the more unruly members of the clans. Just those stories retold in this book include:

Dempsey Brown and Jim Nixon (1896)
The Travis County Dog Wars (1902)
Tom Young (1906)
John Teague (1911)
Bull Creek moonshine raids and the Boatrights (1922–25)
Bud Tracy (1926)
Mountain children rescued from a "demented mother" (1927)
Ernest Thurman shoots a UT student (1931)
Buster and Ellis Young (1931)
Earl Short (1932)
Berry Pierce and Eva Mae Simpson (1933)
Pete and Bruce Young (1935)
Ernest Thurman and Albert Brust (1936)
Ike Young and federal agent Thomasson (1937)

Journalism during this period took white America as the norm. Nothing was said if the victim or perpetrator of a crime was Anglo, but any who were African American or Hispanic were usually identified as a negro or a Mexican. At first, these articles about the hill people didn't label the men involved as white, but as time went on, the stories made clear that these were not ordinary whites—they were "unkempt mountaineers" and "hillbilly moonshiners." They were "those that don't belong to us," according to the story about the rescued children—not a part of Austin that would be acknowledged. And soon, when they emerged from the hills during the 1940s in their pickup trucks loaded with cedar posts, they would be given a name that would clearly identify them as belonging to a tribe apart. They were called cedar choppers.

The 1940s began the period that I have called the heyday of the cedar chopper. Trucks could haul the posts out of the rugged brakes to the cedar yards, and big semis could long-haul them to feed stores and ranches across the West. The demand for posts surged, and there was even government money to clear cedar from the land. Without these factors, the cedar people west of Austin would have disappeared by 1950, forced to leave the hills to join the army or work in town like everybody else.

Instead, they thrived. Some, like Artie Henry, saved the money they made cutting cedar to start a business. Others used that extra money to live large, spending it at bars and driving nice cars. Like some long-dormant insect that morphed into a highly visible, magnificent stage of existence but for a brief period, they emerged from the hills in their ragged work clothes and beat-up trucks—hard, dirty, and aggressive—and the huge disparity between them and the people of Austin was exposed.

This disparity was so large because, while the hill people had hunkered down and remained isolated from mainstream America during the early decades of the twentieth century, Austin had gone in the other direction. Oil money had fueled state government and the University of Texas, and Austin was the beneficiary of both. It became a service town in the middle of a state dependent on natural resources and agriculture—educated, liberal, white collar, and relatively urbane for a town of its size. The stage was set for its phenomenal growth beginning in the 1960s, accelerating with the computer industry and music scene of the 1970s, eventually to become the hip city it is today. It was as if the twenty-first century met the nineteenth century at the Balcones Fault.

Most of the nation had no firsthand experience with hillbillies, for the hollows of Appalachia and the Ozarks were remote from major population centers. It was mainly people living in cities like

Chicago, St. Louis, and Detroit who had experience with real hillbillies, some of the three million refugees from Appalachia who had migrated after the war to work in the factories.[2] But as foreign as the lifestyles of these people appeared to city people, they were transitioning out of hillbilly-hood into the middle class, with a job, a salary, and a house with modern conveniences. The cartoons of the day—the way most Americans learned about hillbillies—almost always portrayed life back in the hills, not the difficult transition to middle-class America.[3] The Beverly Hillbillies were the exception, but they didn't have to work because they had oil money.

But the Austin hillbillies—the cedar choppers—were the real thing, enabled by their earnings to continue their old way of life. They were part of the landscape of the Hill Country and the towns along the Balcones Fault. John Hoover said they "ruled the country" around Liberty Hill and Burnet, but that Burnet was "a little further up the chain of respectability" because it only had 30–40 percent cedar choppers, while Liberty Hill had 60–70 percent.

When the cedar choppers began to frequent Austin in their pickup trucks, they seemed to fit the hillbilly stereotype portrayed in cartoons like Snuffy Smith and Li'l Abner—they were poorly educated, had big families, and were dirty and unkempt. They were renowned for making moonshine—some of Austin's most prominent citizens and statesmen had relied upon them for whiskey for over two decades. Imagine seeing Buddy Brown riding his big white horse on Walsh-Tarlton Road, with his rattlesnake hatband and carrying a rifle; or Homer Teague with his long beard and big black floppy hat, walking with his dog down Bee Cave Road once a week to buy groceries; or Johnnie Pale, with no shoes or shirt and a feather braided into his hair.

These encounters must have been startling to city people in the middle of the twentieth century. The 1950s were about the celebration of middle-class values of home, family, and career—of cars and modern appliances, and education. The world of cedar choppers, with all the blank spaces filled in by images from cartoons, was both shocking and threatening to middle-class whites in Austin. By the mid-1950s newspaper articles were labeling cedar choppers in the same kind of way as they had routinely identified African

Americans and Hispanics, as in "Searchers Find Cedar Chopper," or "Cedar Chopper Pleads Guilty."[4] The response of middle-class whites, as so often when threatened by members of another race or ethnicity, was derision and ridicule. In 1958 the Westwood Country Club, right across the lake from the cedar hills, held a dance with the theme "Hill Country Cedar Chopper." Hot dogs were boiled in a pot on a wood fire, and Austin's elite dressed up in costumes and fake beards. A sign on the wall advised: "Womenfolks are not allowed to fight in this here saloon because it ain't polite."[5]

One last story; this took place a few years later. We were seniors in high school, two couples looking for something different to do on a summer night. We drove out on Highway 183 toward Burnet and came upon the Hilltop Inn, all lit up with lots of cars and trucks parked outside. We pulled in, walked up to the entrance, and opened the door. The people inside—the picture is etched in my mind, like looking through a portal of time—were dancing. There were couples, but there were also women with women and children with children. Some women—I swear—were wearing gingham dresses and bonnets. A man inside stepped in front of us. He looked us up and down. We were wearing shorts, and not just any shorts but the newest rage, Madras plaid shorts. He said, "You're not welcome here," and he closed the door.

We had intruded, unwelcome, into another culture. We had stepped over the divide that separated our conceit from their defiance. We had slipped through a fissure in the Balcones Fault.

I started this project with a question, *Who are these people?* I have tried to answer it by listening to people and putting together their stories. But in the end I realize that the power of culture is such that it is very hard to step out of one and into another. We can describe situations and tell stories that illustrate how people in a culture respond to the world, but we never really understand how they feel and why they make the choices they do.

I'm left with three unanswered questions. I may have the answer to the first. The second is harder for an outsider, and the last remains baffling.

My first question is: *Why didn't they leave the Hill Country for wage jobs like everyone else?* My answer would probably start with who they were as a people, Scots-Irish borderlanders who "valued individual liberty and personal honor above all else."[6] They had moved down through Appalachia and the Ozarks into the Hill Country of Texas, and up against the Llano Estacado, on the edge of nothing. There they found an economic niche that allowed them to make good money with little capital and no boss. They were, in C. W. Wimberley's words, the last of an independent breed.

Not only did they achieve economic independence, but the rugged Hill Country environment and the resources it provided gave them independence from governmental control and the interference of outsiders. They didn't pay taxes or ask for city services, and they had little respect for the law. Their code of honor was strong and personal; there were consequences if you violated it, but it was not the authorities who enforced compliance.

The Hill Country gave the people in the cedar hills more than independence; it helped shape their character. As kids they had the run of a vast expanse of country, free from the restrictions of law and landowners, where they could find secret places in creeks and mountains and caves. The descriptions by Ronnie Roberts and Frank Boatright of their lives while growing up celebrate a freedom that is outside the realm of experience of a city dweller. They became intimate with the land and familiar with both its beauty and its harshness, and in the process they became harder and tougher. John Graves said there was a "rightness" to the relationship between the people and the land—that "the cedar hills and the cedar people were fitted to each other."[7]

But still, after bringing in the load and cooking dinner, there were long evenings to sit back and enjoy the air cooling down and the light changing. The Hill Country was not only where they worked, it was where they had lived for generations and an integral part of every aspect of their life. They stayed in the land of the Violet Crown because it was part of who they were. They stayed as long as they could, until the cedar and the springs gave out and the city people moved in.

My second question is: *Why didn't they use the money they made to improve their lifestyle?* Of course, the question itself implies a hierarchy of lifestyles to which everyone aspires, and time and again we have been told that their way of life—a lack of adherence to conventions concerning property, appearances, or middle-class values—was a choice. Frank Wilson, who was not a cedar chopper but knew them well, was convinced that they were living exactly the way they wanted to live. An old cedar chopper interviewed at his clapboard house near Johnson City in 1965 said, "I wish we lived like we used to. It's hard to say in words how I feel about the way it was. It was a free life, I guess you'd say."[8]

Their lack of concern for property or possessions was yet another form of freedom. To quote the lyrics of "Me and Bobby McGee," they had nothing left to lose. And they knew that whatever came up, they and their friends could cut a few loads of cedar to pay for it, so why worry about tomorrow? Buck Simpson never put any money away for a rainy day; "he just lived in the present," his brother said. Extra money was for having fun, not fancifying a house, so the Shorts bought watches when they couldn't tell time, and Jess Clawson got a saddle when he didn't have a horse. Alice Patterson spoke of her dad Pate: "Dad was a cut-up, I'll tell ya! He would get us, set us down on the ground and play stick guys. That was Dad. He kept us doing things like that. He was a big kid, always. He never got—he never grew up. He had fun, wherever he was."[9]

Edna Patterson is a good example of their spirit of self-reliance. She raised all her children without running water and was still cooking on a wood-burning stove when she died in 1992. Luther offered to help her, to buy her a gas stove or anything to make her life easier, but she declined. They were proud that they could live hard, day-to-day, on the edge. The women were proud of raising their families, and the men were proud that they could work hard and play hard. Their reputation, said an article in 1976, was "earned over a century of cutting posts by day and raising hell by night. And it's a reputation that today's more civilized cedar choppers wear with unspoken pride."[10] The owner of a business on RM 1431 in the heart of Whitt-Maynard-Bonnet country said of the few who were still holding on in 1990, "They're cedar choppers, and that's a high compliment coming from the right person."[11]

My last question is: *Why were they so aggressive and violent?* What was behind the seemingly instinctive resort to extreme aggression in response to perceived injury, without regard for authority or age or power? J. D. Vance, the author of *Hillbilly Elegy*, said his family "could go from zero to murderous in a fucking heartbeat."[12] In neither his descriptions nor my interviews does this seem like a response to their position in society—the result of some tribal inferiority complex.

What is true is that this temperament can be traced back to the Scots-Irish and their descendants in Appalachia and that it appears to be a defining cultural characteristic. Between 1865 and 1915 the homicide rate in the plateau region of the Cumberland Mountains in the heart of Appalachia was 130 per 100,000, ten times today's rate and more than the rate for Honduras, the country with the highest murder rate in the world (90 per 100,000). And, unlike in the northern states, most of these homicides were not associated with another felony but instead were related to interpersonal arguments.[13] That is certainly the case with most of the violence documented in this book.

There seem to be two common elements in confrontations involving cedar choppers. The first is that they had no fear of injury. Through their direct family ties to the Texas frontier, the boys grew up hearing stories of Rangers and Comanches and outlaws, and later of men in the clans who had stood up to the law. These were their heroes, men who had exhibited no fear.

In addition, the boys started working young and got hurt often. They grew up fighting one another, sometimes as ritualized sport, sometimes just in defense. Working with a razor-sharp axe all day, getting beat up in a fight was not the worst injury that could befall a young cedar chopper. When they felt particularly insulted, they might even engage in a rough and tumble form of fighting brought from the southern backcountry called "stomp and gouge," which sanctioned anything you could do with your hands, feet, and teeth.[14] Brucie Young's bad eye was the result of such an encounter.

The second critical element of these confrontations is that they never backed down. It is a refrain throughout this book, and it was more than just "keep on, keep on"—it was an attitude that said *no matter how hard you come on, I'm gonna be harder.* Any cedar chopper could stand up to the physical punishment. The winner was decided by attitude.

No one articulated this attitude better than Simon Ratliff. When I asked him about fighting, and he said he didn't often fight because his adversaries usually backed down. He told this story:

> He was up in eighth grade and I's in the fourth, and my friend, he said, "He's gonna give you a whupping, he's a bully." And I said to him, "He ain't gonna give me a whupping, I ain't gonna fight him." "Yeah, you'll fight him." I said, "No, I won't fight him. I won't have to." Back then I had a good eye and I looked him straight in the eye, you know. Which I fought with my eye. I didn't fight with my fists, I fought with my eye. Like a game rooster. If you didn't look 'em straight in the eye, you're gonna get kicked.

Simon Ratliff's voice is like an echo from the past. Of all the men I interviewed, at eighty-one he was one of the last true cedar choppers. There was no modernity about him—he had cut cedar all his life, mostly with an axe. He said, "Well, I had a big family to raise and I had to have somebody to do it (laughter), and it had to be me." He was a simple man but sharp, and he exemplified an oral tradition where conversations are remembered and repeated word for word; you can download a recording of him telling stories on a spring day in Burnet County, sitting under a tree with a bird singing above.[15]

Simon Ratliff was from the branch of the Teagues who had lived in the western Hill Country for five generations. Elijah Ratliff had come to Texas from Tennessee more than a decade before the Texas Revolution and died in 1836, the year of Texas Independence. His son Tim fought for the Confederacy, and after the war moved to Llano with his wife Hulda Teague, starting one of the three branches of the Teague side of the Roberts-Teague clan. Tim's son Monroe shows up as a thirty-six-year-old cedar cutter with five children in Hayes County in 1900, and in 1930 he was working in a cedar yard in Manchaca. Monroe's son Ben—Simon's father—was born in Bandera and cut cedar in the brakes on the Colorado River where the Scholtens had put in their railroad in the 1920s (chapter 5). In 1940, when Simon was eight, his father was trucking cedar out of San Saba. Simon himself never lived in a city for long, always working west of Austin in Lampasas and Burnet counties.

The Ratliffs were pure Texas Hill Country cedar choppers. There were no frills about them—they were not the type who got in fights in the beer joints outside Austin and defined the stereotype. They raised their families quietly, believing in an austere Old Testament God who could mend grievous wounds, and they survived in the hills in a life mostly unchanged from the past. Like Quanah Parker's Quahadi band of Comanches, they lived a life unpolluted by the invading culture and never "came in" until the very end. They maintained a way of life that had begun long ago and that lasted far longer than it ever should have.

Appendix 1

Voices

Interviews are listed alphabetically in the bibliography. Clarification about referencing of interviews is at the beginning of the endnotes. Conversations not recorded are cited in endnotes and included in this appendix.

Name	Source of Quote	Author/ Interviewer	Date	Location of Source	Classification	Clan	First Cited	Lifespan
Allen, Stanley	Interview	Ken Roberts	2013	SU Library Archives	Cedar chopper	not known	Chap 5	1947–
Bading, Lorenz	Interview	Ken Roberts	2012	SU Library Archives	Farmer	not applicable	Chap 3	1916–2013
Baker, Barney	Interview	Ken Roberts	2012	SU Library Archives	Rancher	not applicable	Chap 5	1938–
Baker, Hollis	Conversation	Ken Roberts	2012	Notes	Newspaper columnist	not applicable	Chap 6	1928¬–
Beard, Benton	Book	Linda Vance	1986	*Eanes*	Eanes store owner	not applicable	Chap 7	1879–1964
Bertling, Kenneth	Interview	Ken Roberts	2012	SU Library Archives	Law enforce-ment/cedar chopper	Bull Creek	Chap 6	1936–2017
Boatright, Albert	Interview	Ken Roberts	2014	SU Library Archives	Construction/ cedar chopper	Bull Creek	Chap 4	1936–
Boatright, Frank	Newspaper	Mark Lisheron	2000	*Austin American-Statesman*	Cedar chopper	Bull Creek	Chap 1	1937–2003
Boatright, John T.	Interview	Ken Roberts	2012	SU Library Archives	Cedar chopper	Bull Creek	Chap 4	1930–2018
Boatright, Marie	Newspaper	John Kelso	2013	*Austin American-Statesman*	Daughter of cedar chopper	Bull Creek	Chap 1	1960–
	Conversation	Ken Roberts	2015	Notes	Daughter of cedar chopper	Bull Creek	Chap 1	1960–
Boatright, Mary	Interview	Ken Roberts	2012	SU Library Archives	Realtor/cedar chopper	Roberts-Teague	Chap 4	1953–
Bonnet, Morris	Interview	Ken Roberts	2015	SU Library Archives	Cedar chopper	Whitt-Maynard-Bonnet	Chap 5	1937–
Cantrell, Lee	Interview	Ken Roberts	2012	SU Library Archives	Cedar chopper	Bull Creek	Chap 5	1934–
Cantwell, Floyd	Interview	Ken Roberts	2015	SU Library Archives	Wrecking yard / cedar chopper	Roberts-Teague	Chap 4	1932–
Cantwell, Keron	Memoir	self	1985	Ancestry.com	Cedar chopper	Roberts-Teague	Chap 2	1913–91
Carlton, Margie	Interview	John Leffler	2000	Balcones Canyonlands	Rancher's daughter, wife of chopper	Bull Creek	Chap 4	1929–
	Interview	Ken Roberts	2013	SU Library Archives	Rancher's daughter, wife of chopper	Bull Creek	Chap 4	1929–

Carlton, Preston	Interview	Ken Roberts	2013	SU Library Archives	Realtor	not applicable	Chap 4	1937–
Dellana, Charlie	Interview	Linda Vance	1986	Eanes History Center	Rancher Eanes	not applicable	Chap 7	1892–1973
Ehrlich, Al	Book	Bill Porterfield	1965	*LBJ Country*	Cedar yard owner	not applicable	Chap 6	1898–1974
Faulkes, Wanda	Book	John Leffler	2000	*Kind of a Hard Old Country*	Rancher	not applicable	Chap 4	1924–2011
Gephart, Willie	Newspaper	Mary Jacoby	1990	*Austin American-Statesman*	Cedar chopper	Roberts-Teague	Chap 8	1948–2015
Gillman, Joe	Interview	Valerie Dunham	1985	Austin History Center	Rancher/cedar chopper	Roberts-Teague	Chap 7	1937–86
Goble, Carole	Conversation	Ken Roberts	2012	Notes	Historian	not applicable	Chap 7	1932–
Graham, Della Edwards	Memoir	self	1976	Eanes History Center	Eanes school bus driver	not applicable	Chap 7	1921–2013
Gumbert, Willie	Newspaper	Irene Van Winkle	2013	*West Kerr Current*	Cedar chopper	Roberts-Teague	Chap 7	1922–2014
Hagood, Charles	Interview	Ken Roberts	2012	SU Library Archives	Rancher/banker	not applicable	Chap 4	1952–
Hawes, Jerry	Conversation	Ken Roberts	2012	Notes	Rancher/feed store	not applicable	Chap 7	1936–
Henry, Betty	Interview	Ken Roberts	2012	SU Library Archives	Farmer	Whitt-Maynard-Bonnet	Chap 4	1929–
Henry, Pat	Book	John Leffler	2000	*Kind of a Hard Old Country*	Farmer	Whitt-Maynard-Bonnet	Chap 4	1931–2005
Hibbitts, Don	Interview	Ken Roberts	2011	SU Library Archives	Camp Wood resident	not applicable	Chap 7	1933–2012
Hoover, John	Interview	Ken Roberts	2012	SU Library Archives	Businessman	not applicable	Chap 5	1932–
Kaufman, Pete	Interview	Ken Roberts	2012	SU Library Archives	Farmer	not applicable	Chap 9	1921–2017
Johnson, Cecil	Memoir	self	1976	Eanes History Center	Eanes resident	not applicable	Chap 7	1922–88
Joseph, Troy	Book	John Leffler	2000	*Kind of a Hard Old Country*	Rancher	not applicable	Chap 8	1919–2011
Johnson City choppers	Book	Bill Porterfield	1965	*LBJ Country*	Cedar choppers	not known	Chap 7	not known

Name	*Source of Quote*	*Author/ Interviewer*	*Date*	*Location of Source*	*Classification*	*Clan*	*First Cited*	*Lifespan*
Kercheville, Genny	Interview	Ken Roberts	2012	SU Library Archives	Rancher	not applicable	Chap 7	1941–
Lavender, Doug	Conversation	Ken Roberts	2012	Notes	Cedar yard owner	not applicable	Chap 7	1961–
Lentz, Milton	Interview	Ken Roberts	2013	SU Library Archives	Power plant/ cedar chopper	Bull Creek	Chap 7	1936–
Marshall, Bruce	Interview	Barbara Langham	1984	Barbara Langham's tape	Artist	not applicable	Chap 8	1930–2015
	Interview	Ken Roberts	2012	SU Library Archives	Artist	not applicable	Chap 8	1930–2015
Maugham, Charlie	Interview	Ken Roberts	2012	SU Library Archives	Cedar chopper	Whitt-Maynard-Bonnet	Chap 5	1933–2016
Maynard, Ozelle	Article	Bob Sherrill	1961	*Texas Observer*	Cedar chopper	Whitt-Maynard-Bonnet	Chap 7	1909–67
McKinnerney, Lee	Interview	Ken Roberts	2013	SU Library Archives	Businessman/ cedar chopper	not known	Chap 6	1948–
Moore, Raymond	Interview	Ken Roberts	2012	SU Library Archives	Cedar chopper	Roberts-Teague	Not quoted	1943–2015
O'Donnell, Guthrie	Interview	Ken Roberts	2012	SU Library Archives	Rancher	not applicable	Chap 5	1928–2018
Old-timers west of Belton	Interview	various	2003	Ft. Hood Oral History	Farmers/cedar choppers	not known	Chap 5	various
Patterson, Alice	Interview	Ken Roberts	2013	SU Library Archives	Construction/ cedar chopper	Patterson-Pierce	Chap 4	1929–
Patterson, Edna	Interview	Bonnie George	1981	Austin History Center	Cedar chopper	Patterson-Pierce	Chap 1	1906–92
Pearson, T. M.	Interview	Ken Roberts	2012	SU Library Archives	Cedar chopper	Whitt-Maynard-Bonnet	Chap 6	1929–2016
Pehl, Pearl	Interview	B. Schlameus	1985	Sophienburg Archive	Farmer	not applicable	Chap 5	1908–2002
Pierce, Luther	Interview	Ken Roberts	2015	SU Library Archives	Quarry/cedar chopper	Patterson-Pierce	Chap 1	1945–
Plummer, Junie	Conversation	Ken Roberts	2012	Notes	City of Austin	not applicable	Chap 7	1955–
Polk, Henry	Article	Gary Cartwright	1977	*Texas Monthly*	Cedar chopper	fictitious name	Chap 3	1928–?
Preece, Andy	Article	Bob Sherrill	1961	*Texas Observer*	Cedar chopper	Bull Creek	Chap 4	1900–89

Preece, Harold	Article	Harold Preece	1932	*Real West*	Writer/cedar chopper	Bull Creek	Chap 2	1906–92
Raley, Olan	Interview	Ken Roberts	2012	SU Library Archives	Cedar chopper	not known	Chap 4	1946–
Ratliff, Simon	Interview	Ken Roberts	2012	SU Library Archives	Cedar chopper	Roberts-Teague	Chap 6	1931–2016
Riley, John	Interview	Emmett Shelton	1978	Austin History Center	Cedar chopper	Patterson-Pierce	Chap 4	1891–1968
Ringstaff, Minnie	Interview	Valerie Dunham	1985	Austin History Center	Cedar chopper	Roberts-Teague	Chap 7	1903–95
Roberts, Ronnie	Interview	Ken Roberts	2012	SU Library Archives	Firefighter/cedar chopper	Roberts-Teague	Chap 1	1950–2014
Russell, Kerry	Interview	Ken Roberts	2013	SU Library Archives	Lawyer/friend of choppers	not applicable	Chap 7	1945–
Shelton, Emmett	Interview	self	1978	Austin History Center	Lawyer	not applicable	Chap 4	1905–2000
Short, Earl	Tape transcript	Emmett Shelton	1978	Austin History Center	Cedar chopper	Roberts-Teague	Chap 5	1908–96
	Interview notes	Linda Vance	1982	Eanes History Center	Cedar chopper	Roberts-Teague	Chap 5	1908–96
Simons, Don	Interview	Ken Roberts	2012	SU Library Archives	Construction/ cedar chopper	Bull Creek	Chap 4	1936–
Simons, Earleen	Interview	Ken Roberts	2013	SU Library Archives	Wife of Cedar chopper	Bull Creek	Chap 7	1943–
Simons, Princeton	Interview	Ken Roberts	2013	SU Library Archives	Son of cedar chopper	Bull Creek	Chap 3	1959–
Simons, Rex	Book	Dot Hatfield	1999	*Medina, Delightful Retreat*	Cedar chopper	Bull Creek	Chap 7	1949–2011
Simons, Willie	Book	Dot Hatfield	1999	*Medina, Delightful Retreat*	Cedar chopper	Bull Creek	Chap 7	1928–2007
Simpson, Leonard	Newspaper	–	1991	*Austin Statesman*	Cedar chopper	Roberts-Teague	Chap 7	1897–1976
Sutton, Mack	Interview	Ruth Ellsworth	1978	Austin History Center	Austin resident	Patterson-Pierce	Chap 3	1914–96
Sutton, Sam	Book	Sam Sutton	1928	*Medina's Early Days*	Ranger/shingle maker	Patterson-Pierce	Chap 5	1850–1941

Name	*Source of Quote*	*Author/ Interviewer*	*Date*	*Location of Source*	*Classification*	*Clan*	*First Cited*	*Lifespan*
Teague, Homer	Tape transcript	Emmett Shelton	1978	Austin History Center	Cedar chopper	Roberts-Teague	Chap 7	1898–1965
Teague, John	Newspaper Interview	– Emmett Shelton	1911 1978	*Austin Statesman* Austin History Center	Cedar chopper	Roberts-Teague	Chap 3	1872–1963
Teague, Stoney	Interview	Ken Roberts	2015	SU Library Archives	Trucker/cedar chopper	Roberts-Teague	Chap 5	1941–
Teague, Tiney	Luther Pierce interview	Ken Roberts	2012	SU Library Archives	Cedar chopper	Roberts-Teague	Chap 7	1918–2002
Teague, Tom	Newspaper	–	1911	*Austin Statesman*	Cedar chopper	Roberts-Teague	Chap 3	1879–1972
Tracy, Bud	Newspaper	–	1926	*Austin Statesman*	Cedar chopper	Roberts-Teague	Chap 4	1886–1962
Turner, Dick	Interview	Ken Roberts	2012	SU Library Archives	Cedar chopper	Whitt-Maynard-Bonnet	Chap 6	1917–2013
Turner, D. L.	Interview	John Leffler	2012	Balcones Canyonlands	Ranchers	Whitt-Maynard-Bonnet	Chap 8	1928–
Turner, Gladden	Interview	John Leffler	2012	Balcones Canyonlands	Ranchers	Whitt-Maynard-Bonnet	Chap 8	1925–2015
Wallace, Arthur Lee	Interview	Ken Roberts	2012	SU Library Archives	Cedar chopper	Roberts-Teague	Chap 4	1966–
Whitt, Katy	Kercheville interview	Ken Roberts	2012	SU Library Archives	Cedar chopper	Whitt-Maynard-Bonnet	Chap 7	1909–86
Willess, Bob	Interview	Ken Roberts	2012	SU Library Archives	Cedar chopper	not known	Chap 4	1937–2015
Wilson, Frank	Interview	Ruth Ellsworth	1978	Austin History Center	Austin resident	not applicable	Chap 1	1908–89

APPENDIX 2

Family Trees, the 1940 Census, and the Austin Paper Online

Individual-level detail from the decennial census is released seventy-two years after its collection, showing for each precinct who is in each household, with age, education, and occupation indicated. The 1940 census data released in 2012 revealed that in the western precincts of Travis and Williamson counties it was common to list "cedar chopper" or "timber cutter" as an occupation (see census on page 217). Every enumerator was different, and a few would indiscriminately write "farm laborer" for any male of working age in rural areas, even those who cut cedar full time. But whenever a man identified as a cedar chopper was not already in the tree, I would look for a relationship through marriage with someone who was.

Teague and Patterson were well-known names along Bee Cave Road and were already in the tree; to find them listed as timber cutters confirmed the value of the census and its classification of occupations. Elmer Morris at the top of the page was not originally in the tree, but his wife Alma was the daughter of a Hutson, a family closely related to the Robertses and the Teagues (see Teague family tree). Because he was a cedar chopper and married to someone already in the extended family tree, Elmer Morris was added to the tree. I would then check to see whether any of his siblings had cut cedar or had married into families of cedar cutters; in this case only Elmer was living in Central Texas and cutting cedar. Thus I would follow individuals in families until they either did something else or moved away from Central Texas. Most did neither, staying in the hills and working in occupations based there, such as cutting cedar or hauling rock.

There is little doubt that the census undercounted the families who were cedar choppers, both because enumerators often lumped occupations together and because people did not really want to answer questions. Wanda Jean Faulkes told John Leffler that her husband was the enumerator for the 1940 census in northwestern Travis County. She said, "There was lots of people up in there, country people up there that didn't really care about having a census made. He used to have quite a bit of trouble."[1]

Nevertheless, of the 171 employed persons in the Eanes precinct, there were 56 whose occupation was listed as timber cutter, rock mason, or quarry worker. All but five of these people were related and in the tree, while those in the other big occupations, farming and construction, tended to be from families that were not in the clans. The cedar choppers were a set of interrelated families, separate from the rest of the community.

Since the focus is on occupation in the year 1940, few women are shown as employed unless they were working for a salary, common enough in central Austin but not in Eanes. So it is unusual to see L. J. Teague, the nineteen-year-old daughter of Jessie Teague, listed as a timber cutter. Though many women worked in the brakes, it was not generally acceptable to acknowledge among good company that women did this kind of work; everybody looked the other way except the cedar choppers, who were proud of what their women could do.

The data in the 1940 census, by including name and place of birth, also allowed me to examine the question of the prevalence of Mexican labor in the cedar business. Mexican labor was so important to Texas agriculture by the early 1950s that farmers and ranchers were granted a special exemption, called the "Texas Proviso," from a law making it a felony to employ undocumented Mexican laborers.[2] I knew from both personal experience and my own research (for a dissertation on Mexican migration) that Hill Country ranchers depended on Mexican labor during the 1960s for hard labor such as clearing land and building fences. In Real County, wrote Gueric Bouchard, "Mexican laborers probably cut more cedar, built more fences, laid more rock . . . than all us 'white boys' put together."[3] But I did not know if persons of Mexican heritage, whether born in Mexico or Texas, were major participants in the cedar industry during the heyday of the cedar choppers.

I found that in most of the Hill Country counties they were not. During the Depression there were massive deportations of Mexicans, and by 1940 Spanish-surnamed cedar cutters were a small minority—less than 5 percent—of the total in seven of the nine Hill Country counties where cedar was important. The first exception was Blanco County, where one locale had a number of Spanish-surnamed cedar cutters and their families. Most were born in Texas and probably cutting on the big ranches that dominated the agriculture of the county. The other was the McNeil precinct of northern Travis County, where there were several heads of household born in Mexico who were working in the local lime factory (now Austin White Lime). Many of the thirty-three Spanish-surnamed cedar cutters were sons of these workers and born in Texas. None of the other six census districts in Travis County where cedar was cut had any Spanish-surnamed cedar cutters. The question of Mexican cedar cutters could not be examined in earlier censuses because enumerators tended to classify cedar cutters as farm laborers. In 1930 there were fewer than thirty persons listed as cedar cutters in all of Travis County.

In addition to clarifying the relationships among the cedar chopper families, building the extended family tree helped the research by providing vital information on the people involved in events. Over time I heard and read stories that I wanted to include in this book, but often the speaker—Emmett Shelton, for instance—was unsure of the name of the person involved, and dates were always uncertain. For major events with known dates, such as the raid on Ike Young's still, I could go to the microfiche files of the Austin newspaper and find an article that described the event, and, with the help of the tree, find information about other participants in the event. But it was tedious to look for follow-up stories in subsequent editions of the paper and impossible if the dates were not known.

This was my only tool to confirm the stories I was hearing until about 2014, when the Austin paper went online back to 1871. Then I could search for an article that would confirm a story using known dates, people, or keywords. For instance, the story written in 1974 called "The Travis County Dog Wars" contained no names, but dates and keywords revealed a 1902 article showing the accused man to be Paul Waechter of the Bull Creek clan (chapter 4). Don Simons's story about his father being burned when his truck overturned filled with whiskey was confirmed by the 1932 article "Driver Is Burned Badly as Truck Overturns." Emmett Shelton's stories about John Teague, Ernest Thurman, and the Youngs were all confirmed by newspaper articles. What I learned from people's stories and from the newspaper usually complemented each other and enriched the tableau. There are no newsworthy stories told in the book that have not been confirmed in print.

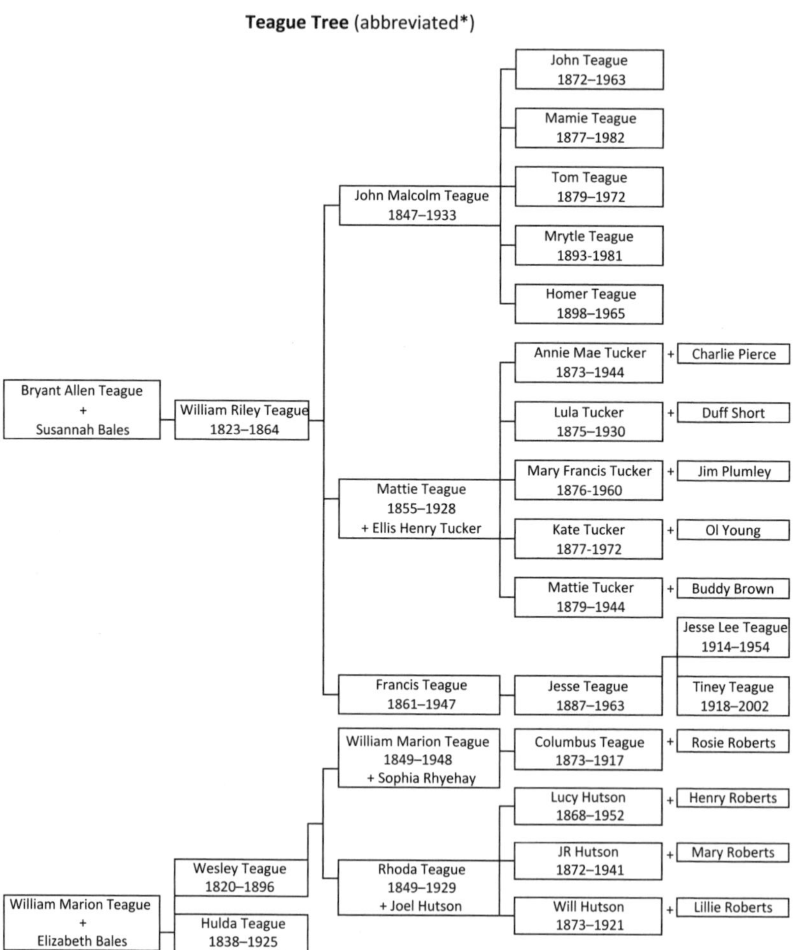

Teague family tree. Corrected from original printing, with thanks to Barbara Phillips.

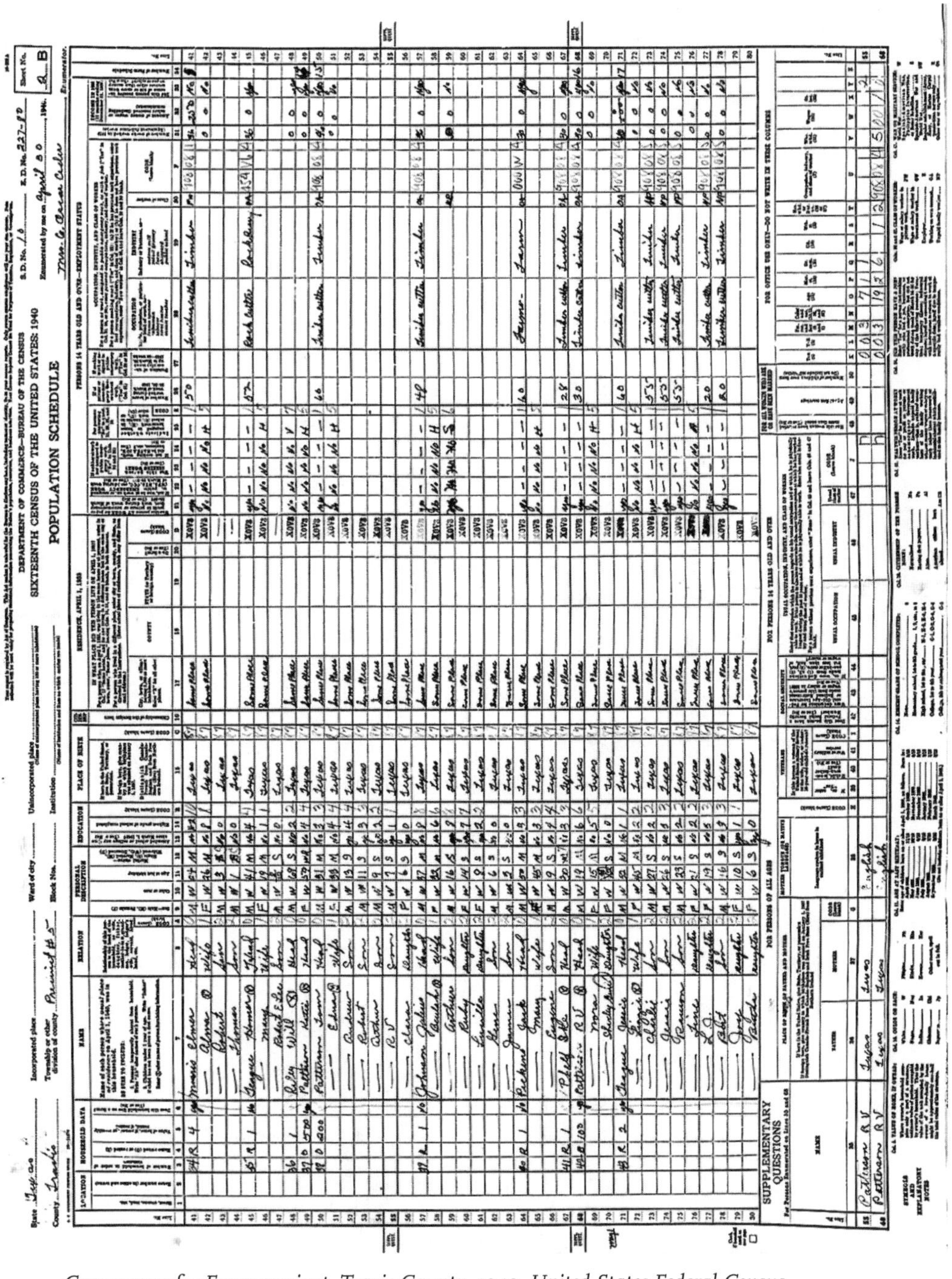
DEPARTMENT OF COMMERCE—BUREAU OF THE CENSUS
SIXTEENTH CENSUS OF THE UNITED STATES: 1940
POPULATION SCHEDULE

Census page for Eanes precinct, Travis County, 1940. United States Federal Census, Ancestry.com, uploaded March 19, 2014.

Appendix 3

Cedar Yards

Austin and Southwest	Company/Owner/Manager
Bee Cave Road and Bulian Lane	
Rosewood Avenue	Dick Simons
South Lamar	F. W. King
South Lamar	Fred Maples and Ruby Roberts
South Congress at bridge	Vaughn
South Congress & Barton Springs	Riley Cedar Company
Jefferson Street	F. W. King
Bull Creek Road	F. W. King
Hooper Switch	Becker Cedar Company
Spicewood Springs Road	Malcolm Reed
South Lamar in Oak Hill	Joe L. Roberts
Hwy 290 in Oak Hill	Al Ehrlich Cedar Company
Oak Hill	Jesse Teague and Elsie Simpson
Northwest and North	
Jollyville at RM 620	Cahill and Hickman Lumber Company
Hwy 183 in Cedar Park	Malcolm Reed
Hwy 183 in Cedar Park	F. W. King
Hwy 183 and RM 1431, SE corner	Buddy Rogers, Nolan Turner, T. M. Pearson
Hwy 183 and RM 1431, NW corner	Dick Boatright
Hwy 183 and New Hope Road	Jack Minnick
Bagdad Road and Crystal Falls Road	Richard Ward
Bagdad Road near New Hope Road	Lester Simpson
RM 1431 near Sandy Creek	Bob Hart

Bertram	Dick Turner, one other yard
Burnet	F. W. King
Burnet	Dick Turner, two other yards
Burnet, Hwy 2341	Eb Masey
Lake Victor	Malcolm Reed, one other yard
Marble Falls	Mack Callahan
Marble Falls	Gerry Noble
Marble Falls	Bob Jay
Marble Falls	Ferguson
Lone Grove (Lake Buchanan)	Forrest Ross
Lampasas	Doug Lavender (still open 2017)
Llano	Al Ehrlich Cedar Company
Georgetown	C. R. Morrison
Brookhaven, western Bell County	John Willis

HILL COUNTRY

Gruene	Willie Simons
New Braunfels	Lee Simons
Kerrville	Joe L. Roberts
Hunt	Cecil Roberts
Ingram	J. T. Stephens (still open 2017)
Ingram	Willie Gumbert
Mountain Home	Mack Callahan
Medina	Rex Simons
Leakey	Floyd Boatright
Leakey	J. W. Ault (still open 2017)
Leakey	O. C. Henderson
Leakey	Ed Thom
Leakey	Jack Cantrell
Kimble County near Telegraph	Preston Wright
Junction near Evergreen School	Bus Carroll
Camp Wood	O. C. Henderson, two other yards

Notes

Referencing of Interviews

This book is based upon oral histories. Because there are so many, all quotes from these recorded interviews are not individually sourced in endnotes. When the person speaking is named, the details in appendix 1, "Voices," help place the speaker in time and social position. If the source of the quote or information is anything other than one of these recorded interviews, it is given in an endnote. The full citations of all sources except unrecorded conversations also appear in the bibliography under the appropriate category: Primary Sources, Online Resources, Interviews, News Articles, or Secondary Sources.

The appendix "Voices" includes date of birth and lifespan, clan (if applicable), and a general classification of occupation or position. The classification of persons in recent generations who were born into a family of cedar choppers, but who pursued something else as their primary occupation, includes both (for instance, the classification for Ronnie Roberts is Firefighter/cedar chopper). "Voices" also includes the name of the interviewer or author, the source of the quote, and the chapter where the individual is first quoted.

Chapter 1

1. Bedichek, "Cedar Chopper," 256.
2. Upton, "Austin Hill Folk," 40.
3. Clarke, "Cedar Posts Fenced a Cattle Empire," 26.
4. Greene, "Mesquite and Mountain Cedar," 317.
5. Winston Bode, "Last of the Charcoal Burners," 2.
6. Sherrill, "Civilization Squeezing out Texas Cedarbilly," 6.
7. Cartwright, "Leroy's Revenge."
8. Langham, "A Man's Got a Right to His Own Mind."
9. Kelso, "Shotgun Funeral for Three Coyotes."
10. Lisheron, "Sundown of the Cedar Choppers."

Chapter 2

1. Fischer, *Albion's Seed,* 630.
2. Shapiro, *Appalachia on Our Mind.*
3. Woodard, *American Nations.*
4. Kirby, *Rural Worlds Lost,* 80.
5. Harkins, *Hillbilly,* 5.
6.Fehrenbach, *Lone Star.*
7. Leyborn, *The Scotch-Irish,* 199.
8. Jordan and Kaups, *American Backwoods Frontier.*
9. Jim Webb, *Born Fighting,* 81.
10. Otto, "Migration of Southern Plain Folk."
11. Jordan and Kaups, *American Backwoods Frontier,* 58.
12. Ibid., 118.
13. Sitton, *Backwoodsmen,* 199.
14. Woodard, *American Nations,* 101.
15. Webb, *Born Fighting,* 68.
16. Jordan, *Environment and Environmental Perceptions in Texas,* 4.
17. Jordan, "Texan Appalachia," 426.
18. Upton, "Austin Hill Folk."
19. Preece, "Where a Dance Still Means the Virginia Reel."
20. Letter to *Texas Highways* from Mrs. Victor B. Fain, January 17, 1985, in Barbara Langham's research notes for "A Man's Got a Right to His Own Mind." For a list including 1937 recordings of Hallie May Preece and David Preece singing several songs, see pages 14–17 at http://traildriver.com/web20content/projects/folklore/loc%201940%20checklists/texas%20checklist.pdf.
21. Kirby, *Rural Worlds Lost,* 80.
22. Roemer, *Roemer's Texas,* 426.
23. Olmsted, *Journey through Texas,* 231.
24. Walter Prescott Webb, *Great Plains.*
25. Quoted from Albert Pike's "Narrative of Journey in the Prairie," in Haley, *Charles Goodnight,* 277.
26. Cantwell West, "Life Story of My Dad, James Thomas (Tom) Cantwell" (Ancestry.com. Public Member Story attached to James Thomas Cantwell: December, 1985).
27. Clara S. Scarbrough, *Land of Good Water,* 5.
28. Roemer, *Roemer's Texas,* 110.
29. Foster, *Forgotten Texas Census.*
30. Olmsted, *Journey through Texas,* 193.
31. Fischer, *Albion's Seed,* 638.

32. While there was cedar being cut in counties like Coryell, Bosque, Somervell, Hood, and Palo Pinto in north-central Texas, it was not by the same people. An examination of the men in these northern counties whose 1940 occupation was "timber cutter" showed they were not kin to the clans on whom I focus, who started in the hills of Austin and spread to the western Hill Country.

CHAPTER 3

1. Preece, "My Grandfather, Dick Preece."
2. Eugene M. Ott and Glen E. Lich, "First Texas Cavalry, USA," *Handbook of Texas Online*, accessed June 6, 2016. http://www.tshaonline.org/handbook/online/articles/qlf03.
3. "1861 Referendum on Secession," *Texas Almanac*, accessed May 5, 2016. Texasalmanac.com.
4. Campbell, *Gone to Texas.*
5. The 1880 census shows the population of the Hill Country as between 94 percent and 100 percent white in Bandera, Blanco, Comal, Gillespie, Kendall, Kerr, Kimble, Lampasas, Llano, Mason, and Edwards counties. The same was true of western Williamson and Travis counties.
6. Kercheville, *Nameless.*
7. Cartwright, "Endless Odyssey of Patrick Henry Polk."
8. "Tom Young on the Gallows," *Austin Statesman*, March 31, 1906.
9. Thompson, "Tumlinson Fort."
10. Parsons, *Taylor-Sutton Feud.*
11. 1890 Veterans Schedules, addendum to U.S. Census of Population and Housing, accessed May 3, 2016, from Ancestry.com, Provo, UT.
12. Fehrenbach, *Lone Star*, 529.
13. Ibid., 451.
14. Ibid., 541.
15. Sowell, "Cox Family as Indian Fighters," 602–606.
16. Rose, *Reckoning.*
17. "Body Found near City," *Daily Democratic Statesman*, March 3, 1878.
18. "The Way They All Go," *Austin Daily Statesman*, June 2, 1886.
19. Scott, "92 Years Young."
20. Miller, *Sam Bass and Gang.*
21. Mrs. Fred Teague, Letter to Dorothy Depwe for Research on *Eanes: History of a Community* (Depwe file 59a, Eanes History Center: July 23, 1976).
22. "A Fatal Shooting Fracas: Dempsey Brown Is Now Dead and Jim Nixon Is Badly Wounded," *Austin Daily Stateman*, May 4, 1896.
23. "An Exciting Elopement," *Austin Weekly Statesman*, March 7, 1895.

24. Ibid.

25. Ancestry.com. Public Member Story attached to James Isaac Nixon (1850–96).

26. The story that follows is documented in the following eight articles in the *Austin Statesman* (see Newspaper Articles section of bibliography): "Brothers Use Guns," March 11, 1903; "John Teague Was Acquitted," June 17, 1903; "Two Are Killed," September 24, 1911; "In Arm's Reach of Gallows," September 28, 1911; "Unwritten Law and Self-Defense," October 8, 1911; "Insanity and Unwritten Law," October 17, 1911; "State to Ask for Death Penalty," October 18, 1911; "John Teague's Fate Rests with the Jury," October 19, 1911.

27. Texas' unwritten law was in fact written in Vernon's Ann. Texas Penal Code Art. 1220, which states: "Homicide is justifiable when committed by the husband upon one taken in the act of adultery with the wife, provided the killing take place before the parties to the act have separated." It was last used in *McGowen v. Travelers Ins. Co.*, 448 F.2d 1315, 1316 (5th Cir. 1971) and was repealed by the legislature effective January 1, 1974.

28. Rosenthal, *Payback*, 47.

29. Nisbett and Cohen, *Culture of Honor*, 5.

30. This story is told by Emmett Shelton Sr., "Cedar Chopper Tapes," Oral History Tape 293, 1978, Austin History Center, Austin Public Library.

Chapter 4

1. Foley, *White Scourge.*

2. U.S. Census of Population and Housing, Historical Census Browser, accessed February 12, 2015, from University of Virginia, Geospatial and Statistical Data Center. http://mapserver.lib.virginia.edu/collections/.

3. Sitton and Utley, *From Can See to Can't.*

4. Sharpless, *Fertile Ground, Narrow Choices*, 167.

5. Sitton and Utley, *From Can See to Can't.*

6. Foley, *White Scourge.*

7. Egan, *Worst Hard Time.*

8. Caro, *Years of Lyndon Johnson*, vol. 1: *Path to Power*, 8.

9. Pugsley, *Imprint on the Land.*

10. Caro, *Path to Power*, 24.

11. Campbell, *Gone to Texas*, 312.

12. Caro, *Path to Power*, 438.

13. Jenkins, "Cedars and Poverty."

14. Margie Carlton Simons, interview by John Leffler in Bertram, Texas, August 24, 2012.

15. This quote, from an interview in 2000 with John Leffler, was used as the title of his report. See Leffler, *Kind of a Hard Old Country.*

16. Toepperwein and Toepperwein, *Charcoal and Charcoal Burners.*

17. Linda Vance, *Eanes,* 52.

18. Kyvig, *Daily Life in the United State.*

19. Caro, *Path to Power,* 117.

20. Fehrenbach, *Lone Star,* 623.

21. Leffler, *Kind of a Hard Old Country,* part III, 9.

22. Sherrill, "Civilization Squeezing out Texas Cedarbilly," 6.

23. Wimberley, *Cedar Whacker,* 25.

24. This story is reported in the following articles in the *Austin Statesman*: "Bud Tracy Captured after Dodging Travis Officers Six Months," July 3, 1926; "Hunting, Fishing Easy Living, Says Tracy," July 6, 1926.

25. Elroy Bode, *This Favored Place,* 123.

26. "Frightened Children Wonder About Future as Mother Is Taken Away," *Austin Statesman,* June 22, 1927.

27. Vance, *Eanes,* 5, 39.

28. This story is documented in Pete Haight, "Shot Down Like a Dog," *Texas Highways,* October, 1974; and "Paul Waechter Dog Killing Case in County Court Yesterday," *Austin Daily Statesman,* January 14, 1902.

29. "Caves in Bull Creek Hills Furnish Safe Retreats for Moonshine Gangs; Officers Get Clue to Nest of Stills," *Austin Statesman,* January 14, 1923.

30. "Sheriff Raids Moonshine Cave," *Austin Statesman,* September 13, 1925.

31. The preceding story is documented in the following *Austin Statesman* articles: "Officers Search Bull Creek Hills," April 12, 1922; "Bull Creek Liquor Traffic," February 4, 1923; "Jurors Wander from Judge's Instruction," March 23, 1924; "Caves in Bull Creek Hills," January 14, 1923.

32. Stoney Teague, interview by Ken Roberts in Sandy Creek, Texas, May 7, 2015.

33. "Boatright on Bond after Liquor Arrest," *Austin Statesman,* August 13, 1936; "35-Gallon Still Is Seized by Federals," *Austin Statesman,* January 22, 1937.

34. Texas State Library and Archives Commission, *Texas, Convict and Conduct Registers, 1875–1945.* Online database attached to a Public Family Tree of Carl Earl Varner (1898–1971) at Ancestry.com.

35. Texas State Library and Archives Commission. *Texas, Convict and Conduct Registers, 1875–1945.* Online database attached to a Public Family Tree of John Thomas Riley (1891–1968) at Ancestry.com.

36. Shelton, "Cedar Chopper Tapes."

Chapter 5

1. "Dobie Offers to Cut Male Cedars," *Austin Statesman*, January 25, 1928. For more on this fascinating professor, see Davis, *J. Frank Dobie*.

2. Patoski, "War on Cedar."

3. Matthew Garriga et al., "Commercial Value of Juniper," 2.

4. Roemer, *Roemer's Texas*, 112.

5. Wimberley, "Cedar Brakes," 229.

6. Olmsted, *Journey through Texas*.

7. Sutton, "Cypress Shingles for Sale," 39.

8. Wimberley, "Cedar Brakes," 230.

9. Haley, *Charles Goodnight*.

10. Robert Adams, personal communication, November 21, 2013. He is the author of *Junipers of the World*.

11. Haley, *Charles Goodnight*, 315.

12. "Local Matters," *Daily Democratic Statesman*, March 7, 1874.

13. "Local Matters," *Daily Democratic Statesman*, April 10, 1875.

14. Emmett Shelton, "Peninsula History," self-made tape, 1979, Emmett Shelton Oral History Collection, Dolph Briscoe Center for American History, University of Texas at Austin.

15. Haley, *XIT Ranch of Texas*.

16. Jordan, "Windmills in Texas."

17. "The Telephone in Austin," *Texas Siftings*, June 4, 1881, cited in SWCA Environmental Consultants, Historical Narrative—Site 41wm892, the Cedar Chopper Site.

18. "Cedar Railroad Ties Wanted," *Austin Statesman*, May 23, 1890.

19. Sherrill, "Civilization Squeezing out Texas Cedarbilly," 6.

20. SWCA Environmental Consultants, Historical Narrative—Site 41wm892, the Cedar Chopper Site.

21. Sherrill, "Civilization Squeezing out Texas Cedarbilly," 6.

22. Stephens, "Lometa Had Boom Town Appearance."

23. "Cedar Choppers Wanted," *Austin Statesman*, November 28, 1908. This was the beginning of a turbulent period when many Mexicans fled across the border. By 1940 most had been "repatriated"—forcibly expelled from the country. For more on Mexican laborers see appendix 2, which examines their presence in the Hill Country counties in 1940.

24. Foley, *Mexicans in the Making of America*, 43.

25. Yarbrough, *Canyon of the Eagles*, 40.

26. Wills, "Uvalde and Northern Railway."

27. Toepperwein and Toepperwein, *Charcoal and Charcoal Burners*, 59.

28. Rissmann, "Charcoal Burner."

29. Rissman, "Charcoal Burning."

30. Rotherham, "The Charcoal Burners."

31. Yarnell, *Southern Appalachians*, 13.

32. Schallenberg, "Evolution, Adaptation and Survival."

33. Toepperwein and Toepperwein, *Charcoal and Charcoal Burners*, 7.

34. Perkins, *Hill Country Paradise*, 127.

35. Toepperwein and Toepperwein, *Charcoal and Charcoal Burners*, 24.

36. John T. Boatright, interview by Ken Roberts in Liberty Hill, Texas, August 11, 2012.

37. Teague, "Letter to Dorothy Depwe for Research on *Eanes: History of a Community*."

38. Coppedge, "Charcoal City."

39. Cantwell West, "Life Story of My Dad, James Thomas (Tom) Cantwell."

40. Toepperwein and Toepperwein, *Charcoal and Charcoal Burners*, 15.

41. Ibid., 17.

42. Tomka and Leffler, *Cultural Overview and Assessment*, 46.

43. Sitton and Utley, *From Can See to Can't*, 257.

44. Ibid.

45. Egan, *Worst Hard Time*, 111.

46. Foley, *White Scourge*, 177.

47. Ibid., 71.

48. Daniel, *Standing at the Crossroads*, 123.

49. Motheral, *Recent Trends in Land Tenure*.

50. Blevins, *Hill Folks*, 118.

51. Lewis, "On the Edge of the Black Waxy," 102.

52. Bettie Edmonds, Kendall County Historical Marker Committee Chairman, "The Engle Store, Bergheim Texas," Texas State Historical Commission, Atlas #5259005329, accessed August 13, 2016, http://atlas.thc.state.tx.us.

53. Dase et al., *Just Like Yesterday*, 1:264.

54. Ibid., 2:1185.

55. Ibid., 2:1120.

56. Jenkins, "Cedars and Poverty," 62.

57. Hollon, "Kerrville Cedar Axe."

58. Sitton and Utley, *From Can See to Can't*, 270.

59. Upton, "Austin Hill Folk."

60. Pryor, "Charlie King."

61. Graves, *Hard Scrabble*, 75.

62. Ibid., 24.

63. Vance, *Eanes*, 75.

64. Ibid., 48.

65. Ibid., 75.

66. Leffler, *Kind of a Hard Old Country*, part III, 4.

67. Earleen Armstrong Simons, interview by Ken Roberts in Bastrop, Texas, May 24, 2013.

68. "Driver Is Burned Badly as Truck Overturns," *Austin Statesman*, June 21, 1932.

69. This story is documented in the following *Austin Statesman* articles: "Officer Slaying Charge Filed," February 15, 1937; "Some of Principals in Thomasson Slaying Case," February 15, 1937; "Hearings Dated in Raid Slaying," February 19, 1937; "Killing Probe Threatened," February 22, 1937; "Young on Trial for Life," June 21, 1937; "Witnesses Put Ike Young in Conspiracy," June 22, 1937; "Sobbing Bride Left Behind," July 7, 1937.

70. "2 Charged after Rum Still Seized," *Austin Statesman*, April 16, 1936.

CHAPTER 6

1. Jordan, *German Seed in Texas Soil*, 165.

2. Cited in Webb, *Great Plains*, 282.

3. Hayter, "Fencing of Western Railways."

4. Liu, *Barbed Wire*.

5. Haley, *Charles Goodnight*, 388.

6. McCallum and McCallum, *The Wire That Fenced the West*, 71.

7. Ibid.

8. Haley, *Charles Goodnight*, 322.

9. McCallum and McCallum, *The Wire That Fenced the West*.

10. Haley, *Charles Goodnight*, 323.

11. Genny Rogers Kercheville, interview by Ken Roberts near Nameless, Texas, June 5, 2012.

12. Lewis, "On the Edge of the Black Waxy," 29.

13. Adams, "Distribution of Juniperus ashei.

14. Hollon, "Kerrville Cedar Axe."

15. Sitton, *Harder Than Hardscrabble*, 100.

16. Graves, *Hard Scrabble*, 34.

17. Lisheron, "Sundown of the Cedar Choppers."

18. Porterfield, *LBJ Country*, 35.

19. Thanks to Dick Kercheville, Genny's husband, for this double meaning of cedar brake.

20. Harris, "Oft-Cussed Cedar Trees."

21. Margie Carlton Simons, interview by John Leffler, August 24, 2012.

22. Mary Lou Ward, conversation with Ken Roberts in Camp Wood, Texas, November 28, 2012.

23. Carole Goble, conversation with Ken Roberts in Burnet, Texas, May 22, 2012.

24. Raymond Moore, interview by Ken Roberts in Ingram, Texas, November 27, 2012.

25. Cartwright, "Endless Odyssey of Patrick Henry Polk."

26. Wimberley, *Cedar Whacker*, 97.

CHAPTER 7

1. Wimberley, *Cedar Whacker*, 25.

2. Doug Lavender, interview by Ken Roberts in Lampasas, Texas, January 15, 2011. He is approximating the diameter of a circle using the formula $C=2\pi r$, where $\pi=3.14$.

3. Lisheron, "Sundown of the Cedar Choppers."

4. Simons, "Cedar's Fed Many a Family," 22.

5. Sherrill, "Civilization Squeezing out Texas Cedarbilly," 6.

6. Simons, "Cedar's Fed Many a Family," 20.

7. Ibid.

8. Webb, *Born Fighting*, 180.

9. Shelton, "Cedar Chopper Tapes."

10. Vance, *Eanes*, 82.

11. Della Edwards Graham, personal memoir, written 1976, in Depwe File 59a, Eanes History Center.

12. Charlie Dellana, interview by Linda Vance in West Lake Hills, Texas, May 8, 1986, Vance notes in Depwe File 59a, Eanes History Center.

13. Earleen Armstrong Simons, interview by Ken Roberts in Bastrop, Texas, May 24, 2013.

14. Kindrick, *Best of Sam Kindrick*, 96.

15. Hollis Baker, conversation with Ken Roberts in Liberty Hill, Texas, May 29, 2012.

16. Lewis, "On the Edge of the Black Waxy," 46.

17. Van Winkle, "Gumberts Made Cutting Cedar a Worthy Trade."

18. Earleen Armstrong Simons, interview by Ken Roberts in Bastrop, Texas, May 24, 2013.

19. Vance, *Eanes*, 25.

20. Shelton, "Cedar Chopper Tapes."

21. Stoney Teague, interview by Ken Roberts in Sandy Creek, Texas, May 9, 2015.

22. Vance, *Eanes,* 67.

23. Webb, *Born Fighting,* 81.

24. Preece, "Where a Dance Still Means the Virginia Reel."

25. Porterfield, *LBJ Country,* 35.

26. "Highly Decorated Austinite Succumbs," *Austin Statesman,* July 24, 1969.

27. Webb, *Born Fighting,* 181.

28. Sherrill, "Civilization Squeezing out Texas Cedarbilly."

29. For an understanding of the importance of extended family in Appalachian culture, see Vance, *Hillbilly Elegy,* 69. He writes, "We didn't live a peaceful life in a small nuclear family. We lived a chaotic life in big groups of aunts, uncles, grandparents and cousins."

30. "Husband Caught as Wife Dies," *Austin Statesman,* May 3, 1933; "Pierce Statement of Wife's Slaying," *Austin Statesman,* October 25, 1933.

31. "Husband Details Slaying of Wife," *Austin Statesman,* December 11, 1930.

32. Shelton, "Cedar Chopper Tapes."

33. U.S. Census of Population and Housing, Historical Census Browser, http://mapserver.lib.virginia.edu/collections/.

34. Vance, *Eanes,* 86.

35. Gregory, *American Exodus,* 130.

36. Ibid., 148.

37. Vance, *Eanes,* 87.

38. Johnson, "Westlake Hills Historical Project," Eanes History Center, 1976, 3 pages.

39. Lewis, "On the Edge of the Black Waxy," 55.

40. Porterfield, *LBJ Country,* 35.

41. Charlie Dellana, interview by Linda Vance in West Lake Hills, Texas, March 28, 1986, Vance notes in Depwe File 59a, Eanes History Center.

42. Zesch, *Captured.*

43. Lisheron, "Sundown of the Cedar Choppers."

44. Ibid.

45. Junie Plummer, telephone interview with Ken Roberts, May 23, 2012.

46. Preece, "Where a Dance Still Means the Virginia Reel." How the son of a cedar chopper became a writer (while in his thirties he was a journalist in Chicago, and later wrote the articles listed in the bibliography and at least one book), is worth telling because it is so unusual. His father Dave Preece worked at the Texas School for the Blind in 1920, where Harold is listed in the census with many other school-age children. He later completed two years of high school. This information is attached to Harold Richard Preece on Ancestry.com.

47. Hollis Baker, conversation with Ken Roberts in Liberty Hill, Texas, May 29, 2012.

48. Vance, *Eanes*, 50.

49. Cantwell West, "Life Story of My Dad, James Thomas (Tom) Cantwell."

50. Public Member Story attached to George Washington Farmer (1869–1947) at Ancestry.com.

51. Tomka and Leffler, *Cultural Overview and Assessment*, 46.

52. Leffler, *Kind of a Hard Old Country*, part I, 16.

53. Carole Goble, conversation with Ken Roberts in Burnet, Texas, May 22, 2012.

54. Vance, *Eanes*, 68.

55. "Highly Decorated Austinite Succumbs," *Austin Statesman*, July 24, 1969.

56. Ibid.

57. Texas State Library and Archives Commission, *Texas, Convict and Conduct Registers, 1875–1945*, online database attached to a Public Family Tree of Harvey John Pearson (1904–58) at Ancestry.com.

58. "Austin Man Is Believed Drowned in Fleeing Cop," *Austin American*, May 7, 1939.

59. This story is documented in the following *Austin Statesman* articles: "2 Brothers Charged in Gun Killing Here," December 9, 1932; "Witness Details Austin Slaying," December 13, 1932; "Fatal Fight Is Detailed," April 11, 1933.

60. Earl Short murder trial documents, Travis County District Court, Criminal Division, Record #20843, 1933.

61. Emmett Shelton Sr., "Homicide Tapes," Emmett Shelton Oral History Collection, Dolph Briscoe Center for American History, University of Texas at Austin.

CHAPTER 8

1. Bouchard, "Role of Cedar in Real County History," 126.

2. Wimberley, *Cedar Whacker*, 23.

3. Kelton, *Barbed Wire*, 82.

4. Porterfield, *LBJ Country*, 35.

5. This quote comes from Wimberley, *Cedar Whacker*, 25.

6. Leffler, *Kind of a Hard Old Country*, part I, 16.

7. Jacoby, "Independent Living."

8. Leffler, *Kind of a Hard Old Country*, part I, 17.

9. Sherrill, "Civilization Squeezing out Texas Cedarbilly."

10. Jacoby, "Independent Living."

11. Webb, *Born Fighting*, 286.

12. Woodrell, *Tomato Red*, 89.

13. Wimberley, *Cedar Whacker*, 231.

14. Graves, *Hard Scrabble*, 34.

15. Sherrill, "Civilization Squeezing out Texas Cedarbilly," 6.

16. Bruce Marshall, interview by Barbara Langham in West Lake Hills, Texas, August 2, 1984.

17. Vance, *Eanes*, 47.

18. Ibid., 68.

19. Margie Carlton Simons, interview by Ken Roberts in Cedar Park, Texas, February 22, 2013.

20. On ranchers in Williamson County, see Linda Scarbrough, *Road, River, and Ol' Boy Politics*, 28; conversations with Jerry Hawes and Hollis Baker were in 2012 (see appendix 1).

21. Wimberley, *Cedar Whacker*, 143.

22. Bouchard, "Role of Cedar in Real County History," 126.

23. Bryson, *Culture of the Shin Oak Ridge Folk*.

24. Ibid., 186.

25. Vance, *Eanes*, 126.

26. Harkins, *Hillbilly*, 105.

27. Hartigan, *Odd Tribes*, 66.

28. Reed, *Southern Folk, Plain and Fancy*, 43.

29. Daniel, *Standing at the Crossroads*, 14.

30. Preece, "Where a Dance Still Means the Virginia Reel."

31. Harkins, *Hillbilly*, 7.

32. King, *Of Outlaws, Con Men*, 8.

33. Isenberg, *White Trash*, 235.

34. Shapiro, *Appalachia on Our Mind*, 104.

35. Reed, *Southern Folk, Plain and Fancy*, 45.

36. "It Happened Here," *Kerrville Mountain Sun*, August 21, 1982, 3; on regional terms, see Hartigan, "Name Calling," 53.

37. Lisheron, "Sundown of the Cedar Choppers."

38. Marie Boatright, conversation with Ken Roberts in Austin, Texas, January 15, 2015.

39. Leffler, *Kind of a Hard Old Country*, part I, 18.

40. "Ol Young Killed by Joe Eppes: Shooting Occurs on Lake Ten Miles from Austin," *Austin Statesman*, September 17, 1917.

41. This story is documented in the following *Austin Statesman* articles: "Examining Trial in Slaying Delayed," September 30, 1931; "Gun Slaying Here Is Described by Girl," October 1, 1931.

42. This story is documented in the following *Austin Statesman* articles:"Kin Charged in Brother's Death," April 15, 1935; "Slaying Hearing to Be Resumed," April 17, 1935.

43. "Plumley Death Probe Continues," *Austin Statesman*, April 16, 1935.

44. Upton, "Austin Hill Folk," 48.

45. Haight, "Shot Down Like a Dog," 7.

46. Ibid. The "grizzled, erect mountaineer" was very likely Paul's brother's father-in-law Lee Boatright, a leader of the clan, who would have been forty-two at the time.

47. Gladden and D. L. Turner, interview by John J. Leffler, February 21 and June 21, 2012, p. 22. See also "Holds Tongue, Must Take Rap," *Austin Statesman*, June 14, 1937.

48. "J. L. Teague Is Charged with Murder," *Austin Statesman*, September 2, 1948.

49. "Teague Case States Witness Charges Intimidation," *Austin Statesman*, October 29, 1948.

50. Leslie Young was stabbed to death in Haskell, Texas, on October 16, 1949 (Texas Death Certificates, 1903–1982, Ancestry.com). Ivey Allen is shown as Convict #3116369, serving two years at the prison at Huntsville, Texas, for a murder in Haskell (Texas, Conduct Registers 1875–1945, Ancestry.com, accessed May 11, 2016).

51. "Charges Filed in Austin Shooting," *Austin Statesman*, March 30, 1927.

52. See *Austin Statesman:* "Youth Badly Cut," March 7, 1926; "Charges Filed in Austin Shooting," March 30, 1927; "Austin Man Cut in Dance Hall Affray," August 22, 1931; "2 Charged after Rum Still Seized," April 16, 1936.

53. This story is documented in a number of newspaper articles, including: "Accused Shooter of Hunter Asks Release," *Austin Statesman*, September 22, 1931; "Ernest Thurman Sought," *Austin Statesman*, October 4, 1931. Emmett Shelton also talked about this case in his "Cedar Chopper Tapes."

54. This story is documented in Emmett Shelton's "Cedar Chopper Tapes" as well as the following articles: "One Killed, One Shot in Feud," *Austin Statesman*, April 30, 1936; "Guards Placed over Duel Victim," *Austin Statesman*, May 1, 1936.

CHAPTER 9

1. "Flywheel Death Ruled Accident," *Austin Statesman*, February 9, 1957.

2. Irene Gibson, "Last Cedar Yards Reminder of Once Flourishing Industry," *Brownwood Bulletin*, May 19, 1961.

3. Vance, *Eanes*, 90.

4. Sherrill, "Civilization Squeezing out Texas Cedarbilly."

5. But only West Lake Hills makes the top ten zip codes of Texas, leading *Texas Monthly* to remark that "the list highlights just how poor the very rich in Austin are." Solomon, "Ten Wealthiest Zip Codes."

6. Cantwell West, "Life Story of My Dad, James Thomas (Tom) Cantwell."

7. Porterfield, *LBJ Country*, 36.

8. The 315 men in my tree born between 1900 and 1925 who were cedar choppers, truckers, masons, and quarry and dam workers lived an average of a little over 69 years. The 94 men who were farmers, mechanics, or in construction lived more than five years longer.

9. Simons, "Cedar's Fed Many a Family."

10. Sherrill, "Civilization Squeezing out Texas Cedarbilly."

11. Harrell King murder trial documents, Travis County District Court, Criminal Division, Record #27201, January 26, 1951.

12. "Two Death Stays Granted by Gov," *Breckenridge American*, March 14, 1952.

Epilogue

1. Upton, "Austin Hill Folk."

2. Isenberg, *White Trash*, 235. Harkins, *Hillbilly*, 194. Harkins cites a 1958 Harper's article titled "The Hillbillies Invade Chicago."

3. To understand just how difficult this transition has been, see Vance, *Hillbilly Elegy*.

4. "Searchers Find Cedar Chopper," *Austin Statesman*, May 15, 1953; "Cedar Chopper Pleads Guilty," *Austin Statesman*, September 26, 1957, 5.

5. "Bechtol, Bourland Wear Hair at Westwood Western Hop," *Austin Statesman*, February 16, 1958. The "Bechtol" in the title is Hub Bechtol, a Texas college football star in the 1940s. I met him when he caught me smoking grapevine at a Boy Scout campout. He ordered all the other boys to take off their belts and line up, hitting me from both sides as I ran through. My Scots-Irish reaction was silent fury and a desire for revenge; thinking of Hub looking silly in a beard goes some of the way.

6. Woodard, *American Nations*, 102.

7. Graves, *Hard Scrabble*, 75.

8. Porterfield, *LBJ Country*.

9. Pate Patterson is a direct link between the nineteenth century and the present—his mother brought him to Travis County to escape the violence of the Sutton-Taylor feud of the 1870s; her sisters Edna and Mary Patterson are the mothers of Luther Pierce and Ronnie Roberts, and I interviewed his daughter Alice.

10. "'Cedar Chopper' Takes Life Easy with No Excuses," *Denton Record*, July 5, 1976.

11. Jacoby, "Independent Living."

12. Vance, *Hillbilly Elegy*, 40.

13. Nisbett and Cohen, *Culture of Honor*.

14. Gorn, "Gouge and Bite, Pull Hair and Scratch."

15. Simon Ratliff stories, https://drive.google.com/file/d/0B02_JxnXt7UWY0xrTmlxbHpOWG8/view?usp=sharing.

APPENDIX 2

1. This quote is from a tape at the Balcones Canyonlands National Wildlife Refuge, Lago Vista, Texas, and is not transcribed or included in John Leffler's report, *Kind of a Hard Old Country.*

2. Foley, *Mexicans in the Making of America,* 138.

3. Bouchard, "Role of Cedar in Real County History," 127.

Bibliography

Primary Sources

Cantwell West, Keron. "The Life Story of My Dad, James Thomas (Tom) Cantwell." Ancestry.com. Public Member Story attached to James Thomas Cantwell, December, 1985.

Fain, Mrs. Victor B. Letter to *Texas Highways* concerning 1936 recordings by Alan Lomax in Austin, Texas. January 17, 1985.

Graham, Della Edwards. Personal Memoir. Depwe File 59a, Eanes History Center, 1976.

Johnson, Cecil M. "Westlake Hills Historical Project." Eanes History Center, 1976.

Teague, Mrs. Fred. Letter to Dorothy Depwe for Research on *Eanes: History of a Community*. Depwe file 59a, Eanes History Center, July 23, 1976.

Online Resources

"1861 Referendum on Secession." *Texas Almanac*. Accessed May 5, 2016. Texas-almanac.com.

1890 Veterans Schedules, addendum to U.S. Census of Population and Housing. Accessed May 3, 2016. Ancestry.com, Provo, UT.

Edmonds, Bettie, Kendall County Historical Marker Committee Chairman. "The Engle Store, Bergheim Texas." Texas State Historical Commission, Atlas #5259005329. Accessed August 13, 2016. http://atlas.thc.state.tx.us/.

Ott, Eugene M., and Glen E. Lich. "First Texas Cavalry, USA." The Handbook of Texas Online. Accessed June 6, 2016. http://www.tshaonline.org/handbook/online/articles/qlf03.

Thompson, Karen R. "Tumlinson Fort." *The Handbook of Texas Online*. Accessed May 5, 2014. http://www.tshaonline.org/handbook/online/articles/uet05.

U.S. Census of Population and Housing. Historical Census Browser. Accessed February 12, 2015. University of Virginia, Geospatial and Statistical Data Center. http://mapserver.lib.virginia.edu/collections/.

Interviews (Tapes and/or Transcripts Available)

Unless otherwise indicated, audio tapes and/or transcripts for all interviews are in the Southwestern University Library Archives in Georgetown, Texas. See appendix 1 for more detail and for conversations not recorded.

Allen, Stanley. Interview by Ken Roberts, Wimberley, January 9, 2013

Auld, Ken. Interview by Ken Roberts, Leakey, November 28, 2012.

Bading, Lorenz. Interview by Ken Roberts, New Braunfels, May 16, 2012.

Baker, Barney. Interview by Ken Roberts, Marble Falls, November 10, 2012.
Bertling, Kenneth. Interview by Ken Roberts, Liberty Hill, August 1, 2012.
Boatright, Albert. Interview by Ken Roberts, Kingsland, Texas, December 18, 2014.
Boatright, John T. Interview by Ken Roberts, Liberty Hill, August 11, 2012.
Boatright, Mary. Interview by Ken Roberts, Liberty Hill, August 11, 2012.
Bonnet, Morris. Interview by Ken Roberts, Liberty Hill, February 26, 2015.
Cantrell, Lee. Interview by Ken Roberts, Liberty Hill, October 27, 2012.
Cantwell, Floyd. Interview by Ken Roberts, Leander, January 30, 2015.
Carlton Simons, Margie. Interview by Ken Roberts, Leander, February 22, 2013.
———. Interview by John Leffler, Bertram, Texas, August 24, 2012. Location of audio and/or transcript: Balcones Canyonlands Oral History Interviews, Balcones Canyonlands National Wildlife Refuge, Lago Vista, Texas.
Gillman, Joe. Interview by Valerie Dunham, Austin, January 30, 1985. Location of audio and/or transcript: Oral History Tape 416, Austin History Center, Austin Public Library.
Hagood, Charles. Interview by Ken Roberts, Junction, October 30, 2012.
Henry, Betty. Interview by Ken Roberts, Cedar Park, August 9, 2012.
Hibbitts, Don. Interview by Ken Roberts, Camp Wood, Texas, March 14, 2011.
Hoover, John. Interview by Ken Roberts, Burnet, May 11, 2012.
Kaufman, Pete. Interview by Ken Roberts, Liberty Hill, June 5, 2012.
Kercheville, Genny. Interview by Ken Roberts, Nameless, Texas, June 5, 2012.
Lentz, Milton. Interview by Ken Roberts, Temple, Texas, July 3, 2014.
Marshall, Bruce. Interview by Ken Roberts, Austin, August 12, 2012.
Maugham, Charlie. Interview by Ken Roberts, Marble Falls, August 11, 2012.
McKinnerney, Lee. Interview by Ken Roberts, Georgetown, May 22, 2013.
Moore, Raymond. Interview by Ken Roberts, Ingram, Texas, November 27, 2012.
O'Donnell, Guthrie. Interview by Ken Roberts, Marble Falls, May 22, 2012.
Patterson, Alice. Interview by Ken Roberts, Lake Buchanan, Texas, May 21, 2013.
Patterson, Edna May. Interview by Bonnie S. George, West Lake Hills, November, 1981. Location of audio and/or transcript: "Interview with Edna May Pierce, Age 75," Austin History Center, Austin Public Library.
Pearson, T. M. Interview by Ken Roberts, Leander, November 15, 2012.
Pehl, Pearl. Interview by B. Schlameus, 1985. Location of audio and/or transcript: Sophienburg Museum and Archives, New Braunfels, Texas.
Pierce, Luther. Interview by Ken Roberts, Jarrell, Texas, March 13, 2015.
Raley, Olan. Interview by Ken Roberts, Junction, October 30, 2012.
Ratliff, Simon. Interview by Ken Roberts, Burnet, June 6, 2012.
Reaves, Leslie. Interview by Ken Roberts, Cedar Park, May 30, 2015.
Ringstaff, Elizabeth Gillman (Minnie). Interview by Valerie Dunham, Austin, January 24, 1985. Location of audio and/or transcript: Oral History Tape 0392, 0393, Austin History Center, Austin Public Library.
Roberts, Ronnie. Interview by Ken Roberts, Dripping Springs, March 25, 2012.
Russell, Kerry. Interview by Ken Roberts, Georgetown, August 11, 2011.
Shelton, Emmett Sr. "Homicide Tapes." Emmett Shelton Oral History Collection. Dolph Briscoe Center for American History, University of Texas at Austin.
———. "Cedar Chopper Tapes." Oral History Tape 293, 1978. Austin History Center, Austin Public Library.

———. "Peninsula History." Emmett Shelton Oral History Collection. Dolph Briscoe Center for American History, University of Texas at Austin, 1979.
Simons, Don. Interview by Ken Roberts, San Marcos, September 7, 2014, and Oak Grove Cemetery, January 25, 2015.
Simons, Earleen Armstrong. Interview by Ken Roberts, Bastrop, May 24, 2013.
Simons, Princeton. Interview by Ken Roberts, Leander, February 22, 2013.
Sutton, Mack. Interview by Ruth E. Ellsworth and Bill Carter, June, 1978. Location of audio and/or transcript: Oral History Tape 236, Austin History Center, Austin Public Library.
Teague, Stoney. Interview by Ken Roberts, Sandy Creek, Texas, May 7, 2015.
Turner, Dick. Interview by Ken Roberts, Burnet, May 15, 2012.
Turner, Gladden and D. L. Interview by John J. Leffler on February 21 and June 21, 2012. Location of audio and/or transcript: Balcones Canyonlands Oral History Interviews, Balcones Canyonlands National Wildlife Refuge, Lago Vista, Texas.
Wallace, Arthur Lee. Interview by Ken Roberts, Junction, October 30, 2012.
Willess, Bob. Interview by Ken Roberts, Belton, Texas, August 10, 2012.
Wilson, Frank D. Interview by Ruth E. Ellsworth, Austin, April 11, 1978. Location of audio and/or transcript: Oral History Tape 227, Austin History Center, Austin Public Library.

News Articles

"2 Brothers Charged in Gun Killing Here: Police Hunting Suspected Couple." *Austin Statesman,* December 9, 1932.
"2 Charged after Rum Still Seized." *Austin Statesman,* April 16, 1936.
"35-Gallon Still Is Seized by Federals." *Austin Statesman,* January 22, 1937.
"Accused Shooter of Hunter Asks Release." *Austin Statesman,* September 22, 1931.
"Austin Man Cut in Dance Hall Affray." *Austin Statesman,* August 22, 1931.
"Austin Man Is Believed Drowned in Fleeing Cop: Austin Laborer Runs from Law, Jumps into River." *Austin American,* May 7, 1939.
"Bechtol, Bourland Wear Hair at Westwood Western Hop." *Austin Statesman,* February 16, 1958.
"Boatright on Bond after Liquor Arrest." *Austin Statesman,* August 13, 1936.
"Body Found near City." *Daily Democratic Statesman,* March 3, 1878.
"Brothers Use Guns: A Serious Shooting Affray Which Terminates in the Wounding of One." *Austin Statesman,* March 11, 1903.
"Bud Tracy Captured after Dodging Travis Officers Six Months." *Austin Statesman,* July 3, 1926.
"Bull Creek Liquor Traffic Amounts to $2000 Per Month." *Austin Statesman,* February 4, 1923.
"Caves in Bull Creek Hills Furnish Safe Retreats for Moonshine Gangs; Officers Get Clue to Nest of Stills." *Austin Statesman,* January 14, 1923.
"Cedar Chopper Pleads Guilty." *Austin Statesman,* September 26, 1957.
"'Cedar Chopper' Takes Life Easy with No Excuses." *Denton Record,* July 5, 1976.
"Cedar Choppers Wanted." *Austin Statesman,* November 28, 1908.
"Cedar Railroad Ties Wanted." *Austin Statesman,* May 23, 1890.
"Charges Filed in Austin Shooting." *Austin Statesman,* March 30, 1927.

"Dobie Offers to Cut Male Cedars." *Austin Statesman,* January 25, 1928.
"Driver Is Burned Badly as Truck Overturns." *Austin Statesman,* June 21, 1932.
"Ernest Thurman Sought on Grand Jury Indictment: Bluff Springs Resident Is Billed for Assault with Intent to Murder." *Austin Statesman,* October 4, 1931.
"Examining Trial in Slaying Delayed." *Austin Statesman,* September 30, 1931.
"An Exciting Elopement." *Austin Weekly Statesman,* March 7, 1895.
"Fatal Fight Is Detailed: Witness Tells of Struggle Which Ended in Death." *Austin Statesman,* April 11, 1933.
"A Fatal Shooting Fracas: Dempsey Brown Is Now Dead and Jim Nixon Is Badly Wounded." *Austin Daily Stateman,* May 4, 1896.
"Flywheel Death Ruled Accident." *Austin Statesman,* February 9, 1957.
"Frightened Children Wonder About Future as Mother Is Taken Away." *Austin Statesman,* June 22, 1927.
Gibson, Irene. "Last Cedar Yards Reminder of Once Flourishing Industry." *Brownwood Bulletin,* May 19, 1961.
"Guards Placed over Duel Victim." *Austin Statesman,* May 1, 1936.
"Gun Slaying Here Is Described by Girl: Effort to Grab Weapon Is Bared." *Austin Statesman,* October 1, 1931.
Harris, Sam E. "Oft-Cussed Cedar Trees Bring Neat Revenue to Ranchers Now." *Austin American,* June 27, 1948.
"Hearings Dated in Raid Slaying." *Austin Statesman,* February 19, 1937.
"Highly Decorated Austinite Succumbs." *Austin Statesman,* July 24, 1969.
"Holds Tongue, Must Take Rap." *Austin Statesman,* June 14, 1937.
"Hunting, Fishing Easy Living, Says Tracy." *Austin Statesman,* July 6, 1926.
"Husband Caught as Wife Dies: Austin Woman Victim of Shotgun Attack." *Austin Statesman,* May 3, 1933.
"Husband Details Slaying of Wife: Mate Shot Her, Thinking She Had Pistol, He Says." *Austin Statesman,* December 11, 1930.
"In Arm's Reach of Gallows Teague Tosses and Thinks." *Austin Statesman,* September 28, 1911.
"Insanity and Unwritten Law, Twin Element of Plea Made in Defense of John Teague." *Austin Statesman,* October 17, 1911.
"It Happened Here," *Kerrville Mountain Sun,* August 21, 1982, 3.
"J. L. Teague Is Charged with Murder." *Austin Statesman,* September 2, 1948.
"John Teague Was Acquitted Yesterday of the Charge of Assault to Murder." *Austin Statesman,* June 17, 1903.
"John Teague's Fate Rests with the Jury." *Austin Statesman,* October 19, 1911.
"Jurors Wander from Judge's Instruction; New Trial Granted." *Austin Statesman,* March 23, 1924.
"Killing Probe Threatened: Warnings Sent by Hill Area, Statesman Learns." *Austin Statesman,* February 22, 1937.
"Kin Charged in Brother's Death." *Austin Statesman,* April 15, 1935.
"Local Matters." *Daily Democratic Statesman,* March 7, 1874.
"Local Matters." *Daily Democratic Statesman,* April 10, 1875.
"Officer Slaying Charge Filed: Federals Push Full Probe of All Angles Here." *Austin Statesman,* February 15, 1937.
"Officers Search Bull Creek Hills for Liquor Stills." *Austin Statesman,* April 12, 1922.

"Ol Young Killed by Joe Eppes: Shooting Occurs on Lake Ten Miles from Austin." *Austin Statesman,* September 17, 1917.
"One Killed, One Shot in Feud: Battle Staged in Hill of County." *Austin Statesman,* April 30, 1936.
"Paul Waechter Dog Killing Case in County Court Yesterday." *Austin Daily Statesman,* January 14, 1902.
"Pierce Statement of Wife's Slaying Told Austin Jury." *Austin Statesman,* October 25, 1933.
"Plumley Death Probe Continues." *Austin Statesman,* April 16, 1935.
Scott, David. "92 Years Young: He Recalls Hosting the James Brothers in 1886." *Austin Statesman,* August 10, 1969.
"Searchers Find Cedar Chopper." *Austin Statesman,* May 15, 1953.
"Sheriff Raids Moonshine Cave." *Austin Statesman,* September 13, 1925.
"Slaying Hearing to Be Resumed." *Austin Statesman,* April 17, 1935.
"Sobbing Bride Left Behind When Young Goes on Long Trek." *Austin Statesman,* July 7, 1937.
"Some of Principals in Thomasson Slaying Case." *Austin Statesman,* February 15, 1937.
"State to Ask for Death Penalty in Teague Case." *Austin American Statesman,* October 18, 1911.
"Teague Case States Witness Charges Intimidation." *Austin Statesman,* October 29, 1948.
"Tom Young on the Gallows." *Austin Statesman,* March 31, 1906.
"Two Are Killed When Desperado Runs Amuck in South Austin." *Austin Statesman,* September 24, 1911.
"Two Death Stays Granted by Gov." *Breckenridge American,* March 14, 1952.
"Unwritten Law and Self-Defense to Be Teague's Pleas." *Austin Statesman,* October 8, 1911.
"The Way They All Go: The Narrative of a Desperado's Killing, as Told by an Actor in the Tragedy." *Austin Daily Statesman,* June 2, 1886.
"Witness Details Austin Slaying: $5000 Bond Is Set after Hearing." *Austin Statesman,* December 13, 1932.
"Witnesses Put Ike Young in Conspiracy." *Austin Statesman,* June 22, 1937.
"Young on Trial for Life: Jury Is Hearing Testimony in Murder Case." *Austin Statesman,* June 21, 1937.
"Youth Badly Cut." *Austin American,* March 7, 1926.

Secondary Sources

Adams, Robert P. "Distribution of *Juniperus ashei* Var. *ashei* and Var. *ovata* around New Braunfels, Texas." *Phytologia* 90, no. 1 (2008): 97–102.
Adams, Robert P. *Junipers of the World: The Genus Juniperus.* Bloomington, Ind: Trafford Publishing Company, 2011.
Bedichek, Roy. "The Cedar Chopper." In *Walking in America,* edited by Donald Zochert, 253–61. New York: Alfred A. Knopf, 1974.
Blevins, Brooks. *Hill Folks: A History of Arkansas Ozarkers and Their Image.* Chapel Hill: University of North Carolina Press, 2002.

Bode, Elroy. *This Favored Place: The Texas Hill Country*. Bryan, Tex.: Shearer Publishing, 1983.

Bode, Winston. "The Last of the Charcoal Burners." *Texas Observer*, August 14, 1959, 2.

Bouchard, Gueric R. "The Role of Cedar in Real County History." In *Wagons Ho! A History of Real County, Texas*, edited by Majorie Kellner, 124–29. Dallas: Curtis Media, 1995.

Bryson, J. Gordon. *Culture of the Shin Oak Ridge Folk*. Austin, Tex.: Firm Foundation Publishing House, 1964.

Campbell, Randolph B. *Gone to Texas: A History of the Lone Star State*. New York: Oxford University Press, 2003.

Caro, Robert A. *The Years of Lyndon Johnson*, vol. 1: *The Path to Power*. New York: Vintage Books, 1981.

Cartwright, Gary. "The Endless Odyssey of Patrick Henry Polk: The Wanderings of a Texas Family on the Road to Nowhere." *Texas Monthly*, May, 1977.

———. "Leroy's Revenge." *Texas Monthly*, August, 1975.

Clarke, Mary Whatley. "Cedar Posts Fenced a Cattle Empire." *Cattleman* 32 (1946): 26.

Coppedge, Clay. "Charcoal City: Turning Cedar into Cash." *Texas Co-op Power*, April, 2011.

Daniel, Pete. *Standing at the Crossroads: Southern Life in the Twentieth Century*. Baltimore, Md.: Johns Hopkins University Press, 1996.

Dase, Amy E., Martha Doty Freeman, William S. Pugsley III, Thad Sitton, and Marie E. Blake. *Just Like Yesterday: Recollections of Life on the Fort Hood Lands*. 2 vols. Austin: Prewitt and Associates, 2003.

Davis, Steven L. *J. Frank Dobie: A Liberated Mind*. Austin: University of Texas Press, 2009.

Egan, Timothy. *The Worst Hard Time: The Untold Story of Those Who Survived the Great American Dust Bowl*. Boston: Houghton Mifflin Company, 2006.

Fehrenbach, T. R. *Lone Star: A History of Texas and the Texans*. New York: Collier Books, 1968.

Fischer, David Hackett. *Albion's Seed: Four British Folkways in America*. New York: Oxford University Press, 1989.

Foley, Neil. *Mexicans in the Making of America*. Cambridge, Mass.: Belknap Press of Harvard University Press, 2014.

———. *The White Scourge: Mexicans, Blacks, and Poor Whites in Texas Cotton Culture*. Berkeley: University of California Press, 1997.

Foster, L. L. *Forgotten Texas Census: First Annual Report of the Agricultural Bureau of the Department of Agriculture, Insurance, Statistics, and History, 1887–88*. Austin: Texas State Historical Association, 2001.

Garriga, Matthew, Amy P. Thurow, Tom Thurow, Richard Conner, and Dale Brandenberger. "Commercial Value of Juniper on the Edwards Plateau, Texas." In *Juniper Ecology and Management*, edited by Charles A. Taylor Jr. Sonora: Texas A&M University Research Station, 1997.

Gorn, Elliott J. "Gouge and Bite, Pull Hair and Scratch: The Social Significance of Fighting in the Southern Backcountry." *American Historical Review* 90 (1985): 18–43.

Graves, John. *Hard Scrabble: Observations on a Patch of Land.* Dallas: Southern Methodist University Press, 1973.
Greene, A. C. "Mesquite and Mountain Cedar." *Southwest Review* (1969): 314–20.
Gregory, James N. *American Exodus: The Dust Bowl Migration and Okie Culture in California.* New York: Oxford University Press, 1989.
Haight, Pete. "Shot Down Like a Dog." *Texas Highways,* October, 1974.
Haley, J. Evetts. *Charles Goodnight: Cowboy and Plainsman.* Norman: University of Oklahoma Press, 1949.
———. *The XIT Ranch of Texas: And the Early Days of the Llano Estacado.* Norman: University of Oklahoma Press, 1929.
Harkins, Anthony. *Hillbilly: A Cultural History of an American Icon.* New York: Oxford University Press, 2004.
Hartigan, John Jr. *Odd Tribes: Toward a Cultural Analysis of White People.* Durham, North Carolina: Duke University Press, 2005.
———. "Name Calling: Objectifying 'Poor Whites' and 'White Trash' in Detroit." In *White Trash: Race and Class in America,* edited by Matt Wray and Annalee Newitz, 41–56. New York: Routledge, 1997.
Hayter, Earl W. "The Fencing of Western Railways." *Agricultural History* 19, no. 3 (1945): 163–67.
Hollon, Gene. "The Kerrville Cedar Axe." *Southwestern Historical Quarterly* 50, no. 2 (1946): 241–50.
Isenberg, Nancy. *White Trash: The 400-Year Untold History of Class in America.* New York: Viking, 2016.
Jacoby, Mary. "Independent Living: Northwest of Austin, Rural Residents Struggle but Shun Welfare." *Austin American-Statesman.* December 17, 1990.
Jenkins, Ross B. "Cedars and Poverty." *Cattleman* 1939, 60–61.
Jordan, Terry G. *Environment and Environmental Perceptions in Texas.* Boston: American Press, 1980.
———. *German Seed in Texas Soil: Immigrant Farmers in Nineteenth-Century Texas.* Austin: University of Texas Press, 1966.
———. "The Texan Appalachia." *Annals of the Association of American Geographers* 60, no. 3 (1970): 409–27.
———. "Windmills in Texas." *Agricultural History* 37, no. 2 (1963): 80–85.
Jordan, Terry G., and Matti Kaups. *The American Backwoods Frontier: An Ethnic and Ecological Interpretation.* Baltimore: Johns Hopkins University Press, 1989.
Kelso, John. "Shotgun Funeral for Three Coyotes." *Austin American-Statesman,* January 15, 2013.
Kelton, Elmer. *Barbed Wire.* New York: Ballentine Books, 1957.
Kercheville, Genny. *Nameless: Its History and Its People.* Kearney, Nebraska: Morris Publishing, 2007.
Kindrick, Sam. *The Best of Sam Kindrick: The Secret Life and Hard Times of a Cedar Chopper.* San Antonio: San Antonio Express News Publishing Company, 1973.
King, Larry L. *Of Outlaws, Con Men, Whores, Politicians and Other Artists.* New York: Viking Press, 1980.
Kirby, Jack Temple. *Rural Worlds Lost: The American South 1920–1960.* Baton Rouge: University of Louisiana Press, 1987.
Kyvig, David E. *Daily Life in the United States, 1920–1940: How Americans Lived*

through the "Roaring Twenties" and the Great Depression. Chicago: Ivan R. Dee, 2002.

Langham, Barbara. "A Man's Got a Right to His Own Mind." *Texas Highways,* February, 1985.

Leffler, John J. *Kind of a Hard Old Country: Oral History from the Balcones Canyonlands and the Surrounding Area.* Austin, Texas: Balcones Canyonlands National Wildlife Refuge, U.S. Fish and Wildlife Service, 2001.

Lewis, Oscar. "On the Edge of the Black Waxy: A Cultural Survey of Bell County, Texas." *Social and Philosophical Sciences,* no. 7 (1948): 1–110.

Leyborn, James G. *The Scotch-Irish: A Social History.* Chapel Hill: University of North Carolina Press, 1962.

Lisheron, Mark. "Sundown of the Cedar Choppers." *Austin American-Statesman,* October 22, 2000.

Liu, Joanne S. *Barbed Wire: The Fence That Changed the West.* Missoula, Mont.: Mountain Press, 2009.

McCallum, Henry D., and Frances T. McCallum. *The Wire That Fenced the West.* Norman: University of Oklahoma Press, 1965.

Miller, Rick. *Sam Bass and Gang.* Austin, Texas: State House Press, 1999.

Motheral, Joe. *Recent Trends in Land Tenure in Texas.* Bulletin no. 641. College Station: Texas Agricultural Experiment Station, 1944.

Nisbett, Richard E., and Dov Cohen. *Culture of Honor: The Psychology of Violence in the South.* Boulder, Colo.: Westview Press, 1996.

Olmsted, Frederick Law. *A Journey through Texas: Or a Saddle-Trip on the Southwestern Frontier.* Austin: University of Texas Press, 1978.

Otto, John S. "The Migration of Southern Plain Folk: An Interdisciplinary Synthesis." *Journal of Southern History* 51, no. 2 (1985): 183–200.

Parsons, Chuck. *The Taylor-Sutton Feud: The Deadliest Blood Feud in Texas.* Denton: University of North Texas Press, 2009.

Patoski, Joe Nick. "The War on Cedar." *Texas Monthly,* December, 1997.

Perkins, Elaine. *A Hill Country Paradise? Western Travis County and Its Early Settlers.* Bloomington, Indiana: iUniverse, 2012.

Porterfield, Bill. *LBJ Country.* Garden City, N.Y.: Doubleday and Company, 1965.

Preece, Harold. "Where a Dance Still Means the Virginia Reel." *Dallas Morning News,* August 14, 1932.

———. "My Grandfather, Dick Preece." *Real West,* 1946.

Pryor, Cactus. "Charlie King." In *Inside Texas: Commentaries from KLBJ-AM.* Bryan, Tex.: Shoal Creek Publications, 1982.

Pugsley, William S. *Imprint on the Land: Life before Camp Hood, 1820–1942.* Austin, Texas: Prewitt and Associates, 2001.

Reed, John Shelton. *Southern Folk, Plain and Fancy: Native White Social Types.* Athens: University of Georgia Press, 1986.

Rissmann, E. J. "The Charcoal Burner." In *The Sunny Slopes of Long Ago,* edited by Wilson M. Hudson and Allen Maxwell, 151–56. Dallas, Tex.: Southern Methodist University Press, 1966.

———. "Charcoal Burning: What Used to Be a Way of Life Now Gone from the Hills Here." *Austin American,* April 10, 1966.

Roemer, Ferdinand. *Roemer's Texas, 1845–1847.* Translated by Oswald Mueller. Austin, Tex.: Eakin Press, 1983.

Rose, Peter R. *The Reckoning: The Triumph of Order on the Texas Outlaw Frontier.* Lubbock: Texas Tech University Press, 2012.
Rosenthal, Thane. *Payback: The Case for Revenge.* Chicago: University of Chicago Press, 2013.
Rotherham, Ian D. "The Charcoal Burners." *Picture Postcard Monthly* 396 (April 2012): 12–14.
Scarbrough, Clara S. *Land of Good Water (Takachue Pouetsu): A Williamson County History.* Georgetown, Tex.: Williamson County Sun Publishers, 1973.
Scarbrough, Linda. *Road, River, and Ol' Boy Politics: A Texas County's Path from Farm to Supersuburb.* Austin: Texas State Historical Association, 2005.
Schallenberg, Richard. "Evolution, Adaptation and Survival: The Very Slow Death of the American Charcoal Iron Industry." *Annals of Science* 32 (1975): 341–58.
Shapiro, Henry D. *Appalachia on Our Mind: The Southern Mountains and Mountaineers in the American Consciousness, 1870–1920.* Chapel Hill: University of North Carolina Press, 1978.
Sharpless, Rebecca. *Fertile Ground, Narrow Choices: Women on Texas Cotton Farms, 1900–1940.* Chapel Hill: University of North Carolina Press, 1999.
Sherrill, Bob. "Civilization Squeezing out Texas Cedarbilly." *Texas Observer,* January 6, 1961, 6.
Simons, Willie. "Cedar's Fed Many a Family." In *Medina . . . A Delightful Retreat, edited by Dot Ferguson Hatfield,* 19–21. Privately published, 1999.
Sitton, Thad. *Backwoodsmen: Stockmen and Hunters Along a Big Thicket River Valley.* Norman: University of Oklahoma Press, 1995.
———. *Harder Than Hardscrabble: Oral Recollections of the Farming Life from the Edge of the Texas Hill Country.* Austin: University of Texas Press, 2003.
Sitton, Thad, and Dan K. Utley. *From Can See to Can't: Texas Cotton Farmers on the Southern Prairies* Austin: University of Texas Press, 1997.
Solomon, Dan. "The Ten Wealthiest Zip Codes in Texas Are Pretty Much Where You'd Expect." *Texas Monthly,* May 15, 2014.
Sowell, A. J. "The Cox Family as Indian Fighters." In *Early Settlers and Indian Fighters of Southwest Texas: Facts Gathered from Survivors of Frontier Days* 602–606, Austin, Tex.: Ben C. Jones and Company, 1900.
Stephens, Lucius M. "Lometa Had Boom Town Appearance When Scholten Railroad Started Construction in 1911." *Lampasas Record,* July 23, 1964.
Sutton, Samuel H. "Cypress Shingles for Sale." In *Medina's Early Days,* edited by Dot Ferguson Hatfield, 39–40. Privately published, 1995.
SWCA Environmental Consultants. Historical Narrative – Site 41wm892, the Cedar Chopper Site, Williamson County, Texas, and the Texas Cedar Industry. Austin: Texas Historical Commission, 2003.
Toepperwein, Fritz A., and Emilie Toepperwein. *Charcoal and Charcoal Burners.* Boerne, Tex.: Highland Press, 1950.
Tomka, Steve A., and John Leffler. *A Cultural Overview and Assessment of Balcones Canyonlands National Wildllife Refuge.* San Antonio: Center for Archeological Research, University of Texas at San Antonio, 1998.
Upton, Elsie. "The Austin Hill Folk." *Texian Stomping Grounds,* no. 17 (1941): 40–48.
Van Winkle, Irene. "Gumberts Made Cutting Cedar a Worthy Trade to Raise Clan." *West Kerr Current,* March 21, 2013.

Vance, J. D. *Hillbilly Elegy: A Memoir of a Family and Culture in Crisis.* New York: HarperCollins Publishers, 2016.

Vance, Linda. *Eanes: Portrait of a Community.* Dallas, Tex.: Taylor Publishing Company, 1986.

Webb, Jim. *Born Fighting: How the Scots-Irish Shaped America.* New York: Broadway Books, 2004.

Webb, Walter Prescott. *The Great Plains.* Boston: Ginn and Company, 1931.

Wills, Fred. "Uvalde and Northern Railway." *Journal of South Texas* 18, no. 1 (2004).

Wimberley, C.W. "Cedar Brakes." In *Wimberley's Legacy,* edited by Williedell Schawe, 229–32. Austin, Tex.: Eakin Press, 1963.

———. *Cedar Whacker: Stories of the Texas Hill Country.* Austin, Tex.: Eakin Press, 1988.

Woodard, Colin. *American Nations: A History of the Eleven Rival Regional Cultures of North America.* New York: Viking, 2011.

Woodrell, Daniel. *Tomato Red.* Houston: Busted Flush Press, 2010.

Yarbrough, C. L. *Canyon of the Eagles.* Dallas, Tex.: Taylor Publishing Company, 1991.

Yarnell, Susan L. *The Southern Appalachians: A History of the Landscape.* Ashville, NC: United States Department of Agriculture, Forest Service, Southern Research Station, 1998.

Zesch, Scott. *The Captured: The True Story of Abduction by Indians on the Texas Frontier.* New York: St. Martin's Press, 2004.

INDEX

Page numbers in *italic* refer to illustrations.